T0312000

Advance Praise for *Creating Value for Leaders*

"Gautam Mahajan has filled a gaping void in the literature on Creating Value. Not just a *tour de horizon* of where the field is today, it is a lovingly-crafted resource that can be used as a field book for academics, business professionals and consultants, as well as a spur to leaders whomever and wherever they are to espouse a value-centric approach. Gautam's key tenet – that the art of leading is actually the practice of creating value *consciously* is an important takeaway for me personally. His book is a non-disguised plea for more conscious business and more conscious leadership – in other words, a message for our times."
                    – Prof. Alon Rozen, *Dean, CEO and Professor of Innovation,*
                                    École des Ponts Business School (Paris, France)

"Gautam Mahajan has displayed by this book why he is considered the leading thinker in the creating value thought process. He has written a comprehensive treatise on value creation, showing its width and depth, its usefulness to people and businesses. The work helps leaders and executives become great value creators and more successful."
                    – Professor Hermann Simon, *Founder and Honorary*
                                    Chairman of Simon-Kucher and Partners, Germany

"*Creating Value for Leaders* is an inspiring book and Mr. Mahajan shares all his experience in addressing holistically the complex world of value. Value Creation has been a hot topic for many years … yet there has been only terse discussion on how to create it. This book by Gautam Mahajan is an exception where he discussed not only the process of value creation in details and for which all stakeholders it should be created and how. This must-read book deep dives in to the nuances of creating value and infuses this thought in to every stakeholder's mind not only for their business but also in their life. There is no doubt that this book will change the thinking of every relevant stakeholder in their idea of purpose in both business and life."
                    – Dr. V Kumar, *Salvatore Zizza Professor of Marketing,*
                                    Tobin College of Business, St. John's University, NY

"Value is one of the most relevant topics for all organizations. Gautam is one of the world's leading experts on the subject, approaching it in a clear and effective way, extremely connected with the demands of companies, professionals and institutions in their most diverse variations. Creating value, sharing value, delivering elements of value to customers and society are fundamental parts of the success of organizations and their respective managers. Gautam's books always bring a relevant perspective on the topic helping professionals in several countries.

This new book *Creating Value for Leaders: Balancing the Interests of Customers, Employees, Investors, and the Marketplace* brings an expanded view of previous books, within a broad market context and its nuances, like conflicts of interest, creating shared value to society, and how to avoid destroying value. Definitely, an essential reading for executives, professionals, and students. There is a space in my personal library for this new book. Enjoy the reading."

— Victor Venancio, *Head of Digital Transformation LatAm at ihm Stefanini Group, Brazil*

"*Creating Value for Leaders* is an inspiring book and Mr. Mahajan shares all his experience in addressing holistically the complex world of Value Management. A must-read to understand how to build meaningful and long-lasting business relationships."

— Paolo De Angeli, CPP, *Head of Customer Experience and Customer Value Management, Borealis AG, Austria*

"This is a "to-go book" for value creation. Mahajan took the concept of value creation from A to Z, from customer side to supplier side to employee side. In addition, the impact of technology in this process is examined. I strongly suggest this book to all practitioners, students and faculty members."

— Dr. Cihan Cobanoglu, *CHTP McKibbon Endowed Chair Professor, and Dean, School of Hospitality and Tourism Management, Muma College of Business | University of South Florida*

"My career has been driven by the mantra, "value is defined by the receiver more than the giver" as our work seeks to create value for all stakeholders Gautam's work captures and extends these ideas in comprehensive, innovative, and relevant ways. The value of this book will be high because users of the ideas will have impact."

— Dave Ulrich, *Rensis Likert Professor, Ross School of Business, University of Michigan, Partner, The RBL Group*

"In this book Gautam Mahajan demonstrates his passion for value and the creation of value in business and in society. He shows that value creation is a complex and multi-faceted process, where many stakeholders and their value-related behaviors are interconnected. For example, value created for employees will transform to value for the business and for its shareholders, and also have the potential to be valuable for society at large."

— Chrisian Grönroos, *Professor, Hanken School of Economics*

"Anyone can argue that creating value is the key to success. In fact, there are various methodologies that claim to be able to create value. However, in order to take advantage of these methodologies, one must have the right mindset.

You will learn the right mindset for value creation by reading this book."

– Youji Kohda, *Professor and Executive Dean of the Graduate School of Advanced Science and Technology, Director of Tokyo Satellite, Vice President of Japan Advanced Institute of Science and Technology*

"Pandemic made us realize the importance of well-being for us. The book gives us various hints to enhance the value and well-being of us and our society."

– Dr. Mari Iizuka, Director, *Doshisha University Well-Being Research Centre, Professor, Doshisha Business School*

"For those who are struggling to understand value creation in the marketplace from multiple perspectives, Gautam Mahajan has the answer. His book, integrating rare insights on how to balance CEO (Customer, Employee, and Owner/Investor) interests, is a *must read* for integrating the importance of ideas and strategies for value creation, with the culture and mindset changes need to engage customers, while enhancing resource fluidity from – and value appropriation for – owners and investors."

– Rajendra Srivastava. *Novartis Professor of Marketing Strategy and Innovation, Executive Director: Centre for Business Innovation (CBI), Executive Fellows Program in Management (EFPM), Indian School of Business*

"Be prepared for a wild excursion that will change your approach to leading your teams, winning and building customer loyalty, engaging your staff and ecosystem, and increasing your own skills and passion. Gautam Mahajan has built on his considerable range of writings and consulting work this opus devoted to defining, creating, and delivering value in its many forms. You might nod knowingly at some of his stories but return to them later for deeper meaning; you will find new material to challenge your thinking, and broaden your horizons."

– Bill Price, *President, Driva Solutions, Former Global VP for Customer Service, Amazon, USA*

Creating Value for Leaders

Creating value is the foundation of all business. It's what sets you apart from your competition, secures long-term customers, and brings distinct meaning to your brand and your stakeholders. Without creating value for your business, your unique offering will be seen as just another commodity in the eyes of your target market. Creating value is in every business leader's vocabulary and uppermost in their overall strategy. In fact, creating value is the purpose of a company according to the Business Roundtable and the World Economic Forum. That is another key reason why more people want to understand and utilize value creation for their benefit and the good of their stakeholders.

Many companies and leaders seek to create value but do not know how to. As a result, they create and destroy value unconsciously. This book shows you how to create value consciously. To create long-term value, organizations need to put in place the mindset, capabilities, and relationships that enable them to meet the needs of their customers and stakeholders.

This book helps executives and leaders understand and use value creation more effectively. The book describes value creation in its various nuances, how it arises, how it is used, and the width and scope of value creation, from how it impacts a company and how that company can become more successful by creating value for customers and other stakeholders. The author also provides tips for CEOs, managers, HR, and other professionals on how to succeed in value creation as a long-term strategy and in day-to-day work. Numerous examples and case studies illustrate the points being made by the author.

Creating Value for Leaders

Balancing the Interests of Customers,
Employees, Investors, and the Marketplace

by
Gautam Mahajan

Foreword by Philip Kotler

Routledge
Taylor & Francis Group

A PRODUCTIVITY PRESS BOOK

First published 2023
by Routledge
605 Third Avenue, New York, NY 10158

and by Routledge
4 Park Square, Milton Park, Abingdon, Oxon, OX14 4RN

Routledge is an imprint of the Taylor & Francis Group, an informa business

ISBN: 978-1-032-46423-7 (hbk)
ISBN: 978-1-032-46422-0 (pbk)
ISBN: 978-1-003-38162-4 (ebk)

DOI: 10.4324/9781003381624

Typeset in Garamond
by Deanta Global Publishing Services, Chennai, India

If you're not creating value for others and customers,
society isn't going to let you be around.

– Charles Koch

Try not to become a man of success, but a man of value. Look
around at how people want to get more out of life than they put
in. A man of value will give more than he receives. Be creative, but
make sure that what you create is not a curse for mankind.

– Albert Einstein

Contents

Foreword by Professor Philip Kotler xiii
Acknowledgements xv
About the Author xvii
Introduction xix
    The Importance of Value.. xix

1 Value.. 1
    Creating Value for Yourself Means Creating Value for Others 1
    What Is Real Value?... 3
    The Impact of Culture on Creating Value.. 5
    The Sense of Value 7
    Using Customer's Bill of Rights to Build a Customer Culture 9
    Value of Belonging: The Orphaned Customer 12
    Why "What's in It for Me" Can Kill Value Creation 14
    What Does Being Secure Have to Do with Creating Value? 16
    Creating Value, Value Co-creation, and Value Destruction 18
    From Value Grabbing to Value Creating: Lesson for Leaders 21
    Is Value Co-creation Always Necessary... 23
    The Value Co-creation Platform... 26
    Wellbeing and Value Creation: Are They Two Sides of a Coin?........... 28

2 Value Creation Education... 31
    Example of Value Creation in Education: At the Michener Center,
        U of Texas, Austin... 31
    Creating Value with Knowledge 33
    Training vs. a Learning Mindset in Value Creation 35

3 Customer Value 39
    What Is Customer Value and How Can You Create It?........................ 39
    The Eight Principles of Customer Value Creation 42
    Some Misconceptions about Customer Value 43

The Memory of Your Experience Is More Important Than Your
    Experience...44
Customer Value and Customer Satisfaction: Two Sides of the
    Same Coin? 46
Can Customer Value Change Customer Behaviour and Vice Versa?.....48
Don't Give Away Too Much to the Customer...51
Steps in Value Creation Implementation: The Customer Department.....55
Customer Value Journey: Making the Journey Easy and
    Meaningful Creates Value..57
Customers as Ambassadors 59
How SMEs Benefit by Creating Value for Customers: A Case Study......61
Does a Customer Seek Customer Experience? 63
Customer-centric Circles, the Self-Directed Approach to Service
    and Mindset Changes 68
Ease and Simplicity Creates Experience and Value.................................79

4   Customer Value Starvation...83
Air India, Whither Goest Thou, and Tata: How to Create Value..........83
Adding More Value Does Not Cost Much; Creating Low Value
    Does Cost You 87
Value Creation Implementation Ideas. Avoid Value Destruction...........89
When Zero Defects Are the Norm, Why Not Zero Customer
    Complaints? 91
Nuisance Value: Value Creation or Value Destruction?..........................93
Value Deprivation 94

5   Employee Value 97
Employee Value Added Is Not What Companies Think!.......................97
Value Creation by Employees...100
Eight Tips for Value Creation for HR Professionals: Become Line
    Managers..101
Employee Journey...105
Using Employees to Build Market Place Foresight and Value
    Creation 107
Do Specialists Create More Value Than Generalists? 110

6   Businesses and Institutions 113
Value Creation Is Output/Input..113
Are Companies Loyal? 115
The Real Sources of Value: Assets and Performance.............................116
Value Creation and Destruction in Customer Value Constellations....118

Four Types of Companies: My Learnings from Value Creation 120
Nine Reasons Why Your Company Isn't Creating Value 125
Building Silos or Breaking Silos? Internal Customer Is a Flawed
    Concept! 130
Management by Creating Value 132
Does Value Creation Need Financial Incentives? 138
Companies Misunderstand Price 140
The Case for Value Creation Centres: Value Councils Go Beyond
    Pricing Councils and Innovation Councils 141
Journey of a Customer Value Creation Evangelist: From
    Companystan to Customerstan 143

7 Profits and Value **147**
How the Pure Profit Motive Destroys Value 147
The Great Balancing Act: You Can Tip the Balance! Increase Profits 151
Death of Profit: Customer Power Requires a Mindset Change to
    Improve Customer Retention and Profits 154
Value Added Stories to Increase Price 155
How Economics Creates Value 156

8 Value Destruction **161**
The Ukraine War Showcases Value Destruction and Learning from It 161
Look at Value Destruction to Create More Value 164
Co-Destruction 170
Value Destruction: Non-Value-Added Tasks Destroy Value 174
Will Value Destruction Ace Value Creation? Big Brother: Google,
    Apple, and Microsoft 178
Power and Value 179
Money and Power: Motivators of Conscious or Unconscious Value
    Destruction 180

9 Leaders, Executives, and Value Creation **183**
Value Creation and Leaders 183
Can Non-Owner Stakeholders Select CEOs to Create Value? 190
To Create More Value, Leaders Should Not Always Lead 191
Fear: Value Creator or Value Destroyer for Leaders 193
Trust Creates Value 194
Should Creating Value Be Part of Leadership and Education 195
Why Leadership Development Programs Fail: A Contrarian View 198
Why Training Does Not Create Great Leaders? 200
The Leadership Skill of Being Able to Unlearn: Create Value
    through Unlearning 201

No Time for Customers? Conduct a Task Audit 203
Are You a Value Creator or a Value Taker? 205
The Chief Creating Value Officer 208
Value Creation Implementation Ideas. Avoid Value Destruction 211

10 Transformation and Value Creation 215
Value Creation for Transformational Growth of an Organization 215
Transforming companies through Value Creation, Not Value
    Destruction: The Balancing Act 217

11 Purpose and Value Creation 221
Our Purpose in Life 221
The Purpose of a Company Defined by the World Economic Forum 222
Why Purpose Creates Value 225
What Is Value Creation and the New Purpose of a Company? 227

12 Sustainability and Value Creation 231
Creating Value through Sustainability 231
Value Washing 239

13 Disruption and Creating Value 245
Creating Value in a Disrupted Marketplace 245
Marketing and Disruption 250
Creating Value Out of Value Destruction by COVID-19 254

14 Marketing and Value Creation 257
Marketing Must Prevent Customer Value Starvation to Increase
    Profits 257
Can Marketing Be a Value Destroyer? 260
Pitching Your Value Proposition: How to Focus on What
    Customers Value 264
De-Commoditizing Commodities: Add Value 265
Customer and Value Migration 267
Value of Being Anonymous? 269
Does Planned Obsolescence Destroy Value? 271
My Terms or Yours: What Creates More Value? 273

15 Value Creation and Technology 275
Why Creating Value Is a Skill Needed for the Future with AI and
    Technology 275
Technology as a Potential Value Destroyer 277
CIOs Can Be True Value Creators 281

16 Value Creation for Suppliers and Partners 283
Are You Adding Value to Your Suppliers and Partners? 283
The Supplier Strikes Back 286

17 Value and Values 289
Driving Businesses from Values: Values Create Value (And Higher
Profits) 289
Value and VBA 291
Corporate Unconsciousness: A Wakeup Call 298

18 Value Waiting to Happen and Innovation 301
Value Waiting to Happen 301

Appendix A: Guide to Customer Value Creation Definitions 305
Index 323

Foreword by Professor Philip Kotler

I am extremely pleased to write this foreword for Gautam Mahajan's new book on Value Creation. No one has done more for value creation globally than Gautam Mahajan. He has singlehandedly built a community of world leaders focused on value creation, started the *Journal of Creating Value* (I am proud to be on the Board), and the Global Conferences on Creating Value where I have spoken, and several value schools and centres around the world.

I have been saying that marketing and management is all about creating value. Gautam proves it in this book, by displaying the many facets of value creation, making it easy for leaders to understand and be educated. Leaders can then follow the techniques and the learnings to become more successful.

Value and value creation are used by many more people in their interactions with others. However, in spite of the body of knowledge that Gautam has increased and collected, value creation has not become mainstream. The Business Round Table and the World Economic Forum (WEF) Davos have stated the purpose of a company is to create value, and many companies are trying to do so. I hope this book will help them and make many more leaders and their companies value creation practitioners and make value creation more central to leaders and companies.

For academics, I suggest they start to work more on value creation and setting up Value Creation Centres and Creating Value Schools. There are Creating Value Schools at Kobe University and Japan Advanced Institute of Science and Technology, a Value Creation Research Centre at Doshisha University, and Value Creation centres in Denmark (Aalborg University), Portugal (Nova University), and the USA (University of Maryland).

Gautam presents the definition and understanding of value, how to implement this in strategy, marketing, HR, technology, and other disciplines, and how to measure value and create it in the marketplace, in ESG (environment, social, and governance), and for employees and customers. The book is replete with examples and anecdotes.

I urge academics and leaders to start more value creating schools and give degrees in value creation.

Gautam's new book will show you how and guide you to greater success.

Philip Kotler

Philip Kotler is undoubtedly the most famous marketing guru in the world. His book *Marketing Management* has been around for about 50 years and is now in its 15th edition.

Acknowledgements

I acknowledge:

Moshe Davidow, for editing and commenting and allowing me to use his comments.

Others whom I have quoted, many of whom I do not know, but thank you for your words of wisdom that I am sharing.

The book is dedicated to my readers who will become value creators, too, and to my supportive family, but mostly to the latest love of my life, my first grandchild, Vidya Lena Mari Mahajan!

About the Author

Gautam Mahajan, internationally acclaimed expert in value creation, strategy, general management, and globalization, is the President of Customer Value Foundation. He is also the Founder Editor of the *Journal of Creating Value*, jcv.sagepub.com. He chairs the Global Conferences on Creating Value and mentors the Creating Value Alliance, creatingvalue.co.

He is the author of numerous books which include: *Value Dominant Logic*; *Value Imperative*; *Value Creation*; *Creating Customer Value Can Make You a Great Executive*; *Total Customer Value Management*; *Customer Value Investment*; *and Customer Value Starvation Can Kill* with Walter Vieira. He is a featured international speaker. His clients included Alcoa, GE, GE Capital, State Farm Insurance, Wisconsin Energies, Sealed Air, Rexam, Reynolds, Viag, Tatas, Godrej, ITC, Birla's etc.

Mr. Mahajan is the past Global President of the Indo-American Chamber of Commerce. He was Chairman of the PlastIndia Committee and Vice President of All India Plastics Manufacturers Association, Trustee Plastics Institute of America. He was also a member of the US–India think tank. Among his honours was a Fellowship from Harvard Business School and Illinois Institute of Technology. He was honoured by the Illinois Institute of Technology with its Distinguished Alumni award. He delivered the first Distinguished Engineering lecture at the Illinois Institute of Technology, Chicago, in May 2012. He has chaired and given keynotes at conferences in several countries. In late 2019, he presented in Japan and the Netherlands. In 2020, he was invited to speak in Denmark, Boston, Geneva, Paris, and Poland all related to Creating Value, which the Business Roundtable has coined as the purpose of a company.. He chaired the International Conference on Creating Value with Technology in Japan (2019) and the Global Conference on Creating Value in Paris in 2020, and a virtual one from Florida in 2021. He co-chaired the Global Conference on Creating Value in Kanazawa, Japan, in 2022. He spoke at Kobe U, Doshisha U, and JAIST virtually in 2021 and 2022, and spoke in all three places physically in 2022.

He has 18 US patents and is the designer of the one piece PET bottles' petal-oid base. His patents include noise control kits and other machinery.

He can be reached at Gautam.Mahajan@gmail.com

Introduction

The Importance of Value

This book is meant for leaders and is also useful for the layman. Leaders become leaders because they create value or have the potential to create value. Executives transform into leadership by demonstrating creating value skills. This book will introduce you to the many dimensions of value and how you can create more value for yourself and others and become really successful. This book will create awareness about yourself and value creation, improve your attitude and mindset, make you more agile and ambidextrous, increase your ability to lead, help you anticipate problems and solutions, and convert all these into action. The book is about leaders exciting people and talent to leverage value creation for generating additional revenue or preventing value leakage and to improve business and society. This book will help you with the human side of value creation: achieving your revenue and cost efficiency targets in a way that enhances your character and improves the humanity that converts growth and progress into value. This book will help leaders to create value for employees and executives and other stakeholders and to become innovative and creative, overcome disruption, and indeed become disruptors.

The book is to remind leaders and other readers about the importance of value creation and help them become better value creators, by increasing their awareness of value, its creation, its use, and how successful it can make you and them.

Moshe Davidow, who helped me edit this book, commented that though everyone is talking about value creation, few are practising it. He cited that Conscious Capitalism which is such an important concept has about 200 listed members from industry and communities. Perhaps ten times more are practising Conscious Capitalism. Yet the numbers are minuscule. Why are the rest not practising the concept? This is a question we keep asking about value creation.

One answer is that most people and leaders create and destroy value unconsciously. Our endeavour is to make value creation a conscious effort.

In the case of value creation, I would guess many more would profess thy use value creation or are value creators. But few can define value, and fewer still can talk about concrete value creation (other than economic) programs. Yes, they can say this effort created value, but not about how value creation made them successful.

Everyone uses the word value, but few truly understand it. Even those who understand it seem to think it is limited to a few areas. In this book we show that value is applicable in so many different fields, and in so many different areas, and how it can help you.

Value has many dimensions. It is used in defining our relationship with, and as also the result of interactions with customers, employees, partners (supply and delivery chains), society, environment, and investors. It has many shades and many aspects from value creation to value destruction, value starvation, value migration, value washing and wasting among others. Value helps you convert ESG (environment, social, and governance) from a cost centre to a profit centre. Cognizance of all these makes you greater leaders, and ahead of the game.

Value is associated with business, wellbeing, education, humanity, society, governance etc. That is why the *Journal of Creating Value* and I have chosen the definition:

Creating Value is executing normal, conscious, inspired, and even imaginative actions that increase the overall good and wellbeing, and the worth of and for ideas, goods, services, people, or institutions including society, and all stakeholders (like employees, customers, partners, shareholders, environment, and society), and value waiting to happen.

The short definition of value creation is doing good and improving wellbeing.

This Book

This very interesting book discusses many of the aspects, their complex and sometimes simple inter-relation with value creation. The book is meant to make leaders think, and get ideas, change, and become more conscious to become value creating leaders.

Spend a few minutes a day reading chapters and build your creating value awareness and expertise. This knowledge will give you new ideas and ways of becoming a greater leader and executive. The book makes you understand that creating value often does not cost much at all. Smiling, working more diligently, and not having to repeat things, all create value at no cost.

The book describes value creation in its various nuances, how it arises, how it is used, and the width of the value creation, from how it impacts an individual and how they can become more successful using value creation, to professionals, students, families etc. The book gives tips for succeeding for CEOs, HR and other professionals, leaders, frontline people, and much more. The book is a rich guide for all of you.

The book has many new ideas such as value wasting, value washing, value depletion, value starvation etc. The chapters represent new ways of thinking and looking at business and value and yourself. It presents a value creating company's organogram.

This book can be used to:

Educate and learn (and unlearn), and increase knowledge and effectiveness of value and its uses
Increase awareness and value creation consciousness
Change mindsets to becoming value creators
Make you a better person and executive and much more successful
Make your companies long lasting and profitable, capable of coping with the fast changing environment, and make you longer-lasting leaders
Help you have a purpose, and better strategy

Revamp your departmental thinking, convert HR to line managers, staff to line, cost centres to profit centres. Learn how to redesign your company and departments like finance and HR. The book helps you refine your thinking and balance the interests of various stakeholders in business, which is an important role of a leader. It helps you in your relationship and priorities with customers, employees, partners, society, environment, and shareholders. It also helps you balance value for yourself and your family versus value for the business. This is also important for executives.

Because of this, the book is of great value for you in your life, in looking at value for yourself and your family and work.

In retrospect, some repetition is necessary for chapters to stand alone: e.g. 8As, the definition of value.

This book will be of interest to scholars and practitioners in the subject of value creation and will create an understanding and knowledge about the width and depth of creating value and make them practice value creation and learn more about value creation.

This book appeals to all people in different fields of learning and teaching, people like you and me, and business and professional managers, leaders, executives, students, scholars, and academics:

1. The only book showing the width and depth of the field of value creation
2. Makes the reader aware of the nuances and impact of value creation

3. Makes them understand how to use it and develop value creation thinking in themselves
4. Helps develop an interest to learn more and use value creation in real life

How to use this book:

First many sections are useful for various disciplines. Thus a section placed in business may be useful for leaders and executives and even non-business people.

This means you could pick and choose your chapters from disciplines outside your own. Use the index and the table of contents to choose the chapters of most interest to you. Remember, you can read the chapters and sections in any order. Read some or all.

You will learn and benefit as a layperson, just as a researcher will find topics to work on, and leaders will find tips to become more successful.

Chapter 1

Value

Creating Value for Yourself Means Creating Value for Others

I gave a talk to BBA and MBA entering students at SGT University in Delhi and then to Model Institute in Jammu some time ago. I asked the students whom they should create value for. Some said for our parents. Others for our company. For ourselves was the answer we all agreed upon. Till you think of creating value for yourself, how can you create value for others?

I told them to create value for themselves, they must create value for those around them, their fellow students, the teachers, and the Institute. Then and only then will these people say that the student is creating value, and also, he or she will notice the value created for him/her by others.

This is true for a company. A company that sets out to create value for itself without creating value for its employees, partners, supply and delivery chain, society, and Customers will not create substantial value for the company. All of these stakeholders together create value for the company. Creating value for yourself without creating value for others could lead to value depletion.

The company and leaders must understand that creating value for the company's stakeholders is a sure way of creating value for the company.

Creating Value for Yourself

Normally, my articles are focused on CEOs and transforming companies to create value. I realize my readers consist of a large number of executives who are trying to move upwards. This section is for them, but my CEO readers will also learn about not only promoting value creation but also helping executives to create value. CEOs, then, will also create value for themselves.

Most of us do not have a strategy for ourselves. We need to ask ourselves what we want out of life, out of work, and what we value at work, and what is our purpose. Is it learning? Is it getting recognized, is it being given responsibility, is it a sense of belonging and being part of a group of people, is it the values of the company, the growth of the company, the reputation of the company, the challenge, the opportunity to achieve, the management, the colleagues, the prospects for advancement, the money? Which are more important? Monetary gains or other monetary advantages such as free courses, travel and an expense report etc. or is it the other benefits?

We call all of this employee value, or what you as an employee value. Value means how worthwhile is it for you to work for this company versus working somewhere else. What is important? The monetary terms or the benefits you perceive you are getting? Which of the benefit terms are most important? So, is money 60% in importance and the benefits 40%, or vice versa?

But you cannot stop here. If you want to go ahead, you have to create value not just for yourself but for your colleagues, your bosses, and your company. In this section, I will focus on the value you can create for your company.

Ask, what will make me a valuable person in this company? What will make the company take notice of me? Is it just doing the expected well or better than others? Or going the extra mile? Or creating ideas, methods, and thoughts that will make the company or your department more valuable? What are these extra steps you can take? How can you get ahead by going beyond what is expected of you and doing extra programs that go beyond just performance expectations?

All this builds your brand equity. You are known by the brand you create for yourself. If your name is Vijay, what is brand Vijay in the eyes of the company? Does brand Vijay mean dependability and reliability and getting the job done? Or brand Vijay means he not only gets the job done, but he thinks of better ways of doing the job and thinks ahead to the next step, something no one else has thought of.

Having good brand equity means people (your colleagues, bosses, suppliers, and customers) want to deal with you. Poor brand equity means they are saying I do not want to deal with him or worse still, keep him out of my way.

So, CEOs how do you create value for your employees? How do you help them create value for your customers and companies? I have written about this in this book in the sections called **Creating Value Is the Key Role of An Executive** and **Why Value Creation is more Important Than Value Extraction?** And **Do Your Employees Feel Valued?**

* * *

What Is Real Value?

Nothing can have value without being an object of utility.

– Karl Marx

Value is created when you do some good for or increase the wellbeing of or worth of yourself or others (widely includes businesses, institutions, people, family etc.). You can create limited value for yourself. More value is created for you when you create value for others, and they in turn create value for you.

But what is value? Is it an economic term? Or is it price, or is it more than that?

Most people use value contextually, in the circumstance or situation they are in. They see a car and ask what is its value? (*Price? Usefulness, Utility?*)

They go to buy a dress and ascertain its value to them. The value is what they perceive it to be. The value is what the car or the dress is worth to them: In use, in utility, in benefits, in usefulness, in style, in getting compliments, in ease of taking care of. So, value creates a benefit for you, but there is a cost to the benefit: what you pay for it, the effort in buying and trying out the dress, the inconvenience etc. So worth or value of the dress is perceived if the benefits in your estimate are greater than the cost as defined above.

That is why we are willing sometimes to buy online, because the cost may be lower than going to a store and spending time and effort. Avoiding the cost of going to the store and your time makes it worthwhile to buy online, and the benefits include saved effort, saved time, and more convenience; the benefits are lowered because you cannot touch or feel the dress. Hence an entrepreneur who can add this feature will create immense value to the customer and perhaps to the seller.

In a broader sense, going beyond business, value is doing good and improving the wellbeing of someone or some item. So, the dress can improve your wellbeing, or buying it may make you feel good. Or buying online may increase the value you perceive.

Value is reciprocal. When you create value for someone, chances are that he will do some good for you (meaning create value for you).

For you, dear reader, *value is doing good and improving the wellbeing of someone or a product or a company*. It could be potential or real; it could happen in the future. Most value comes from embedded perceptions and feelings (noting that transactional value alone is deceptional).

So long-term value is based on embedded feelings of good or of one's wellbeing or worth. Whether useful or not is also a perception, and a person takes all this together in deciding what is of value to him/her. Try it and you will realize why someone or some item creates value for you.

As Gary Mogan, a friend, said, real value is valuable.

Too many people latch on to the meaning of value someone famous has coined, such as value requires to be an object of utility, according to Marx.

Utility can mean useful, helpful, effective, convenient etc.

Utility value is defined in many ways by different people mostly taken from Google:

- Value is how much a person would be willing to pay for a specific level of utility. *So, value is equated to price in this example.*
- It is a measure of satisfaction an individual gets from the consumption of commodities. In other words, it is a measurement of usefulness that a consumer obtains from any good. A utility is a measure of how much one enjoys a movie, favourite food, or other goods. *Here value is equated to Benefits.*
- Utility value is how the task relates to future goals. While students may not enjoy an activity, they may value a later reward or outcome it produces (Wigfield, 1994[1]). The activity must be integral to their vision of their future, or it must be instrumental to their pursuit of other goals.
- Utility and value, in economics, is the determination of the prices of goods and services.
- To find the total utility value, economists use the following basic total utility formula: $TU = U1 + MU2 + MU3 \ldots$ The total utility is equal to the sum of utils gained from each unit of consumption. In the equation, each unit of consumption is expected to have slightly less utility as more units are consumed.

Use value is also defined in Marxist terms by Wiki:

Use value or value in use is a concept in classical political economy and Marxist economics. It refers to the tangible features of a commodity (a tradeable object) which can satisfy some human requirement, want, or need, or which serves a useful purpose. In Karl Marx's critique of political economy, any product has a labour value and a use value, and if it is traded as a commodity in markets, it additionally has an exchange value, most often expressed as a money price. This, of course, is flawed, because with automation, the labour content falls, or with low-cost labour, the labour content is lower, implying the value is lower.

Use value is "real" value, and only labour can create it.

So, one can surmise that use value is a sub-set of utility. Utility is potential value.

---

[1] https://psycnet.apa.org/record/1994-21034-001

As a matter of economics, scarcity is the source of all value, even if it is a combination of "manufactured" scarcity via monopoly control and relative scarcity due to the costliness of extraction and the preferences of consumers, according to Marx.

Marx develops a theory of value in which labour plays a crucial role, but "simply claiming that labour is the source of value," as Kevin D. Williamson[1] does in his *measured analysis* of Marx's work, "misses out the dialectical and historical dimensions of Marx's argument."

Let us not be swayed by what people say but understand what I have said earlier in this chapter about value. And I repeat: *Value is created when you do some good for or increase the wellbeing of or worth of yourself or others (widely includes businesses, institutions, people, family etc.). You can create limited value for yourself. More value is created when you create value for others, and they in turn create value for you.*

* * *

The Impact of Culture on Creating Value

Why Is Culture Important?

Management gurus will tell you culture is important, because culture brings employees and partners in a company together through shared beliefs, traditions, expectations, and goals. The two basic types of culture are material culture, physical things produced by a society, and non-material culture, intangible objects produced by a society.

Culture can be one of Empowering, Innovation, Sales Culture, Customer-centric Culture, and Culture of Leadership Excellence and of Safety. There are other types like a blame culture, blameless culture, a just culture, and so on.

Value Creation and Culture

I want to talk about a Value Creation culture that avoids value destruction (like blaming each other or creating silos and not working together, not taking care of partners and customers etc.).

More importantly, the Business Roundtable announced in 2019 that the purpose of a company is to create value. Davos echoed this in 2020. Now many companies around the world want to create value for stakeholders. A great goal,

---

[1] https://www.nationalreview.com/magazine/2020/08/24/why-marx-continues-to-fascinate -would-be-revolutionaries/#slide-1

but how are they going to do this? The word value has been used loosely in their vocabulary, and value creation (except in the form of profits) has not been a serious goal.

So, I repeat, how are they going to do this? One is to incorporate a culture of value creation:

- Understand what value and creating value means
- Realize what stakeholders want as value
- Learn to measure value for each of the stakeholders
- Find ways of creating and delivering value and extracting a meaningful share

What we want is a culture to create stakeholder value, specifically for employees, customers, partners, shareholders, nature, and society, and measure these. *Do we create more value for the stakeholders, or do they create more value for the companies?* This is important. Generally, companies survive when stakeholders create more value for the company than the company does for them and in fact make a profit from this.

The culture of creating value has to start with the leader who builds a creating value eco-system. The amount of value the company creates for stakeholders (minus the value they destroy) is a measure of leadership.

Leaders and their companies must create more value (this includes the value stakeholders create for the company) than they extract for their company.. Creation must always go ahead of extraction. Creating Social and Environmental value is like banking cash for the future.

In this section I wish to get all of you to understand and establish a culture of value creation for which companies must have:

A stakeholder culture that is your desire to create value for them.
This requires a customer and a stakeholder strategy that then moulds and generates your corporate strategy.

Thus, if your shareholders prefer growing the existing business through various sub-businesses, your corporate strategy should reflect that. If your customer strategy suggests affordability and risk averseness of customers, your corporate strategy must take that into account.

The stakeholder value creation thrust must come from the CEO.

Teaching employees and CxOs that the role of an executive is to create value and not just to perform a job. That is, your people must go beyond their jobs to create value. That value must be created consciously and not unconsciously. Focus also on reducing value destruction. Teach them how to create value. The

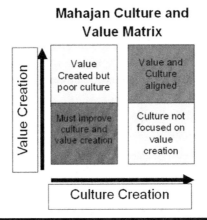

Figure 1.1   Mahajan Culture and Value Matrix

chart shows the relationship between value and culture and makes the best value and culture happen.

This chart shows how value creation and culture must go hand in hand (Figure 1.1), and the culture must lead to value creation; otherwise, the culture does not have so great an impact.

As always, I await your comments.

* * *

The Sense of Value

Developing the sense of value is a two-way street. One is your sense of what value is. The second is whether this value is being created for you, or you are creating value for others. Your sense of value is different in each case.

Do you have a sense of value? What is the sense of value? We all have it but to different degrees. The sense of value includes the feel and intuition and insight of value. We tend to learn what value is (we are taught or told what it is and how to react to it, and this is value expertise). We also build value by feeling or learning from others. This all happens as we develop our intuition of value. Intuitions depend on expertise, experience, and knowledge. Insights help us develop new thinking.

Gut feel is more like intuition.

We also have an instinct of value. This is ingrained in us from our childhood and depends on our expectations and beliefs (should we be prompt, should we keep our promises). Thus, some of us might want an expensive watch, whereas others are happy with a cheap watch. Some prefer a basic car, and others prefer a better car. This instinct of value changes over time, but the basic instinct of what value is remains.

We also have a sense of and instinct for values, our basic beliefs on morals, integrity, honesty etc.

Instinct is different from intuition. Leaders often use intuition to make decisions. We also use intuition to decide what value is. Part of this comes from data, our feel, and our focus.

The way we deliver value is often through people. We educate our frontline people, hopefully to deliver value. Often, we put in thoughts like customers like all customers are not honest.

This thought then impacts intuitive thinking. We want intuitive thinking to be positive.

Are we willing to put more emphasis on intuitive thinking than on the generic rules we set up to handle customers? The company should do this and follow this path to deal with customers is one type of thinking. Eventually we move towards Customer-centricity, intuitively, and then can get more customer loyalty.

Let's examine two types of salesmen selling a B2C item in a shop/store, and a customer walks in (Table 1.1).

So how do we improve this and build the right intuition and curb instincts? How do we develop insights?

Build self-esteem, awareness, anticipation, ability, agility, attitude, and ambidextrousness of the frontline people. Anticipate more.

Form Customer-centric Circles (described in the next chapter) and use self-development and self-directed learning for the customer, thereby exchanging knowledge and building intuition and insight.

These people will have a sense and a feel for what customers want and value.

Table 1.1

Kind of Value	Salesman 1	Salesman 2
Instinctive	Hunt/attack	Hold back/relaxed
Intuitive	Customer will buy Serve fast	Customer will buy/let him browse, be available for questions
Insight	How to convert from a walk in to a buyer	

* * *

Using Customer's Bill of Rights to Build a Customer Culture

In this section, we will discuss the Customer's Bill of Rights, and why they are important in building a Customer Culture.

Customer's Bill of Rights

We have all seen Customer's Bill of Rights. How often are these really fulfilled? More importantly, how many executives/employees know about the Bill of Rights and how to use and uphold them?

I bet in most companies the executives and the Customers do not know the Bill of Rights. So, in one Tata company, at the Customer Centre, the company put the Bill of Rights on the wall behind the executive so that the Customer could see his rights. Very soon they put it also on the wall behind where the Customer sits ... so that the executive could also see it. And what a difference it made.

There are a number of steps in making a Customer's Bill of Rights. Some are self-evident, like the right to get a product to work and honour the warranty. Less obvious are the rights to return a product, get it fixed, access to a knowledgeable, friendly, empathetic service person, no price gouging, no bait and sell, time-bound repairs and delivery etc.

Second, how do you find out whether a particular right is upholdable? Let's say the country you sell in insists on a maximum retail price on the package. So, you put this in your Bill of Rights. How do you prevent someone from selling at a higher price during shortages?

Third, if there is a problem, how do you uphold the Bill of Rights? Let's say the Bill of Rights says a product will be repaired in two days. The frontline person may say that to the Customer also, but does he know that this will happen? This requires all the people responsible for this to ensure this happens. This is the Circle of Promises.

This encourages everyone into focusing on the Customers and engenders teamwork and a Customer focus.

The Circle of Promises

The Circle of Promises is the understanding by people in the company or partners that they are part of a promise to uphold the Customer's Bill of Rights. They have to be in the loop and understand the meaning of their promise. More importantly, they should form a Customer-centric Circle to discuss improvements and

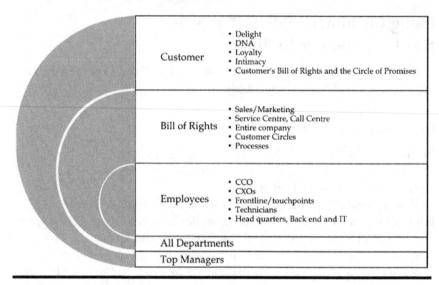

Figure 1.2   The Circle of Promises

where promises were not kept and how to solve problems. This will help change mindsets. This is shown in Figure 1.2.

Continuous Customer Improvement Program

A Continuous Customer Improvement Program (CCIP) is necessary to keep ahead of competition. The Customer-Centric Circles and the awareness through the Customer's Bill of Rights and the Circle of Promises conditionsthe employees to seek more ways to please Customers. This becomes a Continuous Customer Improvement Program.

As the program takes root, we find more and more ideas to improve Customer Value through Customer experience or the Customer journey. Ideas on Customer intimacy, Customer satisfaction, Customer Relationship Management (CRM), Customer delight, Customer customization, Customer channels, and co-creation of value can all be discussed.

Zero Complaints

As we work on the CCIP, we realize that we could actually incorporate systemic changes that could prevent a problem we have noticed from happening with other Customers. Or we could notice that Customers ask the same question … we cannot find your product in the stores. We should then correct this situation, or at least communicate with the Customer where to find the product or offer to deliver it to them.

We have to work towards reducing complaints or getting closer to Zero Complaints. Most people believe this is not possible, but we all agree we can strive towards it. Part of this comes by co-creation and working together with customers to get to zero complaints.

Discussion

In this section, we have taken Customer-centricity and Customer mindset to the next level by allowing the Customer Circles to focus on the Customer's Bill of Rights, understand its importance, and ensure that the promises enshrined in the Bill of Rights are upheld.

This is through the Circle of Promises and ensuring that the people involved understand this. And to build their involvement and mindset, a special Customer Circle including the people in the Circle of Promises is a good idea.

Customer Circles then can embark on a Continuous Customer Improvement Program. This can eventually focus on all aspects of Customer Value such as the Customer Journey, the Customer Experience, CRM, and customization can be worked on.

What items require systemic and procedural changes? How can we get to Zero Complaints?

Total Customer Value Management which includes the Customer Circles and the Customer's Bill of Rights helps all departments and executives to have a Customer focus. It is the foundation of building a Customer culture. Customer strategy and Customer-centric Circles are building blocks of the Customer culture and a Customer mindset. This gives the company a great competitive advantage.

Do It Yourself

Think of where you could set up frontline Customer-centric Circles. Who should be in it? What should be the agenda? What are the follow-up steps, and who has responsibility for it? Who will look for low-hanging fruits? Who will call the next meeting and review what was discussed and the results?

Think of how to set up Customer Circles in various departments like IT and HR. See how they become Customer-centric.

What is your Customer's Bill of Rights? Can you build one?

Can you embark on a Continuous Customer Improvement Program? How will you ensure ideas are cross fertilized?

How does the CCIP look at the Customer Experience, the Customer Journey, and CRM? How can you reduce the Customer Journey?

When you solve a new problem or a different problem for a Customer, do you think this is possibly important for other Customers or could cause them problems? If so, what can we do to prevent these from happening?

What can we do to move towards Zero Complaints?

* * *

Value of Belonging: The Orphaned Customer

Often, I have written about anonymous customers (anonymous because companies do not know them, nor do they make an effort to view their many customers as individuals) and the difficulty of customers in trying to reach anonymous executives. The section resonated with many people that had had difficulty in contacting executives and getting problems solved.

Today I wish to reflect on another aspect of this Customer neglect (or you can call it disregard, inattention, or lack of care).

Take a major Direct to Home TV company (part of India's largest group) that is considered customer focused within the group, but outside the group is thought of as pedestrian. Times of India called them DTH Sigh!

Recently, they were trying to extract more capacity from their satellites. This caused certain channels to go blank. The convenience of the company (maybe they would save costs, read increased profit) came ahead of the convenience of the customers (the convenience of the customers was to be told about the glitch and keeping them in the loop). Television is important to people and they were forced to miss their favourite serial or show with whom they have a sense of belonging and continuity.

The DTH company could have easily broadcast a message to their customers on their TVs. They do this for bill reminders. Here is a case of a company that converted known customers into anonymous ones (we don't know you, they seemed to say).

And then when customers tried to reach them, they were unreachable, because they could not respond to so many people. These calls would have been reduced if they had reached out to customers. One executive told me they thought this was an overnight problem, but actually it took 3 or 4 days to fix. Hell, they could have reached out on day 2 if not on day 1. Or even on day 3.

To me, this is a case of not letting or wanting the customer to belong to a company.

Humans want to belong to or be associated with: a group (religious, political, school, charity, travel), a social organization (Facebook, LinkedIn, college groups, user groups), a product or company, and their family and friends.

Belonging means acceptance as a member. A sense of belonging is a human need, just like the need for food and shelter. Feeling that you belong is most important in seeing value in companies. That is why, company or brand communities like the Harley riders or the wine tasters' group are important. A sense of belonging is important for loyalty creation.

Take your friends or classmates. At some time, there is great interaction and a need for each other. As you leave college, you still think of your friends. Over time, your necessity for the classmate reduces. In a time of difficulty, you might reach out to them again. If they do not respond, you start to drop them. If they respond, it reinforces your friendship.

This is precisely what happens with the customers' association with a company. While buying or first using a product, they need close contact, and as time goes on, they need less interaction with the company. But the moment a problem arises, they expect the company to be there. This is part of the belonging syndrome. And when the company is not available or responsive at this crucial moment, the customer feels let down, and his sense of belonging is affected.. This fits in with Peppers and Rogers's[1] Trustability idea.

And when they are not responded to, customers feel orphaned. They look elsewhere for support.

At the end of the day, people like to connect with things that are really personal to them, says Carla Hassan, CMO of Pepsi. And anxiety, frustration, and not belonging are certainly personal.

Ranjay Gulati of Harvard wrote that companies fall into a competency trap and focus on what they are good at and not what the customer wants. This is why they find it difficult to change. MBA schools teach students to be efficient and good administrators. But they do not teach any real customer or customer value or value creation courses.

Steve DiGioia, a Customer Service Coach (author of *The "Go-To Guy"*), says he has found, time and time again, that along the "ladder of success" comes a withdrawal from the frontline of customer service. As one gets higher in the chain of command, he/she gets lower in the concern of the customer experience and what it's like to be the individual actually responsible for "serving the guest." Numbers, budgets, and marketing take the lead over all else. But, what about the customer?

I say to Steve they must have priorities more important than the customer priority (I couldn't think of one except the ingrained training that profit is God, and not the customer).

---

[1] https://www.businesswire.com/news/home/20120426005497/en/Best-Selling-Authors -and-Thought-Leaders-Peppers-and-Rogers-Publish-Ninth-Book-Extreme-Trust-Honesty -as-a-Competitive-Advantage

Do not be anonymous to the customer. Add value to him by being available when he needs you. Make your company his family/partner in times of his need. Make him belong. Build a relationship. If you, as an executive think through this, you will find a way to keep him in your fold and add value to him and thereby to your company.

Leaders must use value to engender a sense of belonging to all stakeholders and customers.

* * *

Why "What's in It for Me" Can Kill Value Creation

I live in India (what I say about India holds for most countries). People suffer from the "What's in it for me" syndrome, which could be a manifestation of the results of poverty and deprivation (deprivation does not have to be monetary. It can be a lack of love and caring when growing up, it could be lack of attention from teachers etc.), latent selfishness or self-centredness, or it could be just suspicious thinking … what is this person trying to get from me? It could also be a sign of poor self-belief and self-esteem that someone can take away my importance by offering or asking for something. For some, it is an inbuilt filter to look at new requests or changes.

I am not implying that people are selfish, but this could be the first test they use on a new idea or suggestion or request or anything new. "What's in it for me" is a natural tendency for people. But when it becomes a defence mechanism, a way to say no, a closing of one's mind, then we have to work on it and create value for people guided by this question.

This is not to say this ("What's in it for me") is not a worldwide phenomenon, but there seems to be, in many societies, an openness and curiosity to listen to something new and perhaps develop it somewhat more.

"What's in it for me" could also be a manifestation of a desire to seek more value and avoid poor value offerings. It is a combination of what you might get and what you give. Different countries and different people have a different sense of value. Value is subjective and so different to various people.

I deal with many people. Many are takers. Others are willing to give so that they can take. Fewer are just givers. I come across givers, and they do not seem to have a "What's in it for me" attitude. This could be because that is their nature. Or that they have developed from being givers and takers to just givers. I would imagine I would fall into the latter category, as compared to when I was much younger. Remember, giving is a sign of creating value.

Most companies and most of us give so that we can take, or extract. There is nothing wrong with it as long as you do not just take without giving or giving a proportionate amount.

Companies and many people give so that they can get something in return, to create something so as to extract a reward. You give something to a customer or an employee and hopefully take away more than you give (which is profit or a warm fuzzy feeling). When "What's in it for me" is accompanied by a giving attitude, it can be positive and can create value. Giving without any "What's in it for me" is the best giving.

The message business gurus such as Robert E. Quinn[1] states is to have a purpose.

Having a purpose can alleviate the "What's in it for me" thinking. It can make you more efficient in looking at new propositions and ideas, reducing wasted time. The more you think your time is wasted the more you will hide behind the "What's in it for me" thought.

Garrett Gunderson[2] says the same thing and adds that do not play to win, and he says in Forbes, Purpose = Value and Value = Profits. Stop playing to win is the start of giving first and not taking first. When you do this, you stop asking "What's in it for me" as the first question.

Giving and not thinking of taking is a cornerstone of Value Creation. In my life many people have helped and supported me without any expectation … I do not want to single out anyone because I will miss many who did the same. All of you can remember those who gave to you, their time, their advice, or other things, ungrudgingly and generously.

Faisal Hussain,[3] CEO of Synechron Inc. in Huffington Post, discussed why an exit-only strategy kills the creation of value and that is why he said no to a $250 M buy-out.

That is why many start-ups and their investors learn to give (and bleed) so that they can eventually take.

Ask, for example, what most business lawyers are taught to do. They tend to take or extract for their client without much thought of a give and take. Business people have to step in to do this. I had a colleague and a lawyer, when I worked at Continental Can. He thought of give and take and not just about extraction and that is why he became a successful businessman and, later, Chairman and CEO of Crown Cork and Seal.

Reduction of the "What's in it for me" syndrome could be through education (educating to think beyond oneself) to change attitude; it could be incorporating a learning culture, a culture of awareness and anticipation, and one of

---

[1] https://robertequinn.com/

[2] https://www.forbes.com/sites/garrettgunderson/2020/02/15/purposevalue-valueprofits/?sh=6bfcdf08496d

[3] https://www.linkedin.com/pulse/four-pieces-advice-entrepreneurs-tomorrow-post-faisal-husain/

sharing. It is overcoming the curse of knowing it all or knowledge that prevents people from learning and creating value.

What we find is that most people who transcend the "What's in it for me" syndrome are value creators. Leaders for example start as managers and problem solvers, but as leaders, while they continue to solve problems they have to come up with better methods and culture to not worry about the self or to put self-interest ahead of the common good. An example is a CEO who knows he will be rewarded based on quarterly results. He is safe with that. But when he ignores that to seek long-term gains for his company, he may be chastized by the owners.

For us to create such value, we have to assume our customers have the "What's in it for me" syndrome and get to answer that question and how their wellbeing can be enhanced by our offering or how our offering can create value for them.

People seek value for themselves and if marketers can answer the "What's in it for me" question they can create value for such people. Focus on not only their wants but their true needs, and what will benefit them.

Leaders can learn too from understanding the people who are working for them better through understanding the "What's in it for me" syndrome.

* * *

What Does Being Secure Have to Do with Creating Value?

You know people who are secure and others who are insecure. There are many people with low self-esteem.

Security comes from the way you have been treated as a child. But your sense of security and self-esteem can suffer or be enhanced at work.

People who are insecure or have low self-esteem are less likely to create value for themselves, their colleagues, Customers, and for their companies.

Hierarchical companies tend to be feudal and kill security and self-esteem. They tend to cultivate followers rather than leaders or risk takers, or even Value Creators.

When we try to build Customer Value, we find two things are important. These are the pro-activeness of the employees and the sense of ownership of the employee of the Customer. Both these are related to security, self-esteem, and how companies nurture these and employees.

To build the nurturing or developing process, we start Customer Circles (or Customer-centric Circles) in companies. The idea came from quality circles. What we found was that a Continuous Customer Improvement Program (CCIP) became a necessity to foster Customer Value and Value Creation. Customer Circles, typically consist of frontline employees, with some staff people in them, from IT, HR, finance etc. These circles meet once a month or two and discuss what employees should do to create value for the Customer and build a CCIP and try to reach zero complaints.

When we started these Customer Circles, we found that the employees were neutral about being in them. Often, they thought this was a waste of time. They had been told what to do from birth. Mother said drink your milk, eat spinach, or wash behind your ears. Do not put your hand into the cookie jar, do your homework etc., the teacher said, stand up and say Good morning teacher, or stand in the corner, or recite your multiplication tables and so on and on. And then you joined work. Not only did you have to follow the looks and clothes (uniform), and culture, but you were told what to do. Visit three Customers today. So even if you had time to visit a fourth Customer, most would duck the opportunity. Not my job became an inherent characteristic.

And suddenly people like me were asking these people to be pro-active and take charge of the Customers.

So, they looked at us, some suspiciously, and others quizzically. We talked about Customers, and we got stony responses.

When we asked about what they thought of Customers, the answers were non-committal. We then asked them to relate cases when Customers made them happy or unhappy. The unhappy answers came first. Customers are irrational, they get mad for nothing. And we walked through examples of why their Customers got mad, and they started to see that it was due to some acts of omission or commission committed by the employee or the company ... For example, Customer service people visiting Customer's homes said the Customer got angry because they were late and kept the Customer waiting, or they had brought the wrong equipment, or come unprepared for the job. The frontline employees started to see why Customers got mad. And the support employees noticed that they had not given the address properly or the landmarks or the Customer's telephone numbers, or what the Customer really expected from the service people. When employees started to see why the Customer was mad, they were able to devise ways of avoiding making Customers mad, and in fact how they could have made the Customer happy.

The support staff also started to take note of how the frontline person was taking a beating, often because of the inadequacies of the support staff.

The employees then start to examine why Customers are sometimes happy. What did the employees do to make them happy? So, they build the Customer DNA (Do Not Annoy) and delight factors.

And then, when asked what they would like to do to make the Customers happy, the employees come up with great ideas. Letting them enunciate their ideas, and running with them builds their self-esteem. This is followed by an awareness of the Customer. Pro-activeness follows, because they feel more secure and in control.

I have built a personal relationship with many companies, insurance, travel, and white goods. I feel secure dealing with them knowing they will respond and help me. It causes me to be loyal to their companies.

The trick for management and leaders is to create this environment so that employees can feel secure, take control, become aware, get a sense of ownership, understand, Create, and Deliver Value. Make customers feel secure, too. Your comments are welcome!

* * *

Creating Value, Value Co-creation, and Value Destruction

Value has different meanings, and often is seen as economically related to price, cost, profits, and shareholder wealth. Value is actually doing good or improving the wellbeing and worth of people or businesses or institutions. Value encompasses all stakeholders, such as employees, environment and partners.

Values have to do with attitudes and what one has been born with or taught as a child: honesty, integrity, charity, beliefs in God, morality etc.

Value destruction is a characteristic defined in Value Dominant Logic.[1] VDL looks at value creation, co-creation, destruction, and co-destruction.

Peter Stokes et al.[2] say value is generally destroyed by allowing unfair or one-sided creation and wasteful or useless activities and behaviours to prevail. Simple examples can be found here – reading unimportant emails, behaving illegally or immorally, cheating or being unfair, misusing resources, over-staffing, unnecessary travel, and many such examples found in contemporary organizations. All such events represent value-destroying activities and it requires discipline to ensure that they do not permeate an organization. Gautam Mahajan's 2016 model[3] (Figure 1.3) summarizes the dimensions and stakeholders of value creation and their likely impacts in various regards.

Value creation is a global issue and impacts every facet of our lives: economics health, wellbeing, zoology, geography, and education are all affected and can become more effective by creating value for their stakeholders, whether students or practitioners. Examples could be salespeople or politicians using VDL to build their relationships.

---

[1] https://www.amazon.in/Value-Dominant-Logic-Individuals-Companies/dp/0367030578
[2] Stokes, P., Mahajan, G., Lucas, G. J., & Hughes, P. (2018). Creating value: value co-creation and value destruction. Global Focus - the EFMD Business Magazine, 12(2), 44-47.
[3] https://www.amazon.in/Value-Creation-Definitive-Business-Response/dp/9351508978

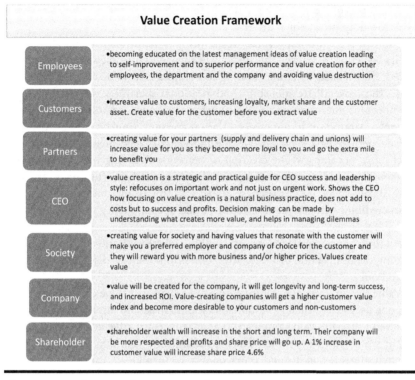

Figure 1.3   Value Creation Framework

The *BS 76000:2015 Human Resource – Valuing People – Management System – Requirements and Guidance* standard produced by the British Standards Institution shows that value is being recognized. This British Standard provides a framework for an organization to create an individually tailored management system, or to align existing systems, to realize the full value (actual or potential) that people provide to the organization through their capabilities, knowledge, skills, networks, experience, behaviours, and attitudes (British Standards Institution, 2015).

I have often discussed when and how and at what specific point value might be created. I believe that value exists around us and is waiting to happen and then fructify or emerge. The value potential has first to be noticed before it can really be created. A classic example is a driverless car: the value it offers existed but was not noticed or taken seriously for a long time by most of us.

After this, value is created in many associated fields, like the sale of driverless cars, financing and insurance, repair and infrastructure necessary; all potential areas of creating more value and for different people and entities. Value is destroyed for professional drivers,

You can see the complex inter-relationship dynamics between a new idea, and its becoming a reality. This new value engenders a whole series of product-related, firm-related dynamics leading to complex and value creating relationships. Thus, overall, relationships and relational dynamics within firms and networks plus inter-dynamics between firms, customers, and other stakeholders emerge as paramount in notions of value co-creation. Implicit in these dynamics, and perhaps less explored, are the individually held beliefs and attitudes which must accompany any creation or perception relating to value creation. Other ways of adding value creation are between the firm, customers, and the firm's stakeholders and encompass empathy, compassion, authenticity, enjoyment, credibility, honesty, empowerment, and accountability to mention but a few.

All this changes and develops our thinking on creating and adding value and avoiding the destruction of value. This comes from the 8As discussed elsewhere in this book.

Value also impacts our thinking on price as part of a value creation process , Also one uses values such as sustainability and fairness to improve value. Thus, we have to measure value and learn that as you create value and you get value, part of which you can extract. Thus spending time and money on improving the environment, and air and water quality in turn create value for the company, and so is not a one-way street. Measurement plays a powerful role and my people and I have learnt to measure value for and to a firm and to and from the environment.

Many unintended consequences can create or destroy value. My work on the plastic PET bottle created value for consumers and was more valuable than glass bottles but had the unintended consequence and value destruction due to plastic waste.

Unintended value creation can occur due to e-distance learning reaching far-flung villages in sub-Saharan Africa to Mongolia, causing great value creation for these kids. It can occur due to COVID, where digitalization and work from home accelerated.

Value creation has to be at the core of the business and human endeavour.

Note, that part of this writing appears in:

Creating value: Value co-creation and value destruction

Partly taken from: *Peter Stokes, Gautam Mahajan, Gerardus JM Lucas,* and *Paul Hughes*

https://globalfocusmagazine.com/creating-value-value-co-creation-and-value-destruction/

* * *

From Value Grabbing to Value Creating: Lesson for Leaders

Delivering Happiness, Giftivism, and Conscious Capitalism all have common messages, one of which is "Give Forward." That is, you create value for someone, often without thinking of a reward. When companies start to understand that they have a greater purpose than just making profits, they move from being value grabbers to becoming Value Creators. They realize the company's purpose is to give to society and the world.

I remember when I came back to India after living in the USA for around 20 years, I was deeply capitalistic. A good friend, an industrialist asked me for some ongoing help, and I suggested we first negotiate what I would get paid. Everything was measured in dollars and cents.

A few weeks later, I went to meet a famous lawyer about helping me with a case. He said he would. I asked him what his fees would be. He got angry. He said I know your family and your grandfather and that he attended my wedding and I cannot take money from you.

I walked out quite dazed and chastened. I appreciated there was something called *Lihaz* (respect and consideration for others, having a concern, and being considerate) in the Indian world.

The lawyer had given it without any expectation from me. He got in me an admirer and a well-wisher in return.

And I learnt also to give forward, without expecting something in return. And it is a satisfying experience.

This lesson is easier for individuals to accept. But when you make a corporate inanimate, it can only think in dollars and cents. But corporates are humans hiding behind the anonymity of the company, and humans trying to be tough and only concerned about profits.

Harvard Business School's Professor, Brian J. Hall calls this Paying Forward. Pavi Mehta in Giftivism echoes the same and gives wonderful examples of giving without expecting returns or anything in return (see https://www.youtube.com/watch?v=p_QLGvp_stI). Brian Hall calls this Value Creating Behaviour and he goes on to say this is a requisite for successful leadership. Winning leaders have a Value Creation mindset where they do good turns on behalf of the organization without expecting any returns.[1]

Value Creation by definition increases value and there is more to go around and share. The pie gets smaller or is shared by fewer when leaders are value grabbers, people who are trying to maintain their place in the organization by any means.

---

[1] https://www.forbes.com/sites/hbsworkingknowledge/2014/09/10/be-a-value-creator-not-a-value-claimer/?sh=60bd163e5501

Value Creators also create happiness, and they share credit and profits. They tend to be team players and work for the team.

Value grabbers tend to be value destroyers in the long run. I remember when I worked with the University of Wisconsin to set up a campus in India, most Indian Professors at Wisconsin were motivated by what they could get out of a campus in India, rather than the fact that an India Campus would create value all around, for the State of Wisconsin, for the university and its stakeholders, and for India and Indian youth. By being value seekers, they played a negative role.

Such people tend to be secretive, they get a sense of security by keeping their knowledge to themselves and not sharing it, because they fear they will lose out or others will become smarter than them. They destroy value. And those who share knowledge encourage people to grow and act as catalysts; those who teach people how to apply knowledge and create value are winners.

And this is true in negotiations. The "I must win at any cost" thinking, the thought of having it all and not leaving anything on the table are value grabbing syndromes.

Conscious Capitalism suggests companies should make the world a better place. Blatant denuding of the earth of its resources for short-term gain (like the illegal mining in the State of Haryana, in India; or the cheating in getting telecom licences in India, or in getting an illegal advantage in coal mining leases; or in the mortgage crisis in the US born of greed) is value and resource grabbing. Large-scale value destruction occurs as a result. Conscious companies or conscious executives will not participate in value grabbing.

Pavi Mehta tells of her family's charitable Arvind Eye Foundation, and eye care hospitals, where every patient is treated equally. His ability to pay has no bearing on the treatment. Everyone pays what they want to or can.

Pavi talks about restaurants where this happens. Your meal is paid for and whatever you want to give for the meal is used to feed someone else. This concept is called paying forward.

Paul Polman of Unilever states that companies with a purpose beyond profits tend to create more shareholder wealth in the long run and have less fluctuation in share prices in the short run. Firms of Endearment,[1] (a term coined by Raj Sisodia, David Wolfe, and Jagdish Sheth), tend to have a purpose and practice Conscious Capitalism and have 14 times greater returns than S&P companies, and 6.4 times the returns of Good to Great companies in 15 years.

---

[1] www.amazon.in/Firms-Endearment-World-Class-Companies-Passion/dp/0131873725

McKinsey in their article on Redefining Capitalism[1] argues that Capitalism has served the world well and has led to growth. However, CEOs and investors are at a crossroad today. Should the role of the business be to make money or advance the good for society? They conclude *the essential role of capitalism is not allocation—it is creation. Prosperity in a society is the accumulation of solutions to human problems.* Ultimately, the measure of the wealth or wellbeing of a society is the range of human problems it has solved and how available it has made those solutions to its people.

Thus, argues, McKinsey, instead of celebrating wealth, we should celebrate innovative solutions to human problems. I would argue, that if done well, the creation of wealth is another result of doing the right things for society and other stakeholders and creates value.

Shareholder value is a result and a measure of how leaders work, not a goal. Such Value Creating leaders create happiness, not just profits, and are greatly successful.

* * *

Is Value Co-creation Always Necessary

Much has been written by experts on value co-creation. Some believe that without co-creation value cannot be provided.

I have a view which is similar to my view on other items. For example, customer experience is not always necessary for value. A journey is not always desired by a customer, so why put him on a journey? Co-creation in my view is not important in many cases, and in some cases, it is extremely important. I have divided co-creation possibilities into four quadrants. The first quadrant is the best for co-creation. The value creation interactiveness is high and so is the product/service experience. The worst is the third quadrant where the product/service experience is low and the value co-creation interactiveness is low.

Below is my matrix on Value Co-creation (Figure 1.4).

Top left quadrant: let me start with the top left box, which is the case for items/services for normal use. Many items are used in a routine, normal fashion. These include salt, soap, and a smartphone for a lay user such as myself. I just want these to work to my satisfaction, and I do not desire interaction with someone in your company. Many of us fall into this category.

---

[1] https://www.google.com/search?q=Redefining+Capitalism+(written+by+Eric+Beinhocker +and+Nick+Hanauer&oq=Redefining+Capitalism+(written+by+Eric+Beinhocker+and+Ni ck+Hanauer&aqs=chrome..69i57.54720j0j4&sourceid=chrome&ie=UTF-8

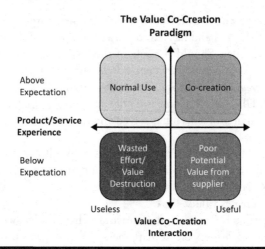

Figure 1.4   The Value Co-Creation Paradigm

Lesson for the supplier of service or product:

1. Make it simple to understand and use (the user should not need to find a knife to open a soap packet, or find a button on a smartphone or put a sim card of a different size into the phone [a micro sim to be put into a normal sim slot or have multiple chargers for multiple phones])
2. Let it work as intended (my smartphone pushes the turn-on image for an incoming call into a small inset on top of the phone, which I cannot easily enlarge, and so I have to go through gymnastics to answer a call. I know some of you are sniggering because you don't have this problem, but those unlucky fellow creatures who have this problem are saying, give us a fix [which requires us to go into the bottom left quadrant, and be made to do a useless task. This is not co-creation; it is the destruction of value])
3. Do not make the user do unnecessary work when using your product (the above is an example)
4. Let the product/service not let the user down (the salt has coagulated in the packet and does not pour easily or my instant coffee from a flexi bag has completely powdered finely from the granules you find in bottles, and the coffee does not taste that good)
5. Make it easy for the user to contact an intelligent person if the user is unhappy or has an idea (so now you have a problem, whom do you complain to? My salt has coagulated. The call centre guy responds, but it is not supposed to …. You idiot customer, how did you let it coagulate … Maybe this lot was chemically different [it cannot be, says the call centre person].

Your option is to throw the salt away and re-buy and find a place in your refrigerator [but first make sure the salt will be ok in the refrigerator. You don't know, but you know you should not put the salt in the refrigerator, but you have no choice. You poor sap, you are only a customer])

Bottom left quadrant: my next quadrant is the bottom left quadrant, which you wish to avoid, but are forced to journey to when you have a problem, and you meet or talk to a company person who knows it all and cannot understand why you are a moron. The soap wrapping is easy to open, and you have spent time in the shower using your teeth to open it. The company guy says you fool you are not supposed to use your teeth ... and you say it did open and he says but it does not need your teeth ....

Lessons for the company:

1. No customer is stupid enough to want to talk to you
2. He must have a genuine problem
3. There must be something wrong or there is room for improvement in your product or service
4. Listen
5. Do not make the customer feel like an idiot

Bottom right quadrant: This is the quadrant which can be used for highlighting problems, getting innovative fixes, in co-creating a better mouse trap ... I had a conversation with LinkedIn that I could not get my California contacts. I was told that they would help and came back saying there was a problem and they would fix it. Now California works, but New Jersey does not.

My wife just got 250 emails from Bharat Matrimony saying she is a registered member. Everyone is introducing himself to her as a potential suitor. The registered member is Radhika and not my wife whose name starts with a V ... There is no way to contact them and to unsubscribe, and the messages keep coming ... Ugh! I have this problem with a big bank. Some guy who has an email ID like gm@yahoo.com has put his address as gm@gmail.com and I keep getting his emails. I cannot make this go away. Help!

1. While you had an opportunity to help in the other quadrants, this is the one you can co-create in and make friends. Take this opportunity to shine (P&G would call it Connect and Develop)
2. You can get ideas not only for improvements but for other products and service
3. So, take the customer seriously and have innovative, knowledgeable, friendly helpful people service him
4. Do not make this a value destruction opportunity

Top right quadrant: here is a real co-creation opportunity, for you to develop a better cell phone (for example, I would like a better search facility that covers the address and the notes. So, if I remember you as Jane's husband, and I have Jane in the contact notes, I want to be able to find this contact).

Or I want my text messages to be easily storable, or I want to get back contacts inadvertently deleted (why can't there be a cache), and I want all my text messages to appear, or I want my call log to be stored let's say on the net so I can pull out the messages I made in Beijing four months ago. I do not want to toggle the on–off switch when I cannot activate an incoming call. Everyone will benefit, though most accept the phone for what it is.

1. Look for opportunities to improve
2. How can you make it easier for me to use your product and love it?
3. How can you co-create disruptive and creative elements?

Friends, companies have an immense possibility to distinguish themselves … but they don't. They end up antagonizing the customer no end, whereas they could make him/her their friend, learn from them and develop, and co-create with them.

Overall, leaders:

Avoid destruction
Seek co-creation opportunities
All opportunities do not mean co-creation

Are you laughing at me or are you with me? (Moshe Davidow commented he was crying with me).

* * *

The Value Co-creation Platform

Welcome to the Platform Economy.

The Value Co-Creation model has been in place for some time, yet most companies have not adopted this powerful way of differentiating themselves.

Early movers were the likes of FedEx who allowed Customers to check the status of packages themselves, without having to contact someone in the company. This created great value (ease of use, sharing of the workload with the customer, putting the customer in control etc.) And the value was co-created for FedEx, as they did not need to have staff to answer status questions.

Others have tried similar approaches, such as setting up service calls, but generally these have not worked well, because tracking of service people is not part of this platform. Imagine if you could track the service person and interact with him. Often problems can be solved without a visit. A platform would help, for delivery, information, and real-time tracking.

Companies that are successful in co-creation understand that co-creation is not managed by the company, but by equal partners in co-creation. So, putting the customer in control or equal control works best. Often co-creation requires the company, the distribution system (or the supply or delivery chain), and the customer to partner in the co-creation of value and ease of doing business.

This requires a change of traditional business practices and models. This is particularly true for and applicable to companies that have moved from being owners to co-creators of value. They have designed platforms where they (take companies like Airbnb, Uber, LinkedIn, Facebook, Amazon) allow customers, service providers, and themselves to connect, interact, innovate, and co-create value and success for each other. These are C2C (Customer to Customer), B2C (Business to Customer), and B2B (Business to Business) all on one platform.

So, we need to look at our business and see how we can set up a co-creation platform, and from the platform connect ourselves to the supplier and the customer. Are we willing to let go? Are we willing to let go of control and our traditional thinking?

The first step is to think about and set up a platform and then make it work.

The easiest platform to form is a co-innovation platform, where the designers and customers can interact. This, of course, involves a small part of your customer base.

This is really an idea generation model that can be refined into a more operational model and result-oriented model.

More complex are sales platforms such as Amazon, where the supplier can participate in the sales (his delivery and guarantees), by customers co-creating confidence in the product through ratings, and co-creating the future requirements of the supplier and the customer. Customers create value for each other, the company for the supplier and the customer, and so on.

So, connect your Customers, and let them "talk" in some way by experiences. So a pesticide company may put in likes and dislikes or ratings of the product, by just punching in a number at the suppliers, or on the platform.

Next help them discuss issues (again this may only mean a rating system) or help each other by suggesting which concentration of the pesticide was best for you. Or what is the best storage method?

Thus, this network of people helps you build customers and connect to them and co-create. Your digital infrastructure should be designed to allow people to participate and co-create.

Next, try to automate your processes and the way people can co-create.

Lastly, measure value and use the platform for continuous value measurement.

It is not just the platform; it is your co-creation of value thinking that is important. You have to rethink your strategy for the product, manufacturing, inventory, distribution, customer interface, and the like and build your digital infrastructure.

GE and Microsoft are making this transition and so should you. Moshe Davidow adds most companies are looking for ways to cut costs and be more efficient. The flip side is it makes it more difficult for the company to solve a higher-order problem (employees are trained only to handle basic complaints. Hopefully, GE and Microsoft can dodge this problem).

Here is an opportunity for companies and leaders to design a value creation and continuous measurement platform for their companies and commercialize this platform to make money.

* * *

Wellbeing and Value Creation: Are They Two Sides of a Coin?

> The GNP (Gross National Product) does not allow for the health of our children, the quality of their education or the joy of their play. It does not include the beauty of our poetry or the strength of our marriages; the intelligence of our public debate or the integrity of our public officials ... it measures everything, in short, except that which makes life worthwhile.
>
> *Robert Kennedy, 1968*

Many countries are looking at wellbeing as a goal, for the country and its people and for education. Japan has set this goal for 2030. India in its 2017 health policy and agenda for 2030 stresses wellbeing.

According to the Oxford Dictionary, "wellness" is "the state of being healthy," especially when you actively try to achieve this. Wellbeing, on the other hand, is considered "general health and happiness, a state of emotional/physical/psychological wellbeing." Wellness is an essential feature of wellbeing. Unfortunately, many authors refer to wellness as being wellbeing. Wellness looks at physical health.

Kai Ruggeri of Columbia University states in a paper,[1] Wellbeing has been defined as the combination of feeling good and functioning well; the experience of positive emotions such as happiness and contentment as well as the development of one's potential, having some control over one's life, having a sense of

---

[1] https://hqlo.biomedcentral.com/articles/10.1186/s12955-020-01423-y

purpose, and experiencing positive relationships. It is a sustainable condition that allows the individual or population to develop and thrive and cope with stress.

Generally, we look at physical wellbeing, financial wellbeing, career wellbeing, social wellbeing, and community wellbeing.

Wellbeing is measured by various factors such as happiness and even economic surrogates such as GDP. Bhutan, for example, measures Gross Domestic Happiness. Wellbeing is also judging life positively and feeling good.

Wellbeing encompasses many different elements. This includes positive emotions, such as happiness, joy, contentment, excitement, wonder, and calmness. It also includes good physical health and positive, meaningful social relationships and connections. The latter is what constitutes social wellbeing (quoting Jenna Sinclair in 2021).[1]

If wellness is physical health, wellbeing is a mindset. In life it is easier to do functional things than to change mindsets. In business, functional work is easier to change than changing mindsets. Thus, conducting HR or marketing exercises is easier than changing the mindset from thinking profits is the most important part of a business to improving the wellbeing of the company's stakeholders.

Wellbeing helps people to function better, be more productive, be better in learning and creativity, and be better socially. Higher wellbeing can lead to longer life, and physical health, and people with wellbeing seem happier.

Miwa Nishinaka, Kagawa University, states there are differences in wellbeing. One is personal wellbeing, which, in a narrow sense, is a state where humans can exercise their potential. The other is social wellbeing, which, in a limited sense, is a social state where you can have opportunities to seize personal happiness, and that state is guaranteed for the future.

Nishinaka shows differences in these types of wellbeing. She gives examples of conflicts of interest that exist between social wellbeing and personal wellbeing, such as a waste incinerator being necessary for society, but not wanting it in your neighbourhood. And conflicts between social wellbeing are things like endangered species that need protection are living in a proposed dam site.

Where does value fit into all this? Many wellbeing gurus suggest wellbeing improves the value people perceive. To me value and wellbeing are similar, perhaps two sides of the same coin, as the definition of value creation is:

Creating value is executing normal, conscious, inspired, and even imaginative actions that increase the overall good and wellbeing, and the worth of and for ideas, goods, services, people, or institutions including society, and all stakeholders (like employees, customers, partners, shareholders, environment, and society), and value waiting to happen.

---

[1] https://www.betterup.com/blog/what-is-social-well-being-definition-types-and-how-to-achieve-it

That is why our parents teach us to be good kids and to do good. But this is soon overtaken by the goal of making a living, of being successful.

This definition shows that creating value is meant to do good and improve the wellbeing of people. Wellbeing people say it increases the value that people perceive.

Obviously, there is a difference between wellbeing and value. Both are perceptions. Value created is felt as something positive and changes as the value changes. Wellbeing is a state of being and feeling and is a result of value creation and changes. As value is perceived, wellbeing and the end result are improved.

Thus, value and wellbeing are very closely related. One has to create value to improve wellbeing and improving wellbeing is valuable to us.

There is a connection between values and wellbeing. It has been shown that personal values such as honesty and integrity that one has can improve the sense of wellbeing.

Is value a proper way to measure wellbeing? Or should we be seeking a correlation between the two? Today we can say value creation leads to wellbeing, and improved wellbeing creates value.

Companies pursue growth, which is generally materialistic. Our sales went up from 1 million dollars to 2. Progress is measured by growth and ethics (discipline, morals, honesty, norms etc.). Success is progress along with humanity, morals, caring and improves wellbeing. Companies need to achieve wellbeing seen as a success.

Paraphrasing Leonard Sweet, the future is something we "create" actively, not something that "happens." Peter Drucker goes on to say the best way to predict the future is to create it. We have to keep creating value to improve wellbeing.

Thus a society seeking wellbeing as a goal, let's say in 2030, has to get its people education in value creation and humanity, moral and ethical mindset, and not train them just for functional work. Value creation has to be taught and people have to understand their role is to create value for the improved wellbeing of people and society. That means our education system has to educate, not merely train. It has to make value creation a way of life and to teach and give degrees in value creation as a means to improve wellbeing.

Leaders must improve wellbeing aka value.

Chapter 2

Value Creation Education

Example of Value Creation in Education: At the Michener Center, U of Texas, Austin

As many of you know, I have been writing about Value Creation in education. Much of the discussion has been generic. That the role of a teacher is to go beyond just imparting knowledge but to create value by showing the student how the knowledge is used by others, what they do with the knowledge, and how the student can use the knowledge and benefit from it and enhance his life and environment (employer, society etc.).

A few years ago, I had the privilege of witnessing this Value Creation in action. This was at the Michener Center at the University of Texas at Austin. The Michener Center has assembled brilliant talent in fiction, screenwriting, poetry, and playwriting. Students in the MFA (Master of Fine Arts) were graduating, and the graduating class spoke about their amazing, life-changing experiences.

The one thing all those graduating said was that the teachers and staff just gave and gave and the students just took and took. The giving was selfless. I wondered what value was being created for the teacher. Was it just satisfaction? Was it more, the pleasure of helping people become creative and successful? And I remembered my article that creative people did not need incentives for creating and helping others create value. Incentivization does not increase creative power but may create the environment (like the grants to the students). But the teachers were not incentivized by higher salaries for creating the value they did. They gave because that is the nature of secure and creative people to give and create more value, and to get satisfaction from doing a better job than others.

The students went on to talk about how their fellow students created value for each other by example, when they wrote or did something well; by witnessing the disappointment and disillusionment and the lows their fellow students experienced and helping each other to get going and try again; by giving emotional support. Much like what the teachers gave them.

The teachers gave them the enthusiasm, the secure environment, and the emotional strength to go through the winning and losing and helped them manage the emotional highs and lows. The staff gave them emotional support in their private lives, their special needs etc. and a sense of being part of a family and being at home.

But what was common was building a sense of security in the students, when they felt insecure, inadequate, and unable to cope, or unable to find that whiff of genius that could help them with a flow of brilliance, and happiness.

What struck me were the enormous emotional bonds that the students had formed with the teachers and their fellow students, their gratefulness to them. Many cried, as they related their story of growing at the Michener Center.

I had written earlier about the need to be secure to create value. Insecurity can come from when you are growing up or in your work or personal environment. And so, the teachers and staff created the environment for fostering talent and security.

One teacher told me that the students were inherently talented, and the teacher's role was to make the student use their talent and grow. An environment of trust, belonging, self-belief, relying on colleagues, and helping each other (creating value for each other), by building emotional strength and bonds helped the students rise to their inherent abilities. And that is what the teachers did. They also helped the students to unlearn so that they could learn faster.

And the importance of unlearning and learning and unlearning.

So, this is an example of Value Creation in education by teachers and students, and how you too can create value.

It is not incentives! It is not self-aggrandizement that makes creative teachers create value. The students too will realize that their creativity will flow despite incentives or lack of it … and as they grow, they will find that if they can create value for their readers, by getting them to learn, or to get an emotional bond with the writer, or making the readers feel good about themselves. Then the writer will become even more successful.

As one teacher said, when you leave, walk backwards so that it appears you are coming in. Or that you are still with us and you belong.

And when you walk away, ask if it is the experience or the memory of the experience that was more important.

And if you as students and teachers consciously start to think of value creation as your role, you will find that all of you will enhance your offerings because now you have added yet another dimension to your creativity and work.

Will you, the student, become a value creator? Will you use the special ability the teachers helped you find and hone to become value creative writers?

With special thanks to some unusual value creators: Jim Magnuson, Elizabeth McCracken, Michael Adams (all of whom I met), and the other students and staff of the Michener Center, University of Texas, Austin.

This has also appeared in my book, Value Dominant Logic.

* * *

Creating Value with Knowledge

To create more value for yourself, you need to create knowledge that enlightens you, makes you do tasks more easily and efficiently, and makes you feel fulfilled. Some knowledge comes from experience, and sometimes from bad experiences or doing things wrong.

Sharing knowledge (and/or experience) which is meaningful to others creates value for others, and this process creates more value for you.

The process of building knowledge starts with:

Knowing you need knowledge
Seeking knowledge. Having awareness of knowledge around you
Sensing and noticing value[1]
Assimilating knowledge that comes your way
Storing such knowledge
Knowledge development. Raw knowledge may not be useful
Retrieving knowledge and sharing it
Enhancing knowledge
Understanding and seeking relevant technology and having a process of knowledge dissemination and sharing
Knowing and measuring knowledge assets
Protecting knowledge and avoiding fake knowledge
Teaching people how to use this knowledge, and determine if it is useful and true
Storing knowledge of processes and ideas that do not work
Avoiding useless or fake knowledge

For successful knowledge management, you need people, processes, content and IT, and strategy to have a proper knowledge flow. People need to know what is relevant

---

[1] From *Value of Values* by Swami Dayanand Saraswati.

to their needs and be able to access it. In due course, AI may become a useful tool for managing, assimilating, detecting, protecting, and disseminating knowledge.

But a very important part of seeking knowledge is to understand what your present and future needs are and how to get to them. Getting knowledge which is dated may not be useful. Dated knowledge may give you some satisfaction, but if you want to be at the cutting edge or are an innovator, you need the latest information, and more importantly what will happen in the future. Therefore, you have to be knowledgeable of the future and make future knowledge bets.

My friend, Prof. Youji Kohda, Dean of Knowledge Science, at Japan Advanced Institute of Science and Technology, adds,

> In the age of AI, knowledge has come to be produced from data. This became a new source of knowledge. But the knowledge produced from data represents the needs of the past and may not represent the needs of the present or future.

At the same time, AI may get predictive capabilities.

Therefore, you must know about technological breakthroughs, and trends and megatrends (all trends cannot be megatrends) in your area of expertise, follow them, and find a way of gaining and sustaining knowledge and value in these areas.

Lastly, your real competitive advantage apart from how you use the knowledge is how you source it. Chinese are past masters at this. Their diaspora and their scientists abroad form a long chain of knowledge gatherers. Many may be unconscious of this. Also, knowledge makes your offering strong if you understand the fundamentals and are fundamentally strong.

Early on my professional career required me to manage the collection of data and systems design for which we used minicomputers. We chose General Automation (GA) after gathering information because it had the best architecture and did not buy Data General or Digital Equipment (DEC). Consequently, when we had used GA minis for data gathering and system design, GA went out of business. Much of our knowledge about GA turned out to be useless. Much knowledge we had gained through experimentation and system design was rendered unusable. We had to buy DEC and restart but could use only part of our past knowledge for DEC systems design. We could also avoid certain programming and other pitfalls.

Prof. Youji Kohda comments the lessons from this example could be a lesson related to "knowledge transfer" (from General Automation computer to DEC computer). He adds, "Generally speaking, knowledge transfer is difficult to accomplish but helpful to make things happen." Knowledge transfer could be one source of competitive advantage.

For many companies, knowledge is a competitive advantage. We once sued a competitor and our former employee who had joined them not to work in competing areas. The competitor's lawyers insisted we reveal to the judge what we thought was proprietary knowledge. The judge demurred. He said the plaintiff (us) does not have to prove they have the knowledge to prevent you (the defendant) from using it. He said even knowledge of what not to do was valuable and proprietary. That is to say, when you are developing something (let's say a product or a device) or doing R&D, you may go down the wrong path which is not usable in the final development of the product or the device. Here your mistakes can save valuable time and money for your competitors if they knew what you learnt not to do.

To protect knowledge and know how, you have to take all possible steps to protect this valuable asset. Then and only then will the law give you protection.

This leads to what Prof Kohda calls knowledge non-transfer, or the knowledge to prevent the transfer of knowledge, and keeping a secret a secret! This becomes important in thinking about privacy, data, and knowledge protection.

Knowledge is an important part of value creation. It creates value for you. You can create value for others. By sharing your knowledge, you can create value for others or co-create it. Hiding knowledge and keeping it away from others can also destroy value. Overly secretive people are guilty of this.

> *Man in his ignorance … needs Knowledge to be visited by doubt, otherwise he would remain obstinate in an ignorant belief and limited knowledge and unable to escape from his errors.*
>
> Sri Aurobindo

* * *

Training vs. a Learning Mindset in Value Creation

> *Future is about creating value. If we have tools to empower each other, more possibility is reality.*
>
> Jessica Jackley

What we want to create is an H2H (Human to Human) environment in our company and with our customers and partners. This is the starting point of education.

Is it the mindset or the training that is more important to our Customers and in Value Creation?

While both are extremely important, I believe mindset changes are overlooked, not because they are not important, but because conventional training does not focus and indeed is not capable of changing mindsets. Often it is said training is for dogs (sit, bark, roll!) and education for human beings. Mindset changes are best impacted by self-introspection. Why do customers get angry? Why are they happy? What is my role in customer behaviour? Realistically, to change mindset, we must first build the self-esteem of people. Once we have done this, we will find they are more open to ideas. Then, we have to build their awareness, which will allow self-evaluation and self-improvement. After this, we can embark on a Continuous Customer Improvement Program (CCIP) led by front-facing employees, not executives. We also let the front-end employees examine the Customer's Bill of Rights. We ask them to comment on how they will ensure this will work and what support they need.

We can also use Mahajan's 8As explained elsewhere in this book: Awareness, Ability, Attitude, Agility, Anticipation, Adaptability, Ambidextrousness, and Action.

For educating and changing mindset, we start Customer Circles, which are led by front-facing employees working with Customers and on the CCIP (Continuous Customer Improvement Program). During the Customer Circle sessions, these employees will also figure out how to keep the promises made by the company and its Bill of Rights (and also by the employees). This leads to massive mindset changes and the taking over of ownership of the Customers by the employees. This also means a change of mindset of the bosses, to let go instead of always telling people what to do and training them. The bosses then let the employees tell them what the employees are going to do and what help they need from the bosses.

(As an aside, people are more likely than not told what to or not to do. As children, we are told not to reach for the cookie jar, we are told to wipe our faces, not to put our elbows on the table, not to talk with our mouths full, to eat the spinach, and so on and on. This continues in school, when teachers tell us to stand up and say "Good Morning, Teacher," or to do your homework. Being told what to do continues at work. Our boss says you will see four customers today. Why would you see a fifth Customer if you had time?)

As mindset changes occur, we also have to ensure that the employees understand the purpose and mission of the company and whether they understand the importance of and how the mission can guide them.

Earlier, I mentioned that for executives to work on mindset changes, they too have to change and learn to let go, and let the employees handle Customers. The executives have to learn that they have to stop directing and ordering (and saying thou shalt …) but actually provide a supportive platform for the employees to perform.

Another reason for not working on mindset changes is that we tend to manage what we measure … the tangibles. We have difficulty working on intangibles because we cannot measure them easily. We have to learn what is important to Customers, not measure only things that companies wish to measure.

What does a Customer want from a billing process? Accurate bills that are easy to correct if they are not accurate. What does a company wish to measure? Are the bills being paid, and past due payments. These do not measure the Customer's concerns. Worthwhile to measure is the percentage of wrong bills, and the percentage corrected in one call.

Chip Conley (founder of Joie de Vivre Hotels and author of *Emotional Equations*) uses the Maslow hierarchy to describe this. He believes Survival, Success, and Transform is the Maslow for the corporation. Transform leads to mindset changes. I believe at Customer Value Foundation, that success often means doing your job and Value Creation means going beyond your job to transform (Figure 2.1).

I have a number of stories of wonderful experiences in airlines and hotels and in other service renditions, and I also have a number of horrible stories. I am sure you the reader have similar great and horror stories. Why is there no consistency? Is it the training or the mindset? I believe with mindset changes, the number of horror stories will go away, and more delight will set in. The routine experience we get as Customers is based on training. But when there is a crisis, mindset has to creep in.

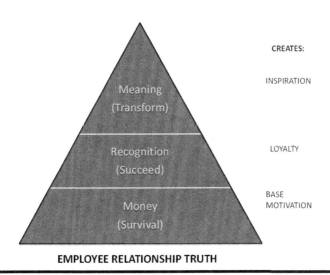

Figure 2.1   Employee Relationship Truth

On top of my horror stories is when employees feel that their role is to protect the company. The company is always right. And so, they lie. They say that (not in so many words) it is not our fault (implying it is the customer's fault). Horror stories include not wanting to help the customer, especially during crises hiding behind policies and rules. An example is when I was downgraded in Brussels on a flight from New York changing planes in Brussels for Delhi, I was told we do not know the rules for a partial refund for a downgrade! Or when we want your money for a flight, you have to pay at once (and no refunds), but when we have to refund, our rules are 30 days.

Don't companies know this is not right? Do they care or don't their mindsets allow them to change?

Customer service departments are trained to solve a customer's problem. When they solve a less-than-usual problem, their mindset does not allow them to initiate a systemic change so that future customers will not face the same issues. For example, with Tata Sky when you want to change an annual plan, you cannot do so without closing and reopening the account. Why can't their system allow the change of a set box serial number? For or without a fee?

But these companies feel they have a Customer-centric mindset, and the Customers do not agree. In fact, 56% of all companies feel they are Customer-centric and only 12% of Customers agree. Whose mindset needs to be changed?

One mindset I wish to change in companies is to get to Zero Complaints. Executives are "trained" to believe that Customers will always complain and so they cannot move to Zero Complaints (or at least attempt to get there). They are trained to forget they too are Customers, and training transforms them from being Customers and behave like and become executives! The executive mindset is often not a Customeric mindset. And if they start to think like Customers, the conversation they will have is Customer to Customer, not B2C.

Most of us will agree. It is true that the intangible of happy employees builds the tangible of business success. Moreover, while we cannot always make everyone happy, we can set the environment and mindset to try to make everyone happy.

What counts? H2H: human to human!

Chapter 3

Customer Value

What Is Customer Value and How Can You Create It?

220,740 views in Customer Think plus 27,529 downloads in 2021 at *Journal of Creating Value* alone

Value has many different meanings. To some value means price (what is the value of this car?), while to others it means benefit (the value I got from this car). It also means the worth of something. That is why you hear some people saying "value for money" (meaning they are price sensitive), and others who prefer "money for value" (meaning they are willing to pay for what they consider as benefits, as from a brand or a better product, or more convenience etc.)

The dictionary meaning of value includes: the regard that something is held, to deserve; the importance, worth, or usefulness of something. Synonyms are merit, worth, usefulness, use, utility, practicality, advantage, desirability, benefit, gain, profit, good, service, help, helpfulness, assistance, effectiveness, efficacy, avail, importance, significance, point, sense.

No wonder, the reader is confused about the value word that s/he uses so often. When used in the vernacular, it does not matter, but when used as a technical term, like Customer Value, the meaning of value must be precise, so that everyone understands what it means, as shown below:

Customer Value is the perception of what a product or service is worth to a Customer versus the possible alternatives. Worth means whether the Customer feels s/he got benefits and services over what s/he paid.

In a simplistic equation form, Customer Value is Benefits – Cost $(CV = B - C)$.

What the Customer pays includes not only price and associated costs (cash, cheque, interest, payment during use such as fuel and servicing for a car, maintenance charges) but also non-price terms such as time, effort, energy, and inconvenience.

The benefits include the advantages or quality of the product, service, image, and brand of the company or the brand of the product, values of the company, experience, success one gets in using the product, and so on.

Values are distinct from value (the plural of value as defined above is value). Values are what someone or a firm stands for honesty, morals, ethics, sustainability, integrity, trust.

Consumers are different from Customers. Consumers use the product or the service, but they may or not buy the product/service. The value the consumer perceives influences the buying evaluation and perception of the decision maker or the Customer. The Customer is someone who buys or makes the decision to buy. The Customer could be a non-consumer. I buy a medicine for my kid: I am the Customer, and the kid is the consumer. A Non-Customer is someone who could buy from us but is buying from someone else.

How Is Value Created and What Does It Do?

Value is created just as much by a focus on processes and systems as much as it is by mindset and culture. Mindset and culture are much more difficult to change, and also difficult to emulate. It is easier to copy processes and systems than to change mindsets and culture. Therefore, for long-term success, mindset and culture are important and lasting. These along with systems improvements create great experience and value.

Value changes during the use of a product or during the Customer Journey. Value is perceived during the purchase intent, the shopping, the actual purchase or buying, the installation or start-up, the use, and even the re-sale. We sometimes call this the waterfall of needs. Needs change during the Customer Journey.

Creating Customer Value increases customer satisfaction and the customer experience. (The reverse is also true. A good customer experience will create value for a Customer.) Creating Customer Value (better benefits versus price) increases loyalty, market share, and price, reduces errors, and increases efficiency. Higher market share and better efficiency lead to higher profits.

How to Create Real Value

You first have to understand the Customer Value concept, what a Customer perceives as value, how a customer's value needs change over time, and how to get

Customer feedback. You must realize that people buy a product or service that *creates the most value over competing options.*

You must know how the Customer views you, your products and benefits, and your competition and its products and benefits. What is important to the Customer in his buying decision? Is price more important or are benefits? Are you good at delivering what the Customer believes is important? Are you able to deliver more than your competition on these factors?

I understand these are general terms, but they will help you to create value as you understand your Customer's needs and perceptions better. Let us take some examples of how to create Customer Value:

1. Giving a price that makes the Customer believe he is getting more than he pays for: the benefits he gets versus competitive offers.
2. Reducing the price, or keeping the same price and giving something extra over competition (this could be service, better attention, an add-on to the product).
3. Making it convenient for the Customer to buy, and how he wants to buy and pay.
4. For B2B, getting a proper price justification, not just a price. Price justification is often more important than price itself.
5. For dealers, the feeling the company will grow and offer new products for the dealers to sell. These are things that the dealer may not have an experience with, but these create value for him.
6. The image of the company, including the brand and the trust in the company or when the Customer appreciates the values of the company including sustainability. These create value for the Customer.
7. Giving the Customer a product that works as it is meant to (as perceived by the Customer) and is easy for him/her to understand and use (so that no unnecessary time or energy has to be expended).
8. Making the Customer feel valued. For example:
    Smiling at and being attentive to a Customer creates value for him
        Ignoring him/her destroys value for the Customer
    Making it easy for the Customer to contact the company, and an assurance that an answer will be given when and how promised (how many times do you have to wait to talk to someone and how often does s/he promise to call back and how often do you get a call)
    Not making you repeat questions or answers, and keep relating the problem
    Receiving a call from a service person confirming his/her visit (the Customer is not kept wondering whether the service visit will take place)
    Not answering queries destroys value

All readers have real-life examples of value creators and value destroyers and can add many more examples. Do add yours. Answer the following:

What could I do to create value for my Customer?
What can destroy value for my Customer?
Does experience create value?

List things that you do not experience but that can create value for you.

Do I look for and solve customer problems not only one by one but also systemically for all customers having the same problem?

If leaders understand this, they can create a competitive advantage and longer-lasting value for the customer and themselves.

* * *

The Eight Principles of Customer Value Creation

To appreciate Customer Value Creation, you must understand the principles of Customer Value Creation. The principles of Customer Value Creation, enunciated by Gautam Mahajan in his book *Value Creation* are:

The First Principle: Customers tend to buy or use those products or services that they perceive create greater value for them than competitive offers. It is essential for executives and leaders to create higher value for their Customers than competition can.

The Second Principle: Customer Value Creation is applicable in all fields, such as business, service, education and academics, society and government, social work, innovation, and entrepreneurship. It impacts humanity.

The Third Principle: Customer Value Creation touches all stakeholders, you, your colleagues, your employees, your partners (supply chain, delivery chain, and unions), and society to create resounding Value for the Customer and thereby for the shareholder. It is the source for creating Customers, retaining existing ones, and increasing loyalty, market share, and profits.

The Fourth Principle: Customer Value Creation is proactively exceeding what is basically expected of you or your job and is going beyond your functional and routine roles to create value in your eco-system. Value Creation can be planned or spontaneous and in both functional and emotional thinking.

The Fifth Principle: Customer Value Creation leverages a person's or an organization's potential, learning, and creativity while making it meaningful and worthwhile for people to belong and perform, both physically and emotionally.

The Sixth Principle: Customer Value Creation presents a very powerful decision-making tool for companies to decide on actions, programs, and strategies for the Customer that can increase the company's longevity and profitability.

The Seventh Principle: Value Creation must exceed value destruction or reduce negative value and be done consciously (not just unconsciously).

The Eighth Principle: Values (what you stand for, integrity, honesty, fairness etc.) create Customer Value (that is, Customers value your values).

These principles form the foundation of the Customer Value Creation strategy and implementation, resulting in great value for you and your company. Leaders can take advantage of these.

* * *

Some Misconceptions about Customer Value

Here are some common ideas posted in blogs, and what is factually correct.

Satisfaction is the reason why people buy: people buy because a product or a service is worthwhile to them versus competitive products or services. Satisfaction is a necessary condition but not a sufficient condition for purchase. Sometimes, we buy even though very dissatisfied. Value is what makes you buy, and satisfaction is one part of buying.

High-value products have low satisfaction: this implies value is price, and that if something is high priced, it has low satisfaction. This is confusing value for price. Sometimes, people pay "money for value" which means they buy high-priced items.

Low-value products have high satisfaction: this implies value is price, and that if something is low priced, it has high satisfaction. This is just not true. It has been proved that at every price point, Customers look for value. What does that mean: if buying a pen, whether a Mont Blanc or a Bic, the Customer is looking for value and buys on value.

Does satisfaction measure Customer Value: Customer Value and satisfaction studies are different. Satisfaction measurements are done on transactions and generally right after the transaction by the user. Normally the top two boxes are measured. Customer Value studies are done a few weeks after the transaction and on the decision maker, not necessarily the end user, so as to get embedded perceptions. *Customer Value studies are done versus competitive alternatives and are ratios.*

Value means benefits: Value is what the Customer gets (benefits) vs. cost (price and non-price) versus competing offers. While colloquially we use value to mean benefit or price, Customer Value is the actual worth of a product versus competing options.

Values and value are the same: Values are what someone stands for, ethics, morals, sustainability. Value is defined above. In fact, values create value.

Customer Value is newer than Customer Experience: both are old concepts. However, the formal usage is more recent. Customer Value as a discipline started in the 1980s with Ray Kordupleski and AT&T, and CX in the 2000s.

NPS is a great measure of what the Customer perceives: NPS only answers a couple of questions on repurchase and recommendation. It does not portray what the Customer thinks of the product and whether he has had a good or poor experience. NPS is better used with other Customer metrics.

Why are these misconceptions propagated and misunderstood? My take is that most people tend to follow what they are told, rather than delving deeply into the actual meaning of, and truly understanding how these concepts should be used. These concepts are used and understood loosely.

My suggestion to the lay reader is to truly understand what each of these terms means, how they are used, and how they should be used. Reflection from one's own experience will show what I am saying makes sense. (Remember your favourite restaurant or airline, and if you are dissatisfied, will you stop using them?)

One reason why companies and executives are not truly becoming Customer-centric is that such loosely used and understood terms confuse companies and do not give the Customer true insight into what will really help. Thus, just measuring NPS and stating that it tells the firm what to do is misleading and will prevent the firm from truly improving.

Leaders, executives, and consultants can lead this change in understanding.

* * *

The Memory of Your Experience Is More Important Than Your Experience

Professor Daniel Kahneman is a Nobel Laureate, psychologist, and expert on judgment and decision-making, behavioural economics, and hedonic psychology. After we see what Kahneman has to say, I will also add what this means to Customer Value versus Customer Satisfaction. Read on:

Kahneman says "there is a big difference between an experience and the memory of an experience." Sounds obvious, doesn't it? But it is not understood by most people such as CxOs, HR, Sales and Marketing, and Customer Experience Executives.

We all know we are "experiencing" things all the time. You are having an experience now by reading this blog. Kahneman calls the experience of experiencing things, like you are experiencing in this reading, "the experiencing self." But Kahneman says we also have a "remembering self."

So let's imagine I experience a telephone call with my bank, and it was not satisfactory. Then I talk about it with my friends, and I say I am unhappy and dissatisfied.

A few weeks later, my memory of the experience would have been modified based on the fact I am more relaxed, the actual incident does not rankle as much, and I have taken subconsciously my other interactions with the bank into account and I do not feel that bad. I think:

- Was the experience really that bad?
- How do I feel now?
- How does this experience compare with other such experiences?
- How is the bank treating me overall?
- Is there anything I remember that stands out, positive or negative?
- How did they perform in comparison to what I think they should have done or versus other banks?

My answers are instantaneous after a transaction, and if I would record them, I would say the bank's system sucks, and they ask me to repeat my account number. My experience becomes less awful after some time, because the memory of the incident is less dissatisfying, and I find they are no worse than others, and I do get some good work from them and I am willing to continue doing business with the bank. This is why value surveys are done much after the event and they measure your memory of the experience perception, whereas satisfaction surveys measure the experience perception instantaneously on transactions.

Consider another example. We were having a Sunday lunch with friends and a wonderful conversation, and suddenly a family with small kids, wailing and screaming, sat next to us and the kids not only shrieked, they ran around and it ruined it for us. Before the family came in, my experiencing self would have said the experience was great. In the end I would say it was terrible, because my memory of the kids ruined the experience.

There is a BIG difference between an experience and the memory of an experience. Most people do not take this into account while designing, measuring, and improving their Customer Experience. That is why they do not understand that satisfaction and value are distinct and measure different things. One measures the experience and the other the memory of the experience.

Remember:

Customers don't choose between experiences
They choose between the MEMORY of their experiences
So learn to work with the memory of the experience.

What are the implications on a Customer Experience?

- To understand a Customer experience, when should you ask for Customer feedback? During the experience or after the memory is formed? Take my restaurant story as an example. If I was asked what I thought of the restaurant before the family with screeching kids came in, I would have given them a 9 out of 10. After the event, with the memory of that experience, I would have given a 5. I see too many companies whose call centres ask for a survey at the very end of their call. I would argue this does not allow people time to form a memory. I would argue this is still part of their experience. How many times have you been very annoyed at something that happened but then "calmed down" after and realized you were being unreasonable? After the call, you may have given them 2 out of 10, but after two days your memory would give them a 5. Therefore, choosing the optimum time to ask for feedback is key. A couple of weeks later, I would forget the distraction and remember our wonderful interaction and give the restaurant an 8 out of 10.
- Are you clear about what part of the experience you are measuring? In my example, if I was asked about the restaurant itself or my experience of eating there, the answers would be very different.
- What are you doing to help create a positive memory of the experience? How can you add to people's memories with positive reinforcement?

After a few days. I called my friends and said I really enjoyed myself, because the memory of the experience was that of our conversation and comradeship. I might have answered differently, had the restaurant called me.

There are many more implications. This is just part of what we call Experience Psychology, which is critical to understand when improving your Customer Experience to drive $$$.

It is essential that you realize your Customers have the "experiencing self" **and** the "remembering self" and they choose between memories of the experience.

What implications do you, as a Leader see coming from this for improving a Customer Experience, or your business, or your dealings with your employees?

* * *

Customer Value and Customer Satisfaction: Two Sides of the Same Coin?

The service management literature argues that customer satisfaction is the result of a customer's perception of the value received … where value equals perceived service quality relative to price… (Hallowell, 1996, p. 29).

- The first determinant of overall customer satisfaction is perceived quality … the second determinant of overall customer satisfaction is perceived value… (Fornell et al., 1996, p. 9).
- Customer satisfaction is recognized as being highly associated with 'value' and… is based, conceptually, on the amalgamation of service quality attributes with such attributes as price… (Athanassopoulos, 2000, p. 192).

How do we measure value: By measuring the satisfaction with the benefits?

As we improve sat, value increases (Figure 3.1).

So, we see in a simplistic sense the satisfaction with products and services leads to satisfaction with benefits. Satisfaction with benefits and cost leads to Customer Value.

Note, I could have replaced the word satisfaction by experience.

Having done this, I find there is no difference between satisfaction and the experience (Figure 3.2).

The key question is when do we measure satisfaction and of whom. In a typical satisfaction or experience study, we measure the satisfaction right after the transaction, and we ask the user or the one experiencing the transaction. Emotions enter into this measurement.

In a value study the satisfaction is measured after some time of the transaction, A few weeks is best. We are then measuring the memory of the experience. More importantly, we ask the decision maker (who may be distinct from the person in the transaction) for his satisfaction of the experience or the benefit. Embedded emotions come into play but not instantaneous emotions.

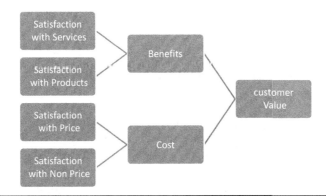

Figure 3.1 Attribute Tree Showing Components of Value

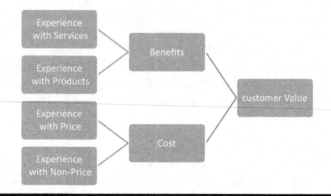

Figure 3.2   Attribute Tree Showing Experience Leading to Value

Thus, value is based on satisfaction, and increasing value means that satisfaction was increased. And increasing satisfaction will increase customer Value. Except that in the Customer Value measurement we prioritize each factor based on the Customer's response, Thus those items of benefits or cost that are important will l increase value accordingly.

So, we come to Cronin's classical paper, where they introduce the concept of BI (behavioural intention). We know Customer Value relates to BI and has been proven. Customer satisfaction which is not based on benefits and cost suffer from not correlating to BI. Lastly, such BI are based on competitive alternatives, and this is taken into account in Value measurement.

Measure Customer Value and be a winner by using the results. Leaders must learn how to measure and understand value to be leaders in their industry or segment.

* * *

Can Customer Value Change Customer Behaviour and Vice Versa?

The answer to both questions is yes. But as I go through articles on changing behaviour, I see very little or no mention of Creating Value for the consumer and society. Why is this? There is no question that Customer Value Creation is a major driver of behavioural change. I think the reason is that Customer Value is not commonly understood or used by many people. Take Keith Weed's article "Change Consumer Behaviour with These 5 Levers," in HBR, November 2012.

He talks about making it (product or service) understood, easy, desirable, make it rewarding, and make it a habit.

You can argue that Customer Value is at the back of these ideas.

Consumer behaviour, according to Wiki, is the study of individuals, groups, or organizations, and the processes they use to select, secure, use, and dispose of products, services, experiences, or ideas to satisfy needs and the impacts that these processes have on the **consumer** and society.

I guess Customer Value lurks somewhere in this statement. Moshe Davidow, Editor of the *Journal of Creating Value*, said the same: it is understood. If it is understood, then why not say it?

Changing consumer behaviour is about adding more value to the Customers. Whether it is Starbucks or cell phones. Very often the value is not easily seen by the Customers as they cannot anticipate the new product, and how to use it. They fear the change and having to get out of their comfort zone. Witness the first telephone … consumer research would have shown it was a loser. Or the cell phone. Who wanted to be connected or reachable all of the time? Who wanted the intrusion? Or having to pay so much for a cup of coffee at Starbucks?

The Customer Value was not apparent, but it was there, even though time and money had to be spent in making these concepts understandable, easy, desirable, and rewarding before they became a habit or a way of life. Customers resist change, they are afraid of loss rather than of gain, and hence their first reaction is not to change. I am one of the late adopters of cell phones. Apart from aversion to change, and loss mitigation, it is also emotions, peer pressure, and a host of other issues that trigger change.

Who would have thought we would use our phones and the net for Uber, for making payments, or that air transport would become a way of life, or that driverless cars are on the horizon or that free energy is a real possibility? They will catch on only if they provide Customer Value, and if the companies can extract value in the future from these ideas.

If we accept that greater value can influence Customer behaviour, then we have to ask how changing consumer behaviour impacts the Customer's value expectation. Will she expect different value parameters? Will her conventional view of value give way to an entirely different set of value expectations?

The answer is yes. No longer will she consider product value from a conventional TV when the flat TV is available. No longer will all face-to-face meetings have a necessarily higher value than a Skype or Zoom meeting.

What we should conclude is that big and massive changes (and also small ones) start with a heightened Customer Value potential. Consumer behaviour people use their expertise to influence behaviour towards the greater value product and service. This in turn changes our value expectations.

Moshe Davidow's comments:

Wiki says that value is a measure of the benefit provided by a good or service to an economic agent. In other words, benefits add value.

According to Weed's article (cited earlier), easy, desirable and rewarding are all clear benefits, while understood and habit are also benefits, although less clear. The value is *implicit* in what he is saying.

His article is talking about sustainable marketing, and he says brands cannot do it alone.

Tobias Webb (http://sustainablesmartbusiness.com/2013/02/two-problems -with-brands-and-consumer) talks about the collaboration between brands and other agents. Now we are talking about adding value to other suppliers as well as to society and consumers.

Why don't we call it value, since at the bottom line we are definitely talking about value? I believe that the word "value" was co-opted by economics, where it does not mean what we think it means. Economic value, market value, fair value. These are all economic terms that mean different things. By the time marketing developed, they were so intent on distancing marketing from economics, that they changed the terminology.

We need to take the term back! Not benefits, but value! Wiki says a **benefit** is something good that comes from something else.

You talk about the fear of change. Kahneman and Tversky talk about "Risk Aversion" or "Loss Aversion," and consumers strongly prefer avoiding losses rather than acquiring gains. They also talk about the "Endowment Effect" where a good that a person owns is worth more than an identical good that they do not own. This has major implications for marketing, consumer behaviour, and change.

The key to change is small increments. Let consumers get used to something and see its real value. They will then want to use it. This is why marketers hand out freebies, offer trial periods, allow test drives etc.

Economic value erodes over time due to changing expectations. Emotional value may remain constant. As consumer expectations increase (a given), the value of a particular product goes down. This might be similar to the discounted value of money over time, but for a different reason. At one point, a car without a radio or air conditioner would have been great for me; now, however, it does not have much value, as my expectations are much higher. I alluded to this when I discussed TV screens. A lot of people no longer have a house phone (great value 15–20 years ago). We no longer call places; today, we call people. Cell phones have eroded the value of a house phone. Is this a form of value destruction? I think so.

Leaders can take advantage of value waiting to happen, and possible behavioural changes, and be winners and ahead of competition.

* * *

Don't Give Away Too Much to the Customer

There has been much talk about giving away too much to the Customer to the detriment of the Company. Companies should be Customer-centric but not *too* Customer-centric, say some (not me). Critics of Customer Value Creation think of Customer Value people as naïve and running the risk of reducing value to the Company. Customer Value is actually used to get the best possible value for the Customer and the company. It also can tell what value the Company gets and when value is being destroyed or reduced for the Company and how to correct this.

Customer-centricity advocates are saying a blanket Customer-centric approach may back fire. How do we correct this thinking?

Let's start with what is evident. Customers buy those products they perceive will give them more value than competitive products. Customer Value is measured by a metric called Customer Value Added (CVA).

$$CVA \text{ is}: \quad \frac{\textit{The Value} \left(\textit{benefits} - \textit{cost}\right) \textit{added by your Company to its Customers}}{\textit{The Value Added by your competitor to its Customers}}$$

Obviously, the name of the game is to add benefits or cut costs or price to increase Customer Value. The easiest thing to do is cut price which can increase Customer Value. But this can get you into a price war, and if carried too far can be deadly. Every time you lower the price by 1%, the Company profit decreases by 10–15%. So, in creating value for the Customer by price cutting you are destroying value for the Company. Or if you add benefits and do not get a price for it, then again value is destroyed for the Company if the benefit improvement has caused a higher cost to the Company. Often, service benefits are for free (doing the right things, having a good attitude), and in this case creating the value for the Customer does not destroy the value for the Company. And if you could get a price improvement, then the value for the Company goes up. Remember, a 1% increase in price can improve your profits by over 10%, generally.

When you conduct a Customer Value Added study, you also get to create a value map. You want to see graphically whether you are adding or destroying value to the Customer, and whether you are giving away value (and just getting Customers to prefer you, and actually destroying value for the Company). The value map also shows graphically the relative value you are adding versus competition to customers.

I am going to show you the same value map twice to make my point. This is real data through market research with Customers. To understand the chart, the Y axis shows the rating on the financials or business returns. As the perception of business returns goes up, the scores increase. The lowest perception of cost is .94 for company BB (which means the cost is perceived to be high) and the highest on the chart is 1.14 on a ratio scale where 1 would be the average perception of business returns scale. The first chart shows Company EE provides the highest value (measured as the distance from the fair value line) compared to Company AA. Company AA started a membership scheme. The chart shows what happens to Company AA's Customers when they become members and more value is added. That boosted the ego of the Customer and improved his sense of belonging and relationship with the brand. The value went up and the willingness to recommend was the highest for this group. But most interesting, the price was not reduced for the AA members versus the rest of the AA Customers. *But the overall perception of business returns for the farmer had gone up (the members perceived a lower cost and therefore higher returns).*

Making them members increased the Customer Value they perceived they received. In this particular case, not much cost was incurred by the Company in making members. They just let it be known they were making members, and members were given badges and recognized at the retail stores by the retailer.

Note high-value Creation for the Customer is to the right of the fair value line (Figure 3.3), and AA, CC, and EE are adding Value to the Customer, and BB is destroying value.

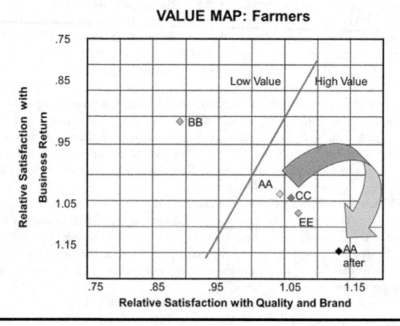

Figure 3.3   Value Map

The second chart (Figure 3.4) focuses on increasing the value to the Company or the profit. Starting with AA members, we notice an immense Customer Value is being created for them (see the distance from the fair value line (the only line on the chart). We can increase the price and thereby reduce business returns (shown by the vertical arrow going up) and reduce the benefits (arrow going to the left), or both (arrow going diagonally towards the fair value line). One could increase revenues by charging a membership fee.

A better way is to increase the price for AA's Customers (members and non-members) or reduce the benefits (such as sales credit, or free delivery).

All these will increase the revenue to the Company and its profit. It is better to ensure we continue to be in the high-value zone and add more value than competitors.

These strategies have worked to increase the value to the Company (Figure 3.4).

In addition, CVA also relates to market share and profits. As CVA goes up and down, market share follows. See chart in Figure 3.5.

Further as CVA goes up, ROI goes up, as we can see in the chart (Figure 3.6).

This section proves to those who believe Customer Value proponents only think of creating value for the Customer that they add value to the company also. In addition, they can do this study for various Customer segments and assess which segments are higher value adding to the Company.

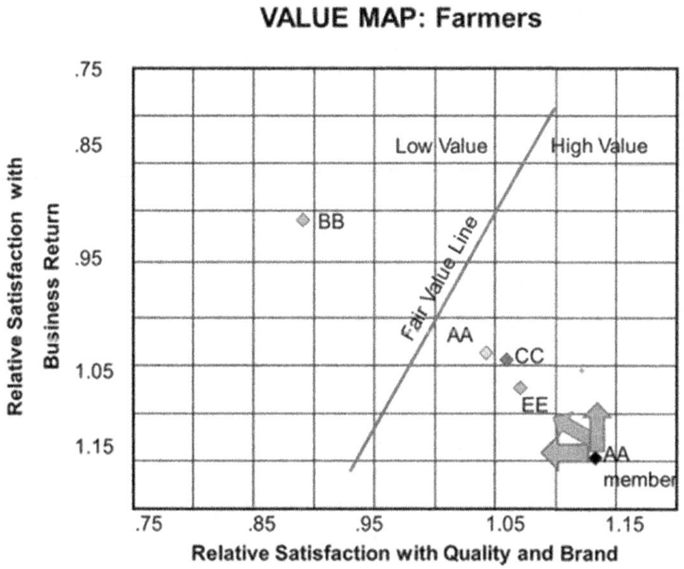

Figure 3.4 Value Map Showing How to Reduce Benefits or Increase Price to Get More Value for Company

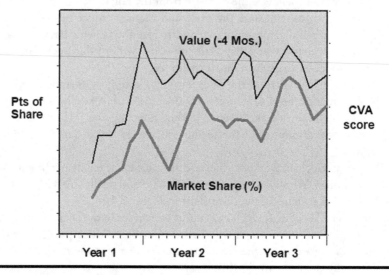

Figure 3.5   Market Share versus Value

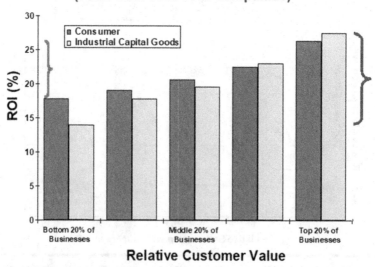

Figure 3.6   ROI vs. Relative Customer Value

Steps in Value Creation Implementation: The Customer Department

The major part of this book is about why Value Creation is important, how it impacts CEO thinking on short term vs. long term, and how companies can add value to customers and employees, and build the Value Creation principles in departments in the company. We have talked about creating value in training and in leadership, and in making the customer your partner and making him your Ambassador. We have suggested to the CEO to change the focus of departments such as HR and IT to become customer focused and become line functions. We have dwelt upon reducing the focus of executives on routine tasks and concentrating on important Value Creation jobs, and "outsourcing" routine work. We have talked about the future, self-tuning companies and awareness, agility, adaptation, anticipation, and ambidextrousness, moving from selling to customers to becoming his buying aide and to get action.

CEOs must have a Value Creation strategy in order to implement all of these. This includes many of the steps mentioned above.

One major step is to change your company, (which should be part of your strategy) is to break silos and make the customer the focus of all departments, and make the customer experience seamless. Your business strategy must be built by first building a stakeholder strategy. For example, what is your Customer strategy? This makes your business thinking and its strategy stronger, more usable, and valuable.

If companies truly wish to give the Customer his deserved place in the company, they have to start a Customer Department. This department will have all functions that are necessary for and/or relevant to the Customer. The functions include product development and products, manufacturing delivery and delivery chain, supply chain, IT, and even manufacturing. For example, the department will work on various aspects of the business and the customer.

Why Is a Customer Department Needed?

First to break silos and unnecessary demarcations in companies where the convenience of the company comes ahead of the convenience of the Customer (let's say the delivery departments focus is on cost cutting and not on working out methods to suit the customer)

Second to have one point of control for the Customer

Customer reporting: the value we added to the Customer, and his value to us. Have these gone up? This is done through measurements

No more billing goof-ups at the finance department, and reducing Customer Value starvation

A proper and dynamic Customer strategy
Continuous Customer Improvement Programs (CCIP)
Promises and procedures to ensure the Customer's Bill of Rights is honoured
Seamless delivery
Customer oriented service department
Customer problem solution group to recognize, understand, and solve customers' problems

How Will the Customer Department Function?

It needs one COO type of coordinator or Chief Customer Value Creation Officer.

Non-customer-related works (like tax, treasury, employee information such as leave due, leave taken, attendance, functional training like finance for non-financial managers) are not part of the Customer Department.

The COO acts as the Chief Customer Officer, whose role is to ensure that Customer tasks are divided within the Customer Department, and the departments become Customeric. Executives are taught to focus on the Customer and his needs. Continuous Customer Improvement Programs are put into place. The COO ensures that the Customer comes first and divides the department and thereby the company. Employee Value Creation programs are started.

The COO reports Customer scores along with an explanation for why scores are improving or not, and correlate this with market share and profits.

The CEO focuses on the Customer Department and non-Customer Departments and reports Customer and financial data to the Board. The CEO assigns key performance indicators and customer score-driven bonuses.

Products and Features Customized for Customers

Products are available where and when the Customer is ready (he may not know he is ready), but your information shows he is inclined to buy, so we will help him buy. An example, I bought tickets for Europe 6 weeks ago. I know I need insurance, but I am not in a rush. If a company selling travel insurance knows this, they could have come to me say 3 weeks ago and given me some options including comparisons and why my insurance is worth it. I bought insurance today, 3 days before my trip. Now all those where I shopped are chasing me, too late!

Help the Customer Buy
Pricing from Customer's point of view
Delivery as he wants it

Relationship he wants
Segment him as he wants
Billing and financing his way
Employees who understand his needs
Customer service and relationship

Establishing New Ideas

Problem Noter and Solver

This is a task very few companies do but is imperative if you do not want unhappy customers. The idea is to get all problems noticed and complaints to be looked at seriously and solved, and solved for the future and for everyone.

Customer-centric Circles

These have been described and should be instituted by the Customer Department. Mahajan's 8As should be taught to and practised by all executives and frontline people. Build self-esteem and then ensure Awareness, Ability, Attitude, Agility, Anticipation, Adaptability, and Ambidextrousness, leading to Action.

All these will help you become Customer-centric.

* * *

Customer Value Journey: Making the Journey Easy and Meaningful Creates Value

I gave a two-day workshop on Value Creation Mapping in Malaysia in April 2014. I found that the concept of value was interpreted differently by different participants. Very few said it meant whether what you got was worth what you paid versus competitive offers. Most participants confused value for either benefits, or value for money, or price. Value is actually a juxtaposition of benefits and price.

I also explained that while we think of the Customer Journey as one journey, it actually has to be viewed as three journeys by the company to be able to make the Customer journey more comfortable, and an enriching experience.

The first part of his journey and the experience is in searching for a product, shopping, buying, taking delivery, or having it delivered, the delivery and installation process (including self-installation), actual use experience, complaint experience, experience of getting something unusual done, getting a call back from the company, billing and payment, maintenance and service etc. The second is the journey that the company makes to the customer, when contacting him for giving information, for getting the customer to buy, for order information, service information, for collecting bills etc. Is this journey that the company makes to the customer a comfortable journey or an experience for the customer? Is it comfortable for the company? Does the company have enough information while making a call? How often do you get a call from a service guy asking for your address, and the model of your TV? Or when you get repeat calls for buying? Or after you have bought it, someone calls you and says when will you buy it? These are unnecessary parts of the journey.

Companies do not view this as a part of the customer journey and often irritate the hell out of the customer and even aggravate the customer.

Lastly, there is the journey the company people make within the company for solving the problems of the customer to make the customer journey comfortable. How often do you hear, as a customer from the company, this is not my department, you will have to call so and so? The company is palming its journey off onto the customer and making the customer embark on a fresh journey.

I just got a call from Citibank cards asking for my date of birth to check a statement (why?). I asked the girl to contact my branch manager to whom I had sent all the information by email. She could not or would not. Could I call him to send her the information?

Companies delegate their work to the customer and make him or her take unnecessary journeys, because the convenience of the company (or its executive) is more important than the convenience of the customer.

All these are Value Destructing. It is important that companies use these journeys to Create Value for the customer, but this is not taught, this is not part of the culture. Too bad, Mr. Customer!

The lessons:

The journey itself cannot be separated from the culture of the company. Are we inwardly focused or do we want to take in the needs of the customer and reduce his pain in the journey and increase the Value Creation, his sense of wellbeing, happiness, and even delight? Is that your culture? If yes, why do these journeys happen in a way to cause some grief to the customer?

Creating Value in the journey should be the cornerstone of the culture and the people.

To do this, a clear understanding of what Customer Value is and how to measure it through the Customer Value Added metric:

$$CVA = \frac{Value\ added\ by\ your\ company\ to\ your\ customers}{Value\ added\ by\ your\ competitors\ to\ its\ customers}$$

Last but not least, build a Business Strategy based on Customer strategy (or even a stakeholder strategy), break silos, and build a Circle of Promises, so that the customer gets a seamless, fulfilling experience during the journey, so that the Customer becomes loyal.

The fact remains that most companies do not implement Value Dominant Logic (or any other Customer-centric strategy). Why not, and what can be done about it?

What percentage of companies today actually implement VDL?

Your comments are welcome!

* * *

Customers as Ambassadors

People mistake the term Customer Advocate. A Customer Advocate is one who works for your company but advocates and works to make the company Customer-centric and customer friendly. An Ambassador is even more dedicated to you and your products and does not work for you.

If the Customer comes first (thanks to your Customer Advocates) and if you are truly creating Value for the Customer, he will reward you with loyalty and referrals. Such people become your Customer Ambassadors.

In today's day and age of social media, your interaction with customers often becomes virtual ones! Social media becomes more important. How do you work with or follow or use social Customer Ambassadors and network with them and get them to refer other customers to you?

Customers with "Social Value": Your Customer Ambassadors

Most companies measure Customer Life Time Value. The equation includes the Customer's current buying, the expected rate of growth of his buying over the years, and the business obtained from the referrals he provides. Very often these referrals are more important than his own purchases. You need these customers as your Customer Ambassadors, and their value as Customer Ambassadors can be immense.

How do Customers become your Customer Ambassadors? The necessary condition is that you create great value for them over what your competition can. As value increases (and value is what it is worth to the Customer to do business with you and includes your products, the relationship, the image and brand, your people and service, and the price and non-price terms). A good Customer Ambassador recommends you to his network. A great Brand Ambassador also has a virtual social network where he can and does refer you.

This last kind of Brand Ambassador has to be nurtured because his referral value can be huge. As an example, if he buys 100 Rupees (Rs) a month but refers ten customers who can buy an average of 60 Rs, he thus has referred 600 Rs to you.

Today, the bulk of referrals are face to face, followed by telephones, and social media is a distinct third but growing. That is why you have to follow your Customer Ambassador there onto the net.

You need a data capture mechanism that captures referrals and Customers referring customers. You can then start a special campaign for them. You could also identify them from surveys as those who would definitely recommend, and by asking how many people have you recommended or can you suggest people we can contact. This can be added to your database.

Ask what made these people my Customer Ambassadors. How can I convert others to become Customer Ambassadors? There are many methods you might have used in the past such as asking for the forwarding of marketing emails, rewards for referrals, or events where such Ambassadors can bring friends. Do something special for your Ambassadors.

Recognize that your best customers are introducing you to their friends and making you part of their social circle. Give them your highest priority and rewards and treat them as special.

Creating Value for Your Customer's Network and Gaining from It

How do you create value from a Customer's Network? We all know that if you have a great Customer Network, it can lead to referral buying. How do you get to referral buying? A Customer Network is your captive one which you normally manage through databases and CRM (Customer Relationship Management) and your website. The bigger database and network is your Customer's Network (the network outside of your day-to-day control).

First, you can see the advantages of a Customer's Network. If you use it intelligently, you can get the customers to come to you directly, circumventing the normal means they would have used such as looking for the product on the net or going to a store to figure out whether they should buy from you or buy your products and services. Instead of this, they might use recommendations from friends, from social media like Facebook or Twitter. They look at what their influencers and friends have to say. They bypass some early buying steps. It is convenient for them and much easier for you to sell to them because they come with some positive pre-determined ideas.

How do you get to this point? First you have to create value for your existing customers. You have to create substantially more value than your competition. Customers then reward you with loyalty and referrals. Creating Value means it is much more worth your customers while to do business with you over competing offers. Your product, services, people, and marketing have to be better your competitions'.

You also have to participate in the Customer's Network. What is the social space your customers use? How do they surf the net looking for merchandise through their Customer Network? How do you become a real (though background) part of this network? Can you become the customers' aide in this interaction with his social space? How do you understand this interaction and how do you derive the data about this interaction or how do you monitor the Customers' Network without invading his privacy? How can you influence him during this phase? An example is the farmers network fertilizer companies set up in India.

Today, your first step is to be part of this social space, become one with them in this space, and become a trusted ally and part of the referral chain. Then price becomes less of an issue in the value equation. You must start to understand what value your customers need in this space and for the customer why he should (and make it easy for him) refer you. And how can you add value (make it easier) for a customer looking for a referral and what do you have to spend to eventually create value from your Customers Network.

* * *

How SMEs[1] Benefit by Creating Value for Customers: A Case Study

Even in today's uncertain economy, some companies are winning big and they are winning big because of three strategies:

They manage for value.
They keep developing human capital.
They get radically Customer-centric.

Here I can take many real examples of well-known companies that followed these strategies and succeeded, even in unfavourable situations.

But have we ever thought about small companies in terms of Customer Value Creation, can they do the same thing by putting "CUSTOMER" at the centre of their business? I would say, "YES" they can.

Let me take a real-life example of an SME Packaging company in Faridabad. When the owner (whom I met) took over this family business, he went into losses. He wasn't able to get new contracts and build a long-lasting relationship with the Customers. He was no different from his competitors.

---

[1] SMEs are small and medium enterprises.

Then he thought of ways to differentiate himself from his competitors, of things that his competitors were not doing nor were they even thinking in that way.

He started getting information such as:

Most of the packaging companies shut down at 5–6 PM in the evening so they can't get orders after 6 PM.

The customer wants prompt delivery even if he places the order at an odd time.

All the competitors were taking orders and executing and delivering the goods during their working hours. They were not interested in increasing their working hours because it was expensive, and there was not much work to do in extended hours.

But Customers work 24 × 7 and need support and product even at night, especially if the Customer forgot to place the order between 10 AM and 6 PM. After this, no competitor was ready to take orders because the Customer would ask for delivery early the next morning.

Such deliveries were rare but were important to the Customer.

So the packaging company owner decided to run his company 24 × 7 hours even though he did not have enough work on the night shift.

Actually what he did was to divide his workers into two shifts, half in the day and half in the night, providing adequate supervision. Guess what happened when no other competitor in the packaging industry was able to answer Customer calls. Our friend was ready and when at last that Customer called, they were surprised the call was answered even at midnight, saying: "Hello sir, how can I help you?" The Customer was amazed; he asked: "Your Company is still running?" And got an answer "Yes sir, how may I help you?" and the Customer placed an order and asked for delivery in the morning. And this SME company delivered.

Several times people called him just to check whether his promise of 24 × 7 service was true. And yes, they found it was, with the managers responding in the same manner with a smile on their face.

What this packaging company owner did was "COVERING THE MISTAKES OF HIS CUSTOMER" and made them feel that "Ok, I made a mistake of placing late order but this guy with his excellent commitment to serve his Customers helped me out." In a way he did the recovery process and created value for his Customers. He had changed the rules of the game!

Slowly Customers started relying on him and a relationship started building and everyone was willing to place orders only with this company.

Initially all the competitors were laughing at him when he decided to run his company 24 × 7 with no assured work, and they missed the train because they did not want to incur the extra expense and did not want to change the rules of the game.

This company has the same material to make the packing boxes as its competitors, has the same machinery as its competitors, and is probably no better in quality than its competitors, but it is far away in **Serving its Customers and taking care of their needs, and creating value for them.**

Contact Customer Value Foundation to know how you can create value for your Customers and earn more profits and trust.

This story came from Narender Kumar.

* * *

Does a Customer Seek Customer Experience?

I, for one, am happy not to get an experience. I do not seek a fantastic experience, but when I get it, I feel great. But what I hate are bad experiences and cannot seem to avoid them. They keep coming.

My parallel example is I do not want to have great health; I just want to be healthy. I do not want to be ill or sick. That really makes me feel bad and makes me remember how good my health was.

All the bad experiences I get, and all of you get too, remind me that they are not necessary. That companies do not care enough and are choosing to seek great experiences for customers and not avoiding bad experiences: call waiting, call cuts, no return calls, problems not being addressed, wrong items being sent, service not being attended to, or me getting an air conditioner manufactured in November 2019 in April 2021. The company would not take it back. These problems are highlighted in my book, *Customer Value Starvation Can Kill,*[1] co-written with Walter Vieira, Phil Kotler's long-time friend.

How many people do you know who ask or seek an experience? Do you seek an experience? Most people want to have a normal experience. It is the bad experiences that cause people to turn away from products and services.

Why then has experience become a buzzword? It has replaced Customer Satisfaction, which was proven not to correlate to customer loyalty.

Customer loyalty can be a result of customer satisfaction, but only along with a lot of other factors.

As an example, if you are a United Airlines frequent flyer, you may have a very poor experience and are highly dissatisfied on your flight from New York to

---

[1] https://www.amazon.in/Customer-Value-Starvation-Can-Kill/dp/1952538580

Chicago. The flight is late, the plane looks tired, and the steward spills coffee on you. You return on American Airlines and everything is perfect. A great experience and you are highly satisfied.

Will you stop travelling United and switch to American? Chances are you will not. At most you might write to United and say I am a frequent flyer; I do not expect this kind of experience.

The real source of loyalty is competitive value created by a company over competition. Just measuring your own performance against yourself (did I get a higher score versus last year?) does not give you the correct picture. The world is competitive. The customer has a choice. You must improve against competition. You must, therefore, also measure what competitors' customers say about them.

You can see in my example of United and American Airlines, we have competitive data. This brings us to the next point. Loyalty is not created by measuring transactions or the experience. It is measured from embedded experiences or the memory of the experience. So, loyalty measurements using value have:

1. Competitive data
2. Measured not by the user but by the decision maker who may not have the experience I described in my example above.
   a. As an example, a parent buys juice for your kid. The kid gets the experience and is the consumer. But the parent is the decision maker.
   b. A company makes a deal with a hotel group for their employees to stay in a particular hotel. The decision maker is the CxO or the Head of Administration. He himself may stay in a different (and better hotel) and so may not have the direct experience of the hotel he selected.
3. Do not focus on transactions but on embedded feelings. Thus, the memory of the experience is more important for gaining loyalty. The difference between customer satisfaction surveys and *customer loyalty* surveys is that customer satisfaction surveys are focused on measuring customers' current attitudes, whereas customer loyalty surveys focus on predicting customer behaviour and attitudes.

I do not know how you measure experience. Through satisfaction type studies? The actual satisfaction study based on the experience can be used for improvements. Through NPS (that gives you no data other than if you will buy again)?

In fact *Gartner is advising to phase out NPS.*[1] I always thought satisfaction was based on the experience in buying, in use etc. Others state Customer Effort Score, which measures how easy the customers found the interaction with your service. However, the list doesn't end here. There are many other metrics. The Customer Health Score scores customers based on the likelihood they'll generate an outcome; the Customer Churn Rate measures the rate at which customers stop doing business with you; also, the Customer Renewal Rate (how many customers cancelled a service vs. how many did not) can give you a sense of the quality of your customer experience. (Partly taken from *Alon Ghelber,*[2] Are we measuring CX the right way?.)

Mckinsey[3] in June 2021 stated: 15% of leaders said they were fully satisfied with how their company was measuring CX – and only 6% expressed confidence that their measurement system enables both strategic and tactical decision-making. Leaders pointed to low response rates, data lags, ambiguity about performance drivers, and the lack of a clear link to financial value as critical shortcomings.

We use the words a satisfied customer, or a loyal customer, not an experienced customer. Our goal is Value Creation which leads to loyalty.

I write this, not because I am against CX. I am for it. But I see the danger that CX will not live up to its promise and go the way of CRM (Customer Relationship Management) or CSat (Customer Satisfaction). Customer satisfaction measurements on transactions are still relevant to make improvements and should be done more often than value studies.

Companies wishing to go into a CX program must ask: how much is it worth to me and how much is it worth to the customer, and how much should I spend? Should I go towards zero complaints first or seek the holy grail of delight instead? They must ask how important CX is in the buying decision and loyalty of a customer. Is it one of many items that makes a person buy? Value, for example, compares competitive benefits (which include experience) and competitive costs as a customer would do when buying. Should I buy this shirt or that one? Is it the colour, how it looks on me, when would I wear it, is it easy to wash and iron, and how much does it cost vs. the other choices I have? I might buy the most expensive one (assuming I can afford it) or the cheapest one. But I buy the one that gives me the most value.

---

[1] https://www.gartner.com/en/newsroom/press-releases/2021-05-27-gartner-predicts-more-than-75--of-organizations-will-#:~:text=Gartner%20Predicts%20More%20Than%2075,Service%20and%20Support%20by%202025

[2] https://www.entrepreneur.com/growing-a-business/customer-experience-is-gaining-traction-but-are-we/371492

[3] https://www.mckinsey.com/capabilities/growth-marketing-and-sales/our-insights/prediction-the-future-of-cx

I thought it is relevant to also understand the definitions of customer experience:

- Customer experience is the impression your customers have of your brand as a whole throughout all aspects of the buyer's journey. It results in their view of your brand and impacts factors related to your bottom line including revenue (see https://blog.hubspot.com/service/what-is-customer -experience).
- Customer experience (CX) is everything related to a business that affects a customer's perception and feelings about it. Customer experience (CX) focuses on the relationship between a business and its customers. It includes every interaction, no matter how brief, and even if it doesn't result in a purchase (see https://www.zendesk.com/blog/why-companies-should -invest-in-the-customer-experience/).
- Smartercx presented by Oracle gives 15 definitions, mostly on transactions (see https://smartercx.com/15-definitions-of-customer-experience/).
- Blake Morgan in Forbes: everything a company does contributes to how customers perceive it, and therefore to the overall customer experience, including the messaging you use, the products you sell, the sales process, and what happens after the sale, plus other internal factors like the inter-working of the company, its leadership, and the engineering of the product or service.
- *CXPA*[1] interviewed an international panel of CX practitioners, consultants, and academics to provide this independent, platform-agnostic introduction to CX. Customer Experience (CX) is the perception that customers have of an organization – one that is formed based on interactions across all touchpoints, people, and technology over time.
- CX Management is the set of practices that an organization employs to meet (or exceed) customers' expectations. True CX management incorporates these key interrelated elements:

  o A Culture of Customer-centricity *Every aspect of the corporate culture – from the top-down – is focused on the customer.*
  o The Realization of the Rewards *Every customer experience gain contributes to positive business performance outcomes.* Holistic Alignment of Systems and Structures. *Every department and employee are united in the quest for customer experience excellence.*

---

[1] Customer Experience Professional Association.

o Evolution of Business Practices Through a Focus on Customer Needs and Engagement *Every thought and action is meaningful, making customers' lives better and showing you care.*

▪ With so many options available, choosing the right resources to advance the success of your organization's CX initiative is a significant decision as you are certain to invest time, money, energy, and attention – all extremely valuable resources. We have addressed common questions in *this section* to help you make better-informed decisions when selecting resources to strengthen your CX practice.

By and large, it is about interactions and customer culture.

Let us end with *Forrester's*[1] findings quoted by Business to Community.

They summarize the four key findings that prove the value of an effortless experience approach:

Finding no. 1: The delight strategy doesn't improve revenue and there is no need for it – loyalty doesn't increase when customers are delighted. And in fact, the book argues that it costs more to delight.

Finding no. 2: Customer satisfaction doesn't predict loyalty as well as brands believe. The book states that 20% of customers who reported being satisfied also reported they intended to leave the company.

Finding no. 3: Customer service interactions drive more disloyalty than loyalty, in general, which emphasizes the need for an effortless customer service interaction.

Finding no. 4: The key to mitigating disloyalty is to reduce customer effort. In fact, 96% of high-effort experiences result in disloyalty, compared to 9% of low-effort experiences resulting in disloyalty.

So, my bottom line is to use CX carefully. Make it a useful tool and do not over-use or over-extend it. Give an experience and a journey where it is needed and minimize both because customers do not have the time and the patience (see *Dave Brock's article*[2]) to look for an experience unless they are on a holiday, and the experience is very important. Otherwise, if I buy a phone, I want it to work, and I want to use it without hassles and extra work. This no-experience is the best for me. When the phone does not work, bad experiences take over,

---

[1] https://www.getfeedback.com/resources/cx/why-an-effortless-experience-isnt-enough-for-customer-loyalty/

[2] https://www.business2community.com/sales-management/how-value-and-value-creation-evolves-02412082

which we want to avoid at all costs. Leaders be sure you understand and not make experience your goal. Make value your goal.

* * *

Customer-centric Circles, the Self-Directed Approach to Service and Mindset Changes

Frontline people are typically trained so as to modify their behaviour and actions. Unfortunately, these training programs do not impact the behaviour, though they are useful in imparting skills.

This paper describes Customer-centric Circles, and the resultant benefits in Customer focus, teamwork, and improved service Value Creation. Much of this is done through mindset changes that occur when frontline people are self-directed and self-motivated.

Customer-centric Circles (shortened to Customer Circles) were started in companies from around 2004. This paper describes Customer-centric Circles; how Customer-centric Circles can create/add value to the firms including their employees and mostly for customers, particularly in the service area and in team-work and Customer focus; Customer-centric Circles are compared to traditional training programs; and how Customer-centric Circles can be implemented and the internal structure/organization and challenges.

Cases of Customer Circles are discussed. The frontline people can be in various disciplines such as manufacturing, administration, sustainability etc.

Training and Customer-centric Circles

Current training programs are effective in teaching specific skills but not in changing mindset. Mindset changes are somewhat intangible, and difficult to measure, whereas traditional training programs focus on specific and (generally) tangible skills that can be measured.

In spite of these training programs, the American Customer Satisfaction Index or ACSI score has remained somewhat static from 1995 (score 74) to 2014 (score 76).

Customer-centric Circle programs were meant to educate and build a platform for self-learning through reflection, and building self-esteem (or self-value or self-worth), confidence, and awareness as the first steps. This leads to pro-activeness, which is focused on creating value for the Customers. As an aside, this process creates value for the frontline employees and the other executives and improves teamwork and service execution. Customer Circles complement traditional training programs.

This is the reason for starting Customer-centric Circles in companies.

Customer-centric Circles: Introduction

The program started because it was realized that frontline people could provide better service if they participated in designing how they should and could help Customers and improve service value. In addition, most of them notice the wrong things companies are doing or espousing and can suggest changes. An example is a complaint that we cannot book two dissimilar rooms such as a suite and a normal room in one online operation in a hotel booking (on some sites it is possible). Most frontline people stop trying to escalate these to the top, because they feel they will not be heard, or nothing will be done.

Frontline people when asked what they should do would tell us at least 90% of what we would have mandated for them (and trained them) to do. Other executives can also get inputs from frontline people and their Customer insight and experience.

Mindset changes are best impacted by self-introspection. Why do Customers get angry? What causes them to be happy? What is my role in Customer behaviour? Realistically, to change the mindset, we must first build the self-esteem of the frontline people. Once we have done this, we will find they are more open to ideas. Then, we have to build their awareness, which will allow introspection and self-evaluation, and self-improvement. After this, we can embark on a Continuous Customer Improvement Program (CCIP) led by front-facing employees, not executives. We also ask the front-end employees to examine the Customer's Bill of Rights. We ask them to comment on how they will ensure the Bill of Rights will be upheld and what support they need. We also help them understand they themselves have personal brand equity that the Customer can recognize, and their brand equity can build or destroy the company's brand equity, and that the Customer Circles will help them build their own brand equity.

Customer-centric Circles: Experiential Learning and Mindset Changes

For making this happen, we start Customer-centric Circles, which are led by front-facing employees working with Customers. In Customer-centric Circles, we do not have a hierarchy. Frontline people learn from Customer problems and service improvement. Why did they happen? What can be done? What should frontline people do to avoid problems in the future? And as they talk to each other, they realize their own role in causing and avoiding problems and finding problem solutions.

This is a form of experiential learning:

- Actually, experiencing and sharing experiences. Trying out and suggesting new approaches.
- Talking about what happened. Reflecting whether what we did was right or wrong or could be improved. Believing that we as employees are adequate and capable of handling Customers. This is the start of the self-esteem program and comes from understanding the Customer's behaviour, and how we can impact it positively and negatively.
- Prioritizing the best alternatives and rolling them out and seeing if they apply to all or only limited situations. Analyse what happened and work on iterative improvements.
- Asking if this works for my team, and how do I apply it?
- Building a better work ethic, better teamwork, ever-improving Customer experience.

During the Customer-centric Circle sessions, these employees will also figure out how to keep the promises made by the company and its Bill of Rights (and also by the employees). This leads to massive mindset changes and the taking over of ownership of the Customers by the employees. This also means a change of mindset of other executives, to let go instead of always telling people what to do and training them. These executives then let the employees tell them what the employees are going to do and what help they need from their supervisors and provide a supportive platform.

As mindset changes occur, we also have to ensure that the employees understand the mission and values of the company and whether they understand the importance of and how the mission and values can guide them.

One of our clients said, "When we put employees into Customer Circles, we find that they take a leadership role, become proactive towards the Customer and devise things to do for him, and go into a self-learning and self-management mode. Continuous Customer Improvement Programmes, better teamwork and awareness of other employees and Customers also ensue:

a. For brainstorming Customer needs
b. For Customer's DNA (Do Not Annoy) and Delight factors
c. For Customer's Bill of Rights and for the Circle of Promises

    d. For Continuous Customer Improvement Programme and to maintain Customer focus

    e. For building and improving employee engagement, and employee and company brand equity

The participants in Customer Circles are asked not only about what to do for the Customer (few companies formally ask their frontline people about their view of the Customer and how to handle them) but also about the pain and pleasure of dealing with Customers. How can they avoid the pain and increase the pleasure? It turns out that most of the factors in doing so vest in the frontline people. This awareness prompts them to suggest and do the right things for the Customer. This cooperative effort can be spread throughout the company.

This bottom-up approach has been tested at Tata Power, Tata Chemicals Crop Nutrition and Agri-Business, Godrej Industries, and other companies through setting up Customer Circles and has brought tremendous enthusiasm and change.

The challenge is not to dampen this new enthusiasm by putting these Customer Circles under traditional project management, but to allow the roll-out to be employee driven and driven by the employees' hearts, thereby changing organizational culture.

Customer-related tasks and initiatives cannot be mandated and instituted using top-down edicts and project-related methodologies. They have to be adopted and adaptable; they require supportive leadership, incentivization, and a change of culture. They call for a bottom-up approach. The analyse/think/aim/fire approach has to give way to the feel/see/believe approach. The approach has to be one of human orientation and not of project orientation, of enabling not ordering, and supporting not mandating. This is accomplished through Customer-centric Circles.

What Helps Customer Circles?

We need to put into play Total Customer Value Management thinking versus the conventional Customer Approach. Unless top management understands this and also ensures that these philosophies are shared with the Customer Circles, the mindset of the frontline person cannot change because he can see the top management mindset is different. Given below are some examples of the Total Customer Value Management (Total CVM) approach.

Please note, that Customer Circles work also in companies where there is no Total Customer Value Management program.

Business Philosophy

The business philosophy has to change in the top-level thinking and has to be reflected in the frontline people thinking (Table 3.1).

Once we have the corporate thinking along with the Total CVM thinking, Customer Circles are easier to set up.

Customer Circles: Rollout and Composition

Assuming the top managers are behind the Customer Circles, we are ready to set one up.

We start with Circle Facilitators/coordinators, Customer champions, discuss with them what is intended and the results, successes, and success factors; why

Table 3.1   Changing the Business Philosophy

Existing Customer Approach	Total CVM Approach
1. Profits are the purpose of business	1. Profits are a result of a higher purpose of the business, to have Customers who are your partners
2. Business strategy is driven from the market assessment	2. The Customer strategy along with the shareholder strategy drives business
3. Price is the main driver of purchase	3. The main driver of purchase is CVA (Customer Value Added, the ratio of the value our company adds to our Customers divided by the value our competitor adds to their Customers). CVA was first described by Ray Kordupleski in the 1980s
4. The bottom line improved by better processes, and a focus on costs	4. CVA builds loyalty, market share, higher profits, and Shareholder Value

these initiatives die, such as diversity of views, discouragement, poor follow-up, lack of action, not timely, no reinforcement, no sharing of ideas, no Customer Circle skills, and the rush to recruit and unaligned teams. Cynicism, being ordered or told to do things, being taught rather than self-learning and organizational structure, all conspire against the success of Customer Circles.

The management appoints a facilitator who can carry the Customer Circle leaders and ensure there is follow-up.

The Customer Circle consists of about 20 frontline people (they have to be carefully selected to be positive and willing to express their views). There can be more or less (we have worked with 60 in a group). Staff people, such as HR, IT, accounts, logistics etc., who can implement the changes required by the Customer Circle are also members. The Customer facilitator has to coordinate the effort.

The process starts by building an awareness of the importance of the Customer. What you'll find is that the group will come up with better ways to handle a Customer. Through this process, Customer awareness in the company and among the employees will invariably increase.

During Customer Circles, we have to ask people why Customers become happy with the frontline people and why they become unhappy. Often, they respond that the Customers' unhappiness is caused by their (the Customer's) unreasonableness or unreasonable expectations. On introspection, the group often reaches the conclusion that it is their own actions or inactions that cause dissatisfaction in the Customer's mind. With this awareness, they search for solutions, including their own behaviour modification, and the support needed to make them more effective. (Such support could be website changes, better coordination with the parts department and the frontline, the ability to call the Customer back and give him/her feedback, better address taking, better coordination of daily service visits to Customer locations.) The group builds its own self-esteem and awareness and decides on action steps, including building the Customers' delight factors and Do Not Annoy (DNA) factors.

The Customer Circles and their members should have a reward and recognition program.

There should be a central coordinator (Chief Customer Officer or the Chief Customer Value Creator) who should have a process to review the progress of meeting including:

The Customer Circles should have:

1. An agenda
2. A review of the tasks set out in the previous meeting, and of achievements
3. The Circles should develop Customer's DNA (Do Not Annoy), Customer Delight Factors, and Courtesy Systems
4. A review of the Customer Bill of Rights, and the Circle of Promises

    a. Promises kept: reinforce them
    b. Promises broken: why broken? Ask if they can be kept. If not, discard. If yes, reinforce
5. Continuous Customer Improvement Program
    a. Process related
    b. Soft or Customer related
6. Set up tasks for various people, including responsibilities for implementation, timelines etc.
7. Establish a date for tasks and next meeting

The minutes of the meeting should be circulated within a day to show the seriousness, and importance of the Customer Circle. Minutes should go to the CCO also. In the following meeting success should be celebrated.

Subsequent or new circles could have some people from the first circle to act as facilitators and to share experiences.

Customer Circles and Shared Visions

But before all this, we must understand the Voice of the Employee, his pain points, and increase his awareness of the Customer. Along with this, we must capture the Voice of the Customer and the Voice of the Competitor.

The frontline people and the staff people must come to a shared vision which should be close to the vision the company and CxOs have.

The problem with a top-down approach is that top management "dictates" a vision and does not build it with a buy-in of key players at all levels, nor is it built on personal and shared visions. This buy-in is important to shared visions and Customer Circles.

Customer Circles and Team Learning

Customer Circles are inter-disciplinary teams. The success of Customer Circles depends on individual excellence and learning, and how well the team members work together. It depends on managing individual skills and merits with team spirit. Unaligned teams waste energy. So, teams have to learn to align themselves and develop the capacity of the Bottom-Up Total CVM.

Customer Bill of Rights

We wish to have a Customers' Bill of Rights, which also translates to promises to the Customer.

Each right enunciated in the Bill of Rights is a promise made by and dependent on the company and the employees. The employee promises what he will do to make the Customers' Bill of Rights a true right. They take ownership of the Bill of Rights and its operation.

Once we publish a Customer Bill of Rights, we have to respect it. The Customer considers it a promise. Everyone in the company has to honour this Bill of Rights. To do this, the people responsible for fulfilling the rights have to promise and commit that they will do all that is necessary to respect the Customers' rights. In return, the company and the managers will have to promise and support the employees to fulfil their commitment to the Bill of Rights and to the Customer. This is the process of enabling the employees.

One client stated:

> The entire process starts with the Customer, and circles through the company back through top management to the Customer as his Bill of Rights! Generally, the promising process happens in the Customer Circles and is an interconnecting Circle of Promises from the company to the Customer, from the employee to the company and from the company to the employees and the support personnel, the support personnel to the frontline people; hence, the Circle of Promises! This is necessary because people who hear Customer problems are generally not the ones that have the responsibility for fixing them.

The Customer Circles will monitor the effectiveness of the promises made. Promises are meant to be kept. Sometimes, they are broken. The Customer Circles, which is a cross-functional team, will examine:

Is the team not able to or not ready to keep the promise? In this case, the promise should be dropped from the Bill of Rights. Is the promise broken because of some let-up or goof-up, or misunderstanding? In this case, we have to reinforce the promise.

Lastly, the Customer Circles of the company should be looking for corrective (and not punitive) action, unless there is some serious infraction of ethics or company policy. The best action is corrective action and punitive action is an extreme step.

These Customer Circles can become a self-learning system. With Customer Circles, the organization is bound to become creative and innovative. People want to be part of such an organization and participate in innovation.

The principle has to be that no one should be too proud to learn. And not too proud to learn from anyone. Continuous learning and participation will lead to Customer excellence.

Customer Circles and Celebration/Recognition

Not only do we discuss what we can do in Customer Circles, but we also have to talk about things we have done wrong. We must celebrate and recognize what we do for Customers and build on this. With corporate communications, we must record Customer stories, where we have done wonderful things for the Customer. These stories should adorn the office walls of the Chief Customer Officer and the Customer Champions and the frontline people should have a copy

Some Customer Value Foundation Case Studies

1. The Tata Power Customer Circles led to the introduction of the courtesy system (smiling and greeting at work). The Customer Circles realized that the Customers were being inconvenienced when they visited the Tata Power office. The Circles designed special signs and put them up for the Customers to get to the Customer Department.

Soon thereafter, at the suggestion of the Customer Circle, an existing office was converted into a comfortable Customer meeting room. The Customer did not have to search for the right Tata Power representative. They just picked up the intercom as they came off the elevator. The person who responded ensured the right person came to meet them and escort them to the meeting room. Individual Customer facing employees started to put Customer-related quotations on their desktops. They made laminated cards they carry showing Customers' DNA (Do Not Annoy). On the reverse side of the card is the Customer delight factors.

Service people who fix Customer problems have started to carry cards showing how to save energy and giving safety tips and leave these with Customers.

Sub-station managers invite important Customers to the sub-station to show the Customers they have dedicated control panels for them with the Customer's names on them, and how they ensure a continuous supply of electricity to them.

Call Centres have better co-ordination on answering billing-related enquiries.

Complaints fell from 9 per thousand to 2.7 per thousand in the quarter following the formation of Customer Circles.

When new Customer offices are set up, the Customer Bill of Rights is put up in the room where the Customer and the executive sit so that they can see what is expected and what executives must do.

When new connections were to be given, Customers had to make several trips to the company's office. During the Customer Circles, most people felt that the Customer should not have to come more than once. But what would happen if they forgot to bring a document? They would be forced to come again.

The Customer Circles went one step further and suggested that Customers should come zero times. In short, the company should visit the Customers. In doing so, prior to their visit, executives would ensure the Customer had collected all the documents needed for a new connection, and therefore the executive would not have to visit the Customer twice.

New connections cannibalized from competition increased 4-fold (a 400% increase in Customers).

Tata Power then set up more Customer Circles:

- An Apex Customer Circle under the leadership of the VP, HR, and the VP of Distribution
- A Core Customer Circle consisting of all Customer Circle leaders (with a convenor, under the guidance of the Customer Care Chief)
- A Customer Management Department Customer Circle (head Customer Management)
- An Administration and HR Customer Circles under the leadership of the Chief Admin Officer. Finance will join this Customer Circle
- A Customer Circle in the Customer Distribution Department
- An IT Customer Circle
- A Customer Circle at the Safety, Health, and Environmental Department and the Corporate Social Responsibility
- A Head Office Customer Circle (Head of Communications, Convenor)

2. At Tata Chemicals Crop Nutrition and Agri-Business, Customer Circles have helped Dealers and Retailers focus on each other and the end Customer, the farmer, and to provide extraordinary service to them.

Eighteen Customer Circles were started, one in each district in one state in India.

Problems of delivery and supply chain, payments, and billing between the dealers and the company were resolved once they started to talk together as equals and team members, listening to each other, accepting problems (and not saying, that's the way it is), and finding solutions. An example is the short delivery of promised supplies from the company to the dealers. Let's say 15 tons were promised, and only 13 tons arrived. The logistic person would shrug it away and say we got a 13-ton truck (trucks were in short supply). What can we do? In the Customer Circles, it was agreed this was a serious problem for the Customer (the dealer) and had to be corrected. Finally, the company worked out a buffer stock to prevent shortages from happening.

3. At another Tata company, the CEO told me that he had spent a month visiting the Customers. They all complained about delivery and the supply chain. I met with the head of logistics, who reported along with the CEO to the group managing director. He told me logistics had improved. In fact, he was getting bonuses. It turned out that his bonus was based on cost effectiveness and not Customer Value!

In discussions in a Customer Circle, it became apparent that there was a problem, and the frontline people asked for an improvement. Changes were then implemented, and the Customer Value Added scores went up and complaints went down.

Lessons for Management

Customer-centric Circles are a good way of improving service, teamwork, and Customer focus. This is achieved by getting frontline people to be self-directed and self-motivated and becoming more Customer-centric.

Mindset: We found that mindset is one of the most important attributes of a frontline person. But just as importantly all executives must have the same mindset. Conducting a Customer strategy is very useful in bringing the entire company and all its departments into being involved with the Customer and building a Customer-centric organization.

Training in itself may not impact mindset changes sufficiently. It is important for diction, manner of speaking, following a script, and for teaching skills.

Requirements for a mindset are self-esteem, awareness and pro-activeness, and self-introspection.

Customer Circle results show an improvement in Customer focus and service and an improvement in business results. How such Customer-centric Circles can be and should be established has been shown. Employee engagement, and employee and company brand equity improve.

We have seen that the frontline people can be self-directed and better motivated to make the Customer happy if allowed to do so in Customer Circles.

Such programs create value for the frontline employees, their supervisors and companies, and mostly for Customers. The personal brand equity of the frontline people also gets built up, improving the brand equity of the company and its service Value Creation. Customer Circles go beyond Customer care to Customer caring.

References

Pierre Gurdjian, Thomas Halbeisen, and Kevin Lane of Mckinsey in "Why Leadership-Development Programs Fail," https://www.mckinsey.com/featured-insights/leadership/why-leadership-development-programs-fail

Ray Kordupleski, Mastering Customer Value Management, Pinnaflex 2003

Gautam Mahajan, Total Customer Value Management, Transforming Business Thinking, Response Books 2011

Gautam Mahajan, Value Creation, the Definitive Guide for Business Leaders, Response Books 2016

Gautam Mahajan, Customer Value Investment, Response Books 2008

* * *

Ease and Simplicity Creates Experience and Value

> Life is not complex. We are complex. Life is simple, and the simple thing is the right thing.
>
> *– Oscar Wilde*

I look for ease and simplicity:[1] that is the best experience I can have.

You can attempt to give the customer great experience, but it is the simplicity that matters. Trying to delight the customer is very difficult and is a hit-and-miss action and costs you a lot. You have to ask, how do I give a good experience with that product, not just by its looks, not its charm, but by its ease of use, its simplicity, not needing help, its proper working, ease of reaching out for help and solving problems, and so forth. See *Simplicity as a Core Value of a Great Customer Experience*[2] and the article in the Harvard Business Review called: *To Keep Your Customers, Keep It Simple.*[3]

Just remember, doing the right things in a simple fashion does not cost you as much as trying to give a great experience, when experience has been proven not to correlate to loyalty. And the cost of losing customers because things become complex.

Somewhere, someone has convinced the marketers we want more, whether it is experience, whether it is choice …. I do not want customer confusion and value confusion. Take air conditioners made by any one brand, Hitachi, Panasonic, or Samsung. In the 1.5-ton size, once you get past the energy efficiency rating and whether you want a split or a window unit, and whether invertor or not (so far easy to understand), there are at least ten products with different product

---

[1] What many people call KISS (keep it simple stupid).

[2] https://nerdcow.co.uk/blog/simplicity-core-value-great-customer-experience/

[3] https://hbr.org/2012/05/to-keep-your-customers-keep-it-simple

numbers with no explanation, and I can't tell the difference between them with the model numbers. This is not experience, this is confusion. The numbers are different. I cannot compare what these are. I cannot tell if it is a 2020 model or a 2021 one. I cannot tell if it has a single swing or dual swing without expending more time in the search. Once I decide I want dual swing, I get three models with different numbers and prices and I have to work to find what they are. Often it is not easy to get the details. So, one lands up buying from Amazon on price!

Another example is buying a lightweight laptop. Many times, the weight is not given. How do I select? Then I get a processor of i5 seventh generation or i9. How the heck am I supposed to know which is better? All to confuse me. Which is the latest processor?

They say customer beware, but if you are like me, a lay customer with minimal knowledge, what do you do?

You do this by making the journey also very simple, easy to understand, easy to find, easy to buy, easy to receive, easy to service, easy to complain, and get rectification. This really is the best experience you can get. I do not want a circuitous route that stops my journey or forces me to abandon my mission and perhaps purchase. You must avoid Customer Value starvation and destruction.

I have managed to find people in many companies who can help me, whether it is an insurance company like Tata-AIG or HDFC Ergo, or Epson for printing, or Acer laptops and getting answers and solutions becomes easier.

Why is this the case? Are these people more in tune to help? More knowledgeable? If this is true, are we wasting time by relegating customer problems to grunt workers? People who have no knowledge continue to say, this is our policy. Or even if you are a registered customer who wants to know the serial number of your air conditioner or your address when they already have it. Waste my time, waste my energy. And it wasted the company's time, effort, and money.

Don't people realize these are value creators when you get a good experience, and that a surfeit of unnecessary experience can overwhelm you and cost you and the company?

Certainly, I want no duplication. The same question is being asked by multiple people. Was your product repaired? Was it repaired to your satisfaction? Have you ever said, no it has not been repaired to my satisfaction, does the person say they will get it rectified?

I have a Hitachi air conditioner, which every now and then starts to leak and send water down the wall. I have to get it fixed. But there is no permanent fix for an air conditioner installed only a year ago. The air conditioner is very noisy. The person comes and says there is no noise. What do I do? Where is the experience?

Some simplicity thoughts. Try to make things simple. Ask customers if they can understand what you are saying and your multiple offerings. Make it simple for them to choose your product. Make sure basic information is available and even more importantly, correct and up to date like contact numbers, addresses; ensure website links work. Make it easy to get more information. Do not confuse giving information to the customer with gathering information from the customer. I just went on the Pidilite company's M-seal site. I wanted to know the different sizes the product was available in. The information did not exist on the website. I found a contact number and asked the question. I had to give them my name, telephone number, email, why I wanted to use M-seal and what my problem was and god knows what else, before the call centre person said you have to talk to our service manager in your area to get this information, as I do not have the information on product sizes. What is your pin code? I then get a number and after failing to connect a few times, I got my information. Phew!

When you make it easy for me to deal with you, you create value for me. I want to do business with you versus with someone who makes it difficult for me. Simplicity is about making it convenient for me and creating value for me and not for the seller.

The tragedy is that sometimes an easy buy may end up with a difficult-to-deal-with product and its service. By this time, it is too late for you. And perhaps for the company because we do not get value from them and it may end up in our boycotting them!

I am sure all of you have examples to share with me. "Simplicity is the ultimate sophistication" (Leonardo da Vinci).

Chapter 4

Customer Value Starvation

Air India, Whither Goest Thou, and Tata: How to Create Value

My first trip with Indian Airlines was around 1954 in a Dakota DC3, and with Air India in 1968, on the much-heralded Boeing 707.

Since then, I have been an Air India fan and a loyal customer. Not to say I did not have some bad experiences, but many more were good. For instance, there was the time we were held up in Paris for a day to change engines and Air India took wonderful care of us (got us great rooms, transportation, and meals and had good updates on the plane departure) or the time the stewardess sat with my wife who was travelling alone because our small child would not stop crying. Or when Indian Airlines staff took care of passengers stranded in Mumbai because of the rains on 26 July 2005. I wrote about this, and the article appeared in 26 newspapers. I wrote to the Managing Director, suggesting he congratulate the staff, but got no reply!

I would defend Air India to my friends as being a great airline even though they would cite poor experiences. Till now, my flight AI173, Delhi to San Francisco, nonstop, a few days ago in May 2022 on Business Class changed all this.

It began with the booking process. The Air India website would show all business class flights to San Francisco were full or not available. Why? I called someone in AI reservations whom I knew, and she said the website was not fully ok and advised me to get to a travel agent who has access to different websites. Through a travel agent, I bought a business class ticket. He had to go to the Air India office twice to assign seats because the system was down.

But this was the beginning of my problems. At the airport, when I checked in, I was asked for information I had filled in during my on-line check-in. (By the way the mobile check-in was more complex. It wanted me to upload my passport etc. Why?) That was a waste of my time and now also a waste of time for the ground staff. I asked the airline representative to make a note of this issue and let the powers that be know. I knew she would not (because this is typical, the frontline staff and their supervisors are not trained to escalate systemic problems), and so I asked for the supervisor. No response! Just ignored the request. At check-in, I requested a change of seats and was told the flight was full. As she was handing me the boarding cards, she suddenly stated seat 14A was non-operative and that she would get me two seats together. Since she had earlier said it was a full flight, I asked how? She said we would get a window and an aisle and not two of the three middle seats, which was fine by me. But all this would happen at the boarding gate, she said. Another woman came and said she promised this and that she would be at the gate. She said her name was Aruna and she was in charge. A promise but no change in the boarding card.

On the way, my wife and I had gone to the AI lounge, and all the food staff were not wearing masks, and I asked them to, but they ignored me. The ground staff should have noticed this, but they did not. The air conditioning was not working. Why did the staff not notice? Or do they care or do they accept all this? Is this a chalta hai attitude?

When we got to the gate, there were two people there at the check-in counter. The young man was busy with a customer. The oldish woman was sitting and ignored us. She finally got up and was leaving and I asked, "Do you work here?" She said, "Yes," and tried to brush me off by saying boarding will start soon. I asked if she was too senior to take care of me. Then I told her my issue, and she checked and we had 8E and 8F, middle seats, and an aisle. I asked for a window and an aisle, but the young man said seven or eight seats were non-functional. Can you imagine eight seats at Rupees 200,000 each or Rupees 430,000,000 over a year if the plane flew 300 days! Not to worry, the plane will get re-furbished soon, said the older woman.

The ground staff did not tell us that 8D, which was next to our newly assigned seats, was non-operative and therefore that seat was empty. They then requested an elderly Sardar and his wife to switch with us and gave us 8G and H. Which was fine except that 8E broke down when the Sardarji was lying on it and was not able to get out of the seat that was now in a prone position for sleeping. He needed a number of crew members to help him off the seat .... So much for the maintenance. As my son, who calls Air India Air Village, said: if the flight is so poorly maintained, how can they manage and maintain systems?

Also, my TV screen and the remote was not working – so much for onboard entertainment!

During breakfast and lunch, my food tray would open at an angle, and never straighten.

The staff on the plane were excellent.

Now, as the Tatas take over AI, I have several suggestions keeping customer value in mind: I work in the area of customer value and creating value. We have a value school at Kobe University in Japan, one at the Japan Advanced Institute of Science and Technology, a Value Research Centre at the Doshisha University, a Value Creation Centre at Aalborg, Denmark, and one at the University of Maryland and the Value Creation Wheel Lab at the Nova Business and Economics School in Lisbon, Portugal. I am the Founder Editor of the *Journal of Creating Value* with Phil Kotler, Steve Vargo, Jag Sheth, and Tata's Mukundan on the Board. We have done customer value work for Tata Power, Tata Fertiliser, Tata Chemicals, SAIL, Birlas, ITC etc.

I mention this to show the world is embracing value. I believe in co-creation and co-operation (two people working or operating together to get a mutually value creating solution).

Also, I suggest my 8As for Creating Value for Air India:

8As for executives holds for leaders also:

Awareness: leaders and executives and frontline people must be aware of things around them, they must be curious, and they must want to know more.

If executives do not notice the staff not wearing masks or poor air conditioning, how can you change the situation?

Attitude: your people must have a super attitude, positive, forward thinking, and multi-dimensional. Able to be strategic and innovative to practical. Some executives are functional in thinking, and this needs to change. Mindset plays a major role.

If you promise, your attitude must make sure you follow through, which Aruna did not. Or you must have the wonderful attitude of the inflight crew.

If you do not try to get things rectified, then problems get larger. If you do not notice (awareness) or do not care (attitude), how can things be rectified?

We have run Customer-centric circles to get frontline people and staff to take charge and talk about problems and solutions. Attitudes change as people become aware of what they are doing wrong and what they should be doing, Customer Circles have worked at Tatas, Birla's, L&T etc.

Ability: much of this is innate, but some come from learning and experience. A great mindset helps here.

Ability is important to be caring

Agility: this comes from a mindset and mental make-up

Adaptability: being able to change with circumstances

Anticipation: being able to be ahead of others by forward thinking and view. Part of this comes from a sixth sense which is developed in your mind

Ambidextrousness: capability of doing more than one thing at a time; capacity to think of different things

Action: convert into action

There is great hope for Tatas at AI. Please do not let things get out of hand. Work on the problems:

1. Appoint a problem noter and a problem solver, particularly on what the customer sees. For example, does the check-in work and is it synchronized with what the check-in counter gets? Does the seat work, does the TV screen work, do the escape jackets work? Is safety in place? Solve these problems pronto. I was told spare controllers for the inflight screens do not exist. Why not? You have no excuse for not having spares on-ground at least.

Also, do not stop at solving individual problems. If the problem is systemic, change the system so that others do not have the same problem.

Remember, that very few customers complain and even fewer do something about it, like I am trying to do.

2. What causes staff to get frustrated? Use Customer-centric Circles to solve their problems, and you will solve many customer problems also.
3. Do not run the airline with bean counters but with a heart. Most passengers will accept problems if they are brought into the loop. Use co-creation and co-operation.
4. See how you can sell faulty seats with discounts (so the customer knows what he is getting into). How can you have full planes? How do you make sure everything works? Prioritize engineering, safety, good planes that take off and land, and happy passengers when they take off and when they land. I am sure Tatas are trying all these.
5. And for attitudes of the ground staff, get this changed. Use Customer-centric Circles approach as told in my book *Total Customer Value Management*.

Get people to be aware and get the 8As. Don't try to get to customer delight on day 1 that may impact only a few customers. That will come with time. However, get the basics right and you will reach the top. Work on this!

As my son said to me, imagine if you were flying cattle class.

You can reach the author at Mahajan@CustomerValueFoundation.com for your comments.

* * *

Adding More Value Does Not Cost Much; Creating Low Value Does Cost You

This doesn't make sense, you think. Doing less cannot cost more.

You have to look at the net cost. Many actions that add value do not cost much. Smiling, being courteous, listening to customers, keeping promises, going the extra mile, wanting to help, being on time, not making the customer anxious, not making him wait, not making him spend energy, not insulting his intelligence, not destroying his self-image, being prompt, being knowledgeable, etc. can all add value.

And that adds up to a higher relationship, better retention, higher sales, better prices, and ROI.

The reverse is not caring and adding less value. The net cost is loss of sales, loss of brand ambassadors, loss of referrals, loss of customers, and loss of profits and ROI. This all leads to value destruction. You must manage value destroyers (or what I call **DNA [Do Not Annoy]** factors).

The cost of poor experience and bad service leads to not being able to charge higher prices or loss of sales.

Let's take an example of airlines. Some of them are full fare and some of them are low cost. Note they do not say high class and low class, nor do they say high value and low value. Full fare connotes certain givens like free baggage allowance, free food, and faster check-in for business class. Low cost means none of these.

So, if you do not want the hassle of paying for your luggage or seat, and the cost is not that important you go full fare.

Let's say you travel low cost. Your experience beyond what you expect of poorer check-in and luggage may still be good. I just took a Ryan Air flight. I had prepaid for my luggage. The flight was on time, the seats were ok, the price was great, the staff smiled, and the luggage was retrieved fast, all adding to the value.

The other day I took a full fare airline. One bag was a hair over 23 Kg, the allowed weight limit, and the other was 12 Kg, and I was asked to take things out of one and put them into the other. The food was bad, and my luggage came late. The value was awful and the cost of this poor value is high to the customer and the airline.

Let's take a person who flies mostly by high-cost airlines. He is used to higher prices. Let's look at his value tree (Figure 4.1):

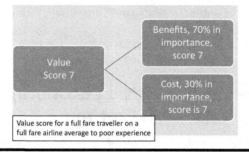

Figure 4.1   Value Attribute Tree and Scores for Full Fare Airline

He finds the value is 7 which is about average.

Now imagine this traveller has to use a low-cost airline. His expectations are lower. His price is low. But the airline staff is friendly and they handle him well. So, he is happy.

When you compare the value score, it is very high at 9 versus 7 (Figure 4.2). It did not cost the airline more to increase the value. They performed better than normal and the cost was low. So, he may consider the low-cost airline in the future. (Note the importance of cost was less [30%] for him!)

A third example is a low-cost person travelling on a low-cost airline. His expectations are low, and he is price conscious. On this flight, the airline did not insult him or aggravate him. They were ok to him. His score is 8, even though the experience was average. Note price has become 70% in importance (Figure 4.3).

The above example tells you the following:

1. Segmentation is important to position your product
2. Much of your offer is based on Customer expectations

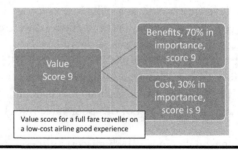

Figure 4.2   Value Score for Low Cost Airline

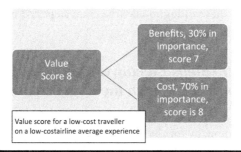

Figure 4.3   Value Score for Low Cost Traveller on Low Cost Airline

3. When expectations are high, you have to perform better. Poor service, poor food, or unhappy or unsmiling staff lowers the benefits and the value. Cost to airline has not gone up
4. When expectations are low, performing better (like staff being polite and helpful, which costs nothing) increases value
5. In this example if the normally full fare flyer found the low-cost airline gave more value than his normal high-cost airline, he may use the low-cost carrier more often than he had in the past, a loss to his full fare airline

Remember, adding More Value does not Cost Much; Creating Low Value does Cost You.

* * *

Value Creation Implementation Ideas. Avoid Value Destruction

We have talked about many ways of Value Creation, and why Value Creation is important.

How do executives create value for themselves and their organizations? By·

Differentiating themselves,
Being on time, reliable, and timely, and
Becoming knowledgeable about the company and the customers so that others in the company seek them for help, or government rules and regulations. In short become the acknowledged resident expert in something the customers want.
Being accessible to your colleagues and your customers.
Doing things right
Keeping promises

The above may sound like motherhood statements, but they are made because executives do not always follow these. Executives and frontline people are often casual, lackadaisical, not willing to take the extra step, and not willing to keep customers informed.

Examples of Extra Steps Executives Can Take (Of Course, This Depends on Your Role in the Organization)

Get to know your customer and his needs better. Become the preferred source of contact in your company for the customer. Have you noticed how you often want to deal with a particular salesperson in a store, retailer, or customer service person? This is generally because you have more faith in them, believe them a little bit more, find them reliable, and think they will give you good and genuine information and advice.

If you do something special for a customer, ask yourself if this problem is genuine or germane to other customers. How can you flag it for systemic changes? For example, if a customer calls and says your website does not give proper information on your branches, don't just give the customer the information but see how you can initiate the program for making a permanent change. Or if you find a customer cannot get options available in the company on the net, let the right people know. For example, if you are told by a customer, he cannot input his passport number because it does not fit in the required field, and you help him, can you prevent this for other customers by increasing the required field to accept more digits?

Your boss asks you set a meeting for 10 days from now. You do it. On the day of the meeting, you confirm with the person your boss is to meet that the meeting is on at the right location. Then confirm with your boss. This adds value to your boss.

If you are taking an address, take it carefully. And if you are sending someone for a service call, make sure he gets the right address and directions. This is a serious issue in India. The customer has to keep giving directions.

Examples of Value Destruction That Can Be Avoided

A major company advertizes their addresses on the net. Some of the offices have moved location, but the net information is not updated. Value is destroyed for the customer who goes there. If you are told about this, do not just apologize and get the information updated. Even more, make a check on other locations.

If you are a car dealer, and your customer wants a test drive, and the information has been taken (like customer name and address, type of car he wants to test drive, and at what time), do not re-ask these questions when you call to check if the test drive had been done.

A customer calls and wants to know your CEO's name. Do not ask why, who are you, etc. His name is public information, and you will just get the customer to do extra work to get the name, and also get him irked.

Do not answer a question with a question.

I get so irked when a courier company calls to say am I sure my address is right. Where is your office? Don't courier services have means to find address information?

The car dealer service people call you for an appointment two days after you got the car serviced.

Notice many value creation ideas are doing things right. Notice when people add value to you and when they destroy value.

Try answering these:

1. Someone calls your extension asking for another person in your office.

Should you hang up?
Tell him this is the wrong number?
Or tell him it is the wrong number and I will transfer the call?

2. You walk into your coffee room and see it is messy:

Walk out
Get your coffee and leave
Either get the responsible person to clean up or do it yourself

3. You send an email and it bounces:

Do nothing
Call the party and say the email is bouncing
If you cannot call, do you send this by snail mail or courier?

You can be a value creator today! Leaders do get people to think like this. Setting up Customer-centric Circles (described elsewhere) helps in changing these attitudes and mindsets.

Your comments are welcome.

* * *

When Zero Defects Are the Norm, Why Not Zero Customer Complaints?

There was a time when there was no such phrase as "zero defects." It was accepted that some defects would always remain. But management Gurus convinced management that zero defects were possible and also would create a competitive advantage.

Today, it is accepted that customer service is necessary, and good customer service creates a competitive advantage. Unfortunately, customer service efficiency is measured by customer satisfaction that measures transactions and not embedded feelings over a period of time, measured by customer value. Another measure is complaints per thousand interactions. Many companies are happy to have ten or fewer complaints per thousand, or 1%. Some companies achieve 0.1% complaints. And they rest on their laurels.

Whenever a complaint gets escalated upwards to management, the general thought is to solve the complaint (and not always to the customer's satisfaction). No one thinks about systemic means to change processes and set procedures. And the cost of time and energy is not considered.

Much of this happens, because the job of the managers is to solve the problem. They do not, or are not asked to, reach zero customer complaints. If they were to look at the problem from this viewpoint, not only would the problem be solved, but also in future the complaint or customer problem should not happen.

Let me give you an example from some of the most admired and large Indian companies.

I just bought overseas travel insurance on the net. Unfortunately, I had to extend the length of stay and consequently the number of days of insurance. The insurance was due to start a month from this time. I got on the phone and found one phone number did not exist. The other one was difficult to get and when I would get on and was made to answer many questions and listen to many unnecessary "ads," I would be put on hold for the next available agent. And then I would get disconnected. I had to go through a few iterations before I got to talk to an agent. No, the policy could not be extended (he did not know how). The best would be for me to cancel the policy and get a new one for a longer time period. So, I requested cancellation. The agent could not tell me when I would get my refund. Almost 20 days later, I managed (through influence) to get the number of a senior executive. He was very apologetic. A few days later, I still did not have a refund. So, I sent an email again. This time an executive working for the company called me because his boss had asked him to help me get a refund. I had to fill out a form for a refund. I told him I had not filled out any form for getting the policy, why now, and why the call centre had not told me about the form. To cut a long story short, he said he would arrange for a refund. The executives would never go back and get the problems corrected using software, processes, and procedures so that others would not have a problem, which would lead to zero customer complaints.

I urge companies to embrace the concept of zero customer complaints and work on reducing problems for customers. What a different customer experience zero customer complaints would be!

* * *

Nuisance Value: Value Creation or Value Destruction?

Nuisance Value: value, importance, or usefulness arising from a capacity to annoy, frustrate, harass, or injure (Merriam-Webster dictionary).

I'm sure that you are all familiar with how pearls are formed. An irritant (could be a grain of sand) works its way inside the oyster and begins to irritate the soft inside, similar to us having a splinter. The oyster, in order to protect itself, begins to form layers around the irritant, out of the same material as its shell. The oyster keeps adding layers and layers and the result is often a beautiful, perfectly formed pearl.

Perhaps we should take a lesson from the simple oyster. Sometimes we are plagued with irritants from the outside (inside too). Somehow these things work their way into our psyche and they begin to annoy us and bother us. It may be the tiniest thing, something that others may not even notice, but for us, boy, are they irritating. We may think that we are able to ignore them and they will "go away," but most of the times they remain and sometimes even begin to grow and grow until they can be ignored no longer (Irritants and Pearls from andie33 in Meandering thru Life, November 15, 2010).

Maybe we should just deal with them the way that an oyster does. It takes work to turn an irritant into a beautiful pearl, but once the pearl is formed, the oyster can live with it inside its shell. We need to turn those sharp, piercing annoyances into something smooth and round and certainly something that we can then live with in peace. Sometimes we cannot rid ourselves of the problem. Sometimes we have to face it, work with it, and transform it. And then, the product is something that we can be proud of. The oyster is different after the pearl is formed, and so are we. It doesn't happen overnight, it is a process, but one that yields a beautiful result.

Sunanda Ghosh, who is VP of Sales at Sage, my Publisher said in a Sage meeting with me that she wasn't really part of the meeting and wondered why she was there. "Nuisance Value" that's why I'm here.

This got me thinking. Was nuisance value bad or good? Does it create value or not? Sunanda always had a viewpoint, and mostly she had good ideas in her viewpoint. She was enthusiastic, and it showed in her point of view. She clearly was creating value.

I have two clients in the agri input field. Both giants. One of the companies' executives insisted they could not do anything new because it was the selling season. The other one wanted the engagement because it was the selling season and what they learnt about creating value would help them sell more.

You might have a customer who is a nuisance value, but he can help you develop a pearl of a service.

When I look at nuisance value, I think of the Aam Aadmi Party (AAP), the Indian phenomenon which could blossom or fizzle out. AAP came to power in Delhi because of the nuisance value it created for the incumbent government. The AAP destroyed value for the incumbent and got elected by promising the creation of value for the ordinary citizen. For the Voter, this nuisance held out the chance of true Value Creation. So, AAP was voted in much to the surprise of all political pundits, and market researchers.

But after they came into power, they continued their nuisance value ways, and continued agitation, in spite of being the governing party. This nuisance value is veering towards value destruction in the worst possible way. The citizen is not getting the government's attention (its attention is on agitation). Transport is being curtailed (a value destroyer for working people). Three to four thousand police people are being deployed to safeguard the agitators. True nuisance value and value destruction.

"Interesting philosophy," Richard Rorty writes in *Contingency, Irony and Solidarity*, "is rarely an examination of the pros and cons of a thesis. Usually it is, implicitly or explicitly, a contest between an entrenched vocabulary which has become a nuisance and a half-formed new vocabulary which vaguely promises great things ... it [the half-formed new vocabulary] says things like, 'try thinking of it this way' – or more specifically, 'try to ignore the apparently futile traditional philosophical questions by substituting the following new and possibly interesting questions'."

Nuisance Value is good as long as it leads to Value Creation. Let it not become a value destroyer.

Your comments are welcome.

* * *

Value Deprivation

I have written about value destruction and how it can be turned into a value creating opportunity. Value destruction assumes that value was or is available to you. Elsewhere, I have written about customer frustration when customers are value starved. But a more basic issue we as humans and marketers must look at is value deprivation.

What happens when value is not available to you because of circumstances or because you have no control?

Why is this important to companies and marketers? Very often, some people are deprived of common goods available to a higher economic class of consumers. Those, who are being value deprived, used mud instead of soap; charcoal instead of toothpaste; having only one change of clothes instead of a wardrobe;

no recourse to quality or even minimum education; not getting two square meals a day; having to work in someone's house; and being deprived of an alternative future.

Many of these can be converted into opportunities; small bars of soap, sachet shampoo, or toothpaste etc. Or products with fewer features and a lower price point. I will leave the reader to think through these.

Deprival value is based on the premise that the value of an asset is equivalent to the loss that the owner of an asset would sustain if **deprived** of that asset. So, imagine the deprival value of lost education.

Much of this happens because people who can do something have closed their consciousness or trained it to ignore such things. Ayn Rand in 1966 wrote in *The Voice of Reason: Essays in Objectivist Thought*:

> Men's consciousness is the least known and most abused vital organ
> … the loss of control of one's consciousness is the most terrifying
> of human experiences … and yet men abuse, starve and subvert
> their consciousness … She says this leads to the question, Who is
> to blame? All those that are afraid to speak, or who know better
> are willing to compromise, temporise and thus to sanction such
> happenings?

Examples of Value Deprivation

Value Deprivation occurs when you are clearly eligible to be selected for a national team, but because of vested interests or quotas you are not selected. Yet another example is a worthy candidate who cannot get admission to a good school because of reservations. Or worse still, rich people who "bought" admissions for their kids to the detriment of deserving but less connected candidates.

An orphan, deprived of parental love is a case of value deprivation.

A worker being paid less than minimum wages in cash by greedy industrialists who use their black money for this purpose and simultaneously deprive the worker of social benefits apart from paying lower wages. During demonetization in India, these industrialists sacked the workers depriving them of jobs, the economy of growth, and then blamed their actions on the government. Had they been paying by check, this would probably not have happened.

A poor guy who is unable to get recourse to justice or bureaucrats is value deprived. Do the clerks and bureaucrats notice this?

Value deprivation occurs when you live in a village in India and have no opportunities. You reconcile yourself to this and do not want to do something or become someone. Then we in big cities wonder why these people are that way and not ambitious.

I met a villager who wanted to get more opportunities for his son and decided to send him to Canada. They went to touts in a bigger city, who arranged admission to unknown colleges and with large payments. This is one consequence of value deprivation: making people do things out of desperation.

The worst example is the financial community who in their greed has perpetuated great value deprivation in the guise of value creation. By making people who were marginal buy homes with cheap mortgages without worrying about the buyer's viability or the mortgage viability, they first deprived such people of long-term value and peace of mind and finally caused value destruction for them and society in a big way (value was destroyed for 6 million people who lost their homes and 8 million people who lost their jobs as an aftermath of the 2008 financial crisis. No financial company officer had any value deprivation from this crisis or went to jail).

So, What Can Leaders Do?

The first and last is to become conscious and aware of value deprivation. Recognize it. Point this out in your circle of friends or your company. Avoid it.

Your innate ability may then suggest possible solutions for those you can impact, or those your circle of friends and your company can.

A focus on value deprivation will increase value to people and society and improve the good and wellbeing of people all around. Your company will sound more fair!

Marketing people can look at their products that are deprived of people because of affordability, and they can come up with smaller sizes, lower featured products for such people and bring them into their fold.

This will all lead to the reduction of value deprivation and increase value.

Chapter 5

Employee Value

Employee Value Added Is Not What Companies Think!

This section will help you create value for yourself and your employees.

Google "employee value" and you will find it is the value the employee adds to the company, generally based on Initiative, Judgement, Loyalty, and Cost Efficiency. Just like companies look at Customers on how they can add value to the company, they look at employees as worth having as employees or not. Always the company's viewpoint!

Yet all of the time companies talk about employee engagement and customer engagement.

Can there be a change where companies look at the stakeholder (employee and customer) viewpoint?

It will happen when companies realize that they have to give to get. They have to create value before they can extract value.

How do you create value for yourself? By being seen as someone who creates value for others; someone others can rely on; someone who is creative and wants to get the job done. Someone who adds value to his employees and Customers.

The role of HRD is to create value for employees. How do you do that? The first step is to understand what creates value for the employee and enhance this value. Have you ever tried to do this consciously?

Total Customer Value Management and common sense require that you must also add value to the employees, your partners (supply and delivery chain), and society if you wish to add value to the Customer. Value added employees can and will add value to Customers and the company. This increases Customer

DOI: 10.4324/9781003381624-5

Value, which in turn increases loyalty, market share, wallet share, and profits as we learnt earlier.

To add value to the employee, we must learn what the employee values. Ask yourself what is important to the employee.

One significant way of figuring out employee value is to measure a parameter called Employee Value Added (EVA). We can just measure employee value with our employees, but it is always desirable to also measure the value your competition adds to its employees. We can then compare the value we add to our employees to the value competition adds to its employees.

Employee Value Added Is

$$EVA = \frac{\textit{Value we add to our Employees}}{\textit{Value our competition adds to their employees.}}$$

We first have to build attribute trees of Benefits and Financials as follows (Figure 5.1).

Of course, you should modify this attribute tree for your particular case, and the employee segment you are looking at.

Advantages of Employee Value Added

It is a measure of what your employees value, and what motivates them

Tells you what is most important to them in their work life

Reveals whether you are delivering what they value

Helps you improve Employee Value

Measuring competitive data tells you whether your company is adding more or less value than competition and if you are a desirable company to remain in. If you add less value, employees will migrate to a higher value adding company.

Helps you find the causes of employee churn and to reduce it.

How to Use Employee Value Added for Your Benefit

First, employ a Chief Employee Value Creator. The Chief of HRD should be renamed the Chief Employee Value Creator. Value added employees add value to Customers.

Employee value: X + Y = 100%	Benefits: X%	The job content
		On the job learning and external learning opportunities
		Image of company
		Emotional and psychological factors
		Other people (bosses/colleagues)
		Progression/exposure
	Financials: Y%	Salary
		Learning opportunities
		Other perks/travel
		Reward for performance/incentives
		My time required and pressure on me

Figure 5.1   Employee Value Attribute Tree

The **Chief Employee Value Creator** or the head of HRD has to learn to add value to the employee and not just police the employee and be the management spy or hatchet person in the eyes of the employee.

Reducing employee churn has high financial benefits (reducing hiring and replacement costs, training, lost time, and efficiency).

We are talking of big changes that might be out of your scope of work.

In Conclusion

You can see that employee value added helps you in your Total Customer Value journey.

It helps create value for employees and thereby improve value for Customers. Customer-centric Circles create value for employees and Customers.

It reduces churn and increases your company's efficiency. Lost employees and replacing them cost a considerable amount to the company.

Do you consider yourself a value added employee? Why? How much of this has to do with you and how much is dependent on the company?

Are you adding value to your employees? How?

How could the company increase value for you?

How could you increase value for yourself, your colleagues, your partners, and society? And for Customers?

How will they know that value is being increased?

Do you need to communicate value?

* * *

Value Creation by Employees

For months, people like me and members of the Board of the Value Creation Journal have been promoting Value Creation as an imperative, and that Corporates have to transform themselves to become Value Creators. That means the CxOs (CxO stands for heads of functions like marketing, manufacturing, strategy, operations…CMO, COO or the like) should lead the charge and aid and abet their employees to become Value Creators.

I recently discussed this with Donovan Neale-May, the CEO of the CMO Council, who turned my thinking on its head (so to speak).

He suggested we need to work with executives, and that they would embrace the idea of Value Creation. Not only do they need to know what Value Creation is, but also what will Create Value. They need to recognize: how can I know whether I am Creating Value, how do I measure my Value Creation, how do I Create meaningful Value (and for whom?), and how do I see the impact of Value Creation and what it does for me? So, this takes us into the realm of ingenuity, imaginativeness, pro-activeness and initiative taking, and implementation. And how do organizations transform themselves into helping Value Creators?

First, I think, companies have to recognize Value Creation is an important role for the executive. They have to set an environment for Value Creation. So, they need an enabling organization, and they have to let go (not ask for conformists). They have to subtly promote Value Creation while discussing what Value Creation will do for the Value Creators and the company. How, what, and where to Create Value? And to understand Value Creation means change of mindsets from functional thinking to value thinking.

Donovan also wondered whether culture and regions had to do with Value Creation propensity. Or was management support more important than the culture of the country or the culture of the company? Could culture curtail Value Creation? He was interested in seeing if Indian executives were better/worse than executives in Canada/Thailand/USA/Europe.

Eric Orts, a Professor at Wharton on Legal Studies and Business ethics, writes in his book *Business Persons* that executives Create Value for the shareholder. He mentions the concept of principal agents and that management is sometimes perceived as principal agents of shareholders. But he goes on to discuss about people coming together and forming teams to Create Value. But the corporate fraud issue, especially with respect to some accounting issues, partly has to do with (I quote) "incentives that are created by asking managers to only manage [with regard to] short-term shareholder value. The theory is ... that managers should manage [in a way that increases] shareholder value." At one time creating fraud was the role of managers/accountants to Create Value for the company, but that is changing. And if we accept that people Create Value, then employees become important as do business partners for whom value is to be created.

Management has to create wealth for everybody, not just shareholders. Wealth just does not mean money but also could be social or other improvements. In fact, the State of Delaware allows corporations to state their purpose of not only making money about also having a social objective, such as improving the environment or alleviating poverty.

Therefore, managers have to look at the long term and not miss opportunities. Shareholders Create Value by understanding that retained earnings are the major source of growth and corporate wellbeing and therefore should eschew short-term motives. He gives examples of Google that has successfully built companies by avoiding short-term thinking.

So where does this fit in with Donovan's thoughts? Well, Prof. Orts goes on to state that individuals from the bottom up have to Create Value and innovate for the firm's prosperity.

So here are two people coming to the same conclusion on Value Creation being the role of an executive. Donovan's thoughts focus on the individual and that they should learn to Create Value. Prof. Orts focuses on the wellbeing of the firm and comes to the conclusion that Value Creation should be encouraged to make the firm stronger, and not just look for short-term gains.

* * *

Eight Tips for Value Creation for HR Professionals: Become Line Managers

Have you ever asked yourself why HR is considered a staff function? Have you ever asked why most HR Professionals do not become CEOs?

Because historically they were administrators, managing the policies of the company and conducting HR jobs such as labour management, hiring, firing, performance reviews, raises etc., all functional work.

I gave a seminar on converting HR to a line function. We also worked on Creating Value in HR. Attendees included top HR managers from companies like Tata, Ernst and Young etc. They all agreed there was a need for HR to be more strategic and to become line managers. I think they are more strategic today but follow the business strategy instead of leading it.

How do HR professionals become line managers (other than managing their departments)? First, they have to understand they must influence the most important assets of the company to give the company more returns. To make this asset, the employee asset perform better, you have to create value for them. Many HR managers understand this. I was at the Randstad employer awards, and every HR manager talked about Creating Value. They had generic methods of Creating Value. Walk the talk, have values etc. But there was no real concentrated method or focus on Value Creation. What creates value for the employee? How is this value created, and communicated?

And to create value for the employee assets, actually the HR head has to become the Chief Employee Value Creator. This means his other work has to become subservient to Creating Value and not the reverse. It is a change in mindset, which has been honed over the years to create value for the company, cut costs, show limited raises are sufficient, police policies and benefits, and manage employees for the company with their departments and their bosses.

The second reason is that most companies are in the people business, because they deal with employees and customers. They are not in agri-businesses, or hospitality but in the people business. And who is better equipped to influence this people business than HR? One more reason for HR to be a line function.

The third reason stems from HR's Value Creation role. For too long, companies have felt that shareholder wealth is really created or influenced more by CEOs, CxOs etc. maybe 20 people in all. But if we get employees to create value, and this value creates value for customers, then the combined influence on the business and shareholder wealth will be much more than what would be created in the old top-led regime that felt only a few people can influence shareholder wealth. By getting employees to create value meaningfully, the HR department becomes the most important line department.

How can these people turn on their head and become the opposite of what they have been doing traditionally?

They have also to teach the employee to create value, which is what he does in return for the value you create for him. You have to increase his individual brand equity to increase the company's brand.

There is an objection that having a Chief Employee Value Creator will act as a deterrent to getting everyone involved. But the Chief Employee Value Creator works with the Chief Value Creator (the CEO) and aligns the entire company to create value for employees, by building employee strategies and revamping the culture.

Perceived investment in employee development by the employee is very important, but when an employee perceives value is being created for him, he is powerfully stimulated. Value Creation for the employee includes the employee's beliefs about the organization's commitment to improving his competence and enhancing his marketability, both internally and externally. This is what I have called brand equity. Building the employee's brand equity creates a belief in greater control personally of his development and future. Lee and Bruvold proved that in healthcare morale and dedication to the level that emotionally binds them to the organization and encourages them to stay on improved considerably (Lee and Bruvold:* Creating Value for Employees).

John Ingham in a blog states that Creating Value requires that people are put first, not just current business objectives. In other words, my take is that look at Creating Value for employees and brand equity of employees as coming first. Business results follow in the form of value creation for the company. This is different from looking at business results first and what to do next.

To make this happen, I propose an Employee Value Creation strategy which is managed by various departments and bosses, and the EVA and CVA are metrics for success and bonuses of the bosses (Employee Value Added and Customer Value Added) where

$$EVA = \frac{Value\ added\ to\ your\ employees\ by\ you}{Value\ Added\ by\ your\ competitors\ to\ their\ employees}$$

$$And\ CVA = \frac{Value\ added\ by\ you\ to\ your\ customers}{Value\ Added\ by\ your\ competitors\ to\ their\ customers}$$

And so, the first place to measure the employee value creation impact is on the customers. All such measurements are versus competition. Business results will follow if customers are happier with your company. Note you must be measured against competition, because if all of the companies are the same, the employee and the customer will have nothing to differentiate between them. They want to work where they perceive they will get more value, and if that is your competitor, that's where they will want to go. Work on differentiating yourself by building the next practices described here.

Value is the juxtaposition of financial benefits and non-financial benefits. A financial benefit may be non-financial in nature (they provide me with unpaid maternity leave for a longer time).

The HR head by becoming the Chief Employee Value Creator impacts the Value Creation for the customers and thereby for the company, the HR head becomes an extremely important line manager, shedding his staff garb, and finding a higher purpose!

---

* Lee, C. H., & Bruvold, N. T. (2003). Creating Value for Employees: Investment in Employee Development. *The International Journal of Human Resource Management*, 14(6), 981–1000. https://doi.org/10.1080/0958519032000106173

As Gitte Larsen and Erica Skafdrup Hornemann stated:

The value-creating employee is the foundation for the working life of the future. In the industrial society it was about making the capital productive, and in the knowledge society it is about people being productive – it is people that Create Value. This makes it necessary to redefine the way we organize companies, organizations, management, and working life.

They are making a strong case for ousting age-old beliefs in working hours, employee expectations (discipline) etc.

Watson Wyatt in his book, *The Human Capital Edge*, says:

"Focus on the basics. People are more alike than different." It seems counter-intuitive when researchers use detailed data to identify the unique factors that make people tick, but we suggest that companies stop looking so hard for differentiating factors. I think this is important in an organization-wide Value Creation approach born out of measuring the EVA. Basics and fundamentals must be in place to Create Value and Values. This includes the values of the company and the culture for Value Creation.

An example is when Joie de Vivre Hospitality took over Hotel Carlton in San Francisco, they decided to give the housekeepers new vacuum cleaners every year. The cost was minimal, but the housekeepers felt cared for and performed better, proving the age-old belief that happy employees perform better.

The lesson is if your Value Creation Culture is not in place, customizing Value Creation for each individual employee is useless.

But successful companies go beyond the generic set-up to find differentiating factors for different individuals. This will get Value Creation to take hold. David Zinger suggested giving people hints about the sorts of factors which may engage them (this approach also helps people understand the variety in the sorts of things which engage different people and work with them on customizing).

All this builds the employee's brand. The Chief Employee Value Creator is then also seen as contributing to the company's brand, another line function.

To recap, there are eight steps HR has to take:

1. Recognize the purpose of a business is to Create Value for the customer and thereby for the company and most businesses are people businesses
2. To do so the company must Create Value for the employee
3. Build an Employee Value Creation strategy and involve various departments. As employees create more value for customers, shareholder wealth will increase
4. The HR department has to reinvent itself with the HR head becoming the Chief Employee Value Creator and help the company, various departments, and managers to Create Value, and to believe that they are in a people business

5. Measure Employee Value Added and Customer Value Added. Understand what value the employee is looking for
6. Build a basic Value Creation Culture and Values
7. Customize or individualize Value Creation
8. Correlate employee value, Customer Value, and company financial metrics

Before we end, let us understand Value Creation better:

Value Creation is the primary aim of any business entity. Creating Value for customers helps sell products and services, while Creating Value for shareholders, in the form of increases in stock price, and ensures the future availability of investment capital to fund operations. From a financial perspective, value is said to be created when a business earns revenue (or a return on capital) that exceeds expenses (or the cost of capital). But some analysts insist on a broader definition of "Value Creation" that can be considered separate from traditional financial measures. "Traditional methods of assessing organizational performance are no longer adequate in today's economy," according to Value-Based Management. "Stock price is less and less determined by earnings or asset base. Value Creation in today's companies is increasingly represented in the intangible drivers like innovation, people, ideas, and brand." Create Value for employees!

So, we have learnt HR managers can reinvent themselves to become line managers and transform themselves by becoming the Chief Employee Value Creator, by transforming companies to think of their business as a people business, and to help employees Create Value for themselves, the customer, the company, and the shareholder.

* * *

Employee Journey

The employee journey is a working life-long journey. The customer journey is sporadic within a company. The employee journey cannot be viewed as just a series of various journeys within a company. The journey must be viewed in totality by companies.

In this section the principal focus is the employee journey and the employee's journey (interaction with, working for) with the customer. What other factors influence the employee journey? What is an employee journey? Why is it important?

First and foremost, the employee is an asset and a people asset that can appreciate or depreciate during the journey. Employee assets like all assets need to be maintained. The brand equity of the employee is seen during the journey by colleagues, peers, bosses, and customers, and this brand equity of the employee impacts the brand and performance of the company.

Second, only a value added employee can contribute (add value) to the company and add value to the customer. Companies can add or destroy value to the employee through this journey.

So, an understanding of the employee journey is crucial to the performance and health of the company. Too many people define this journey narrowly as being interviewed, hired, performance appraised, motivated, skills developed, promoted, or retired (leaving). Others think it is just the interaction with HR, the employee, and his boss and his external contacts. Some parts of the journey are given below:

The family and social journey

The journey for self-improvement

The journey to help customer: sometimes a one way journey; you cannot contact the customer or the customer cannot contact you

The journey to help the customer navigate the company: an internal journey

The journey with colleagues and bosses, 24/7 availability through cell phone and email

The journey to break silos and frustration

The 'politics' journey, be honest or loyal

Employee touch points, be it accounting, bosses, HR

If you really want to have employees perform, then the wellbeing of the employee is important. His wellbeing is impacted by his problems outside of work. The Japanese had recognized this and had tried to help the employee as a family member. I am not suggesting we do this, but we have to recognize this.

How do we do this? By understanding the employee's self-esteem that is influenced by his journey inside or outside the company. If the employee has poor self-esteem, his awareness, pro-activeness, and performance are affected. So, we have to look at the employee journey differently.

Self-esteem can be impacted by expectations from the company, starting with expectations of his 24/7 availability in the company (your time belongs to us ... that is why companies are suggesting no email or work to be done outside the office and office hours).

There is yet another journey that the employee makes, of self-improvement. Many companies can help and do help.

The next journey is the journey of interacting with the customer externally and internally in helping him navigate the company. Very often the employee's journey is thwarted by silos, by rules, by regulations, and thou shalt or shall not do this. So, he prefers to not take the journey in its entirety and leaves the customer stranded. He needs help in this journey. The silos, hierarchy, and rules can cause frustration during the journey.

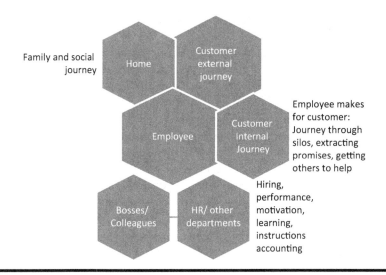

Figure 5.2 The Employee Journey

Then is the journey with his colleagues and his bosses, and in office politics. Should he appear honest or loyal? Should he bend the rules for the sake of the company?

And then there is the journey which is impacted by company touch points, by having multiple people to contact, rather than having one single point of contact, accounting for expense reimbursement, boss for time off, HR for education, motivation (bosses? colleagues) .

A much wider employee mapping is necessary to know his needs and to make his journey well worth it.

This section should give leaders ideas on value creation in the organization. Actually the HR head, if he were an Employee Chief Value Creator should be cognizant of and taking care of what we have said (Figure 5.2).

* * *

Using Employees to Build Market Place Foresight and Value Creation

I talk to many companies about Customer Value and Value Creation. And many say this is important. And many are ready to engage me.

What I find strange is that these clients expect a magic wand. There is a wealth of data from frontline people that they have. Is this data really sought out and collated in a systematic fashion? Is there a pro-active procedure to analyse this data and act on it?

Data is now being collected in a larger fashion and often analysis shows clues to future trends or changes in the marketplace. If management is not willing to listen to expressed opinions, specific impending issues, the changing comments from the marketplace and customers, and pending problems of customers and staff, will they really get to collecting data and even analyzing it to predict future trends, problems, and opportunities as seen from the eyes of the customer or channel partners in the market place? Will they be quick enough to respond, or will they be followers? Serious questions you have to ponder on.

The global trend is that more and more future-thinking leaders are looking at collecting data and analyzing it. And they realize the frontline people are a great source for such data. They have often an entirely different and actionable insight into customers. Often the frontline people know why there is a problem, whereas what the problem perception in the back end of the company might be different. For example, bills may need to be corrected is the what of the problem, but the why of the problem may be the billing process itself, which frontline people could educe. So correcting the bills is not really the long-term solution. Customer Circles described in earlier chapters help greatly in this process.

This is what we call Value Creation: the smarts inside or inside intelligence, which we can use effectively. So set into motion such insight to build foresight by first recognizing you have a pool of data collectors. Second, you should recognize that employees may be reluctant to come forward, particularly when in the past they have been ignored. Then you have to find a process to get this information in-house and analyse it and use it.

After you act on the data you got from the employee, you have to go back to the frontline people and tell them how the data was used, and how problems were solved or forestalled. Reward them for their insight.

Lastly, this has to be ongoing because the culture of talking to each other, of capturing data has to be worked on. The customer successes have to be repeated over time through such analyses and prognoses, and actions. Reward employees and recognize them. Recognize you are at the start of a winning teamwork and spirit that can keep you ahead of the competition and have engaged employees. You will then also create value for your employees and your customers.

Zappos gives us some ideas on how to create value for employees. Zappos has a Wow! Employees program based around:

Understand What Your Employees Think and Want
Build a Trust Culture
Practice Open Communication
Provide Clear Career Paths

Demonstrate Appreciation for Contributions
Inspire Employees Beyond Turnover
Communicate Your Employee Focus

They also have special programs such as apprenticeships; new employee scavenger hunt; shadow programs where new employees shadow experienced one; Zappos $$$, where employees earn Zollars that are given to them by bosses and co-employees, which they can use on internal programs; Grant a Wish program, where co-employees and the company can help out an employee; and Co-worker bonus, where employees can give bonuses to co-worker through the company. All great ways to Create Value and engagement. Then employees are willing to openly talk about what the customer is saying and defend the customer, because there is a sense of belonging and trust, and customer data gets captured and used!

Your employees are, after all the Number 1 Source to Collect Valuable Information about Your Business

A key takeaway from here is to gain input towards better understanding your customers and find the time to listen to the voice of your frontline employees. If you don't, you'll know less about your customers than you should.

Several ideas come to mind to help make this work:

Schedule time for management to be with frontline employees on a regular basis.

In a call centre, the supervisor may work with a customer service person by alternating calls.

Manufacturing facilities offer many ways for first-hand observation to take place … nothing better than to see a manager actually working in the plant.

Restaurants need more than the occasional manager coming up to customers asking if their meal and service were excellent.

Management from time to time needs to actually "wait" at the tables or be a *food runner*. This will add value to their inputs both to their employees and "up the chain" of management.

Management in department stores needs to be out front instead of in their offices or storerooms. A little bit of interaction with a customer, merchandising and working in the fitting rooms, will go a long way to giving them a greater pulse on the action. In the fitting rooms, one hears first-hand the perception that customers have about the store and product.

Another area that you have to look at to "Unlock customer Value" is segmenting your customer base. Learn and differentiate what makes up that "super elite" group of loyal customers that you have. The more accurate you are in defining that special group, the greater will be your overall customer satisfaction rate. Take for instance a program that Apple perfected ....

Apple has had a program that they developed which involves alignment of the customer with a key ingredient within their overall formula for success. The program is by invitation only to select customers and asks for routine feedback up to 2X per month. This "selective" process by invitation only allows you to gain specific feedback to focus on the type of customer that you are keying on. For example, when Apple puts together a number of factors to come up with its "premier" customer, they can see better ways to engage and partner with them if they know what makes these "premier" customers tick.

As you gain confidence in the insights and observations of your frontline people, you will gain a much greater pulse on your environment and business. Never forget that a focus on quality and customer satisfaction is good business. Everything happens at the "frontline"!

* * *

Do Specialists Create More Value Than Generalists?

On the face of it, it would seem that specialists add more value than generalists. But the facts are generalists generally do add more value than specialists.

Specialists tend to be good performers but not great value creators. A generalist is a better value creator. A generalist understands business better than a specialist and has many more areas of knowledge. Take two accountants at the same level, one a specialist and the other a generalist. Both perform well, and the specialist might understand accounting better. The generalist on the other hand may come to the boss and say we need to think differently with Brexit coming around the corner. He is adding more value.

Even more interesting is that specialized and experienced accountants have more difficulty adjusting to new accounting laws than novices. This is true of expert chess players where rules are changed versus beginner players' rules.

David Epstein in "Range" says highly specialized experts can become narrow minded and may become worse with experience (which makes them more confident) as they tend to become single minded. He goes on to say specialist cardiologists are likely to put in stents more often than necessary and you may be better off with a generalist in cases where stents are not required, to avoid the insertion of unnecessary stents.

There are more specialists though in the USA than general physicians and this is due to the better income levels of specialists.

Epstein talks about a study on Nobel Laureates. He states these people have hobbies like dancing or singing or gardening, which instead of dissipating their deep knowledge strengthens it. Experts who do not make it to the Nobel Prize are single minded in their work and specialization.

Being a generalist gives you a better chance in a variety of markets. (In my case, early on in my career, I found companies were interested in my specialist skills rather than my generalist outlook.) Later on, in their career, generalists have "career flexibility" more than early on. HR people miss this when they try to match someone's background to a job. Learning and unlearning are becoming important traits in the future.

On the corporate front, as the world becomes increasingly interconnected, organizations are valuing generalists for their ability to multi-task, see the bigger picture, and work with different departments to solve issues. Generalists also have more transferable skills – a critical aspect in ensuring business scalability.

The biggest disadvantage of being a generalist, however, is the trade-off between depth and breadth. Having knowledge of several things prevents one from mastering a single discipline to the best extent possible. This could make generalists more replaceable and increases job insecurity.

Generalists in today's digital economy have to rely on specialists for data and analysis, but they (generalists) are able to make much better decisions.

Does when you start specializing impact your success and value creation? Many people have researched this and have found whether you start specializing early on (like Tiger Woods and golf) or much later (like Roger Federer and tennis), you are likely to succeed. Similarly, the length of specialization does not matter, and the generalized experience before specializing is very useful.

Learning, according to this, is better to be done slowly, even if it means poor test scores (according to Epstein). These people are smarter eventually in what they have learnt.

So, we have to ask how rote education rates with flexible education. Closed skills are acquired fast, whereas open skills are also required. Thus knowledge, experience, early agility, and mental exercising are all important in education. So, in colleges perhaps open teaching is better, to thinking beyond experiential learning. Self-education techniques are worthwhile.

Doctors during training rotate and get generalized training before specializing.

The best innovators are those who can use analogies from their different domain experiences and splice together and synthesize, through their diverse knowledge.

There is much to be said about being an outsider and having a breadth of knowledge in innovating and solving tricky problems. Many generalists have solved problems using knowledge from some other field in the problem. Generalists do not get bogged down by details that generalists tend to.

In innovating meetings, I would always tell people to look at solutions and not to say they will never work or they are too expensive. Better to see how to make them work or reduce the cost (costs come down as products become popular and are sold in larger quantities).

Thus, should we look for a specialist or a generalist (this is a general question and not a specific one)? Or Generalizing–Specialists and Specializing–Generalists? That is a specialist who develops a wider range of interests is more valuable. Also, there is a risk of specialization, and that is you can become outdated, or your skills are no longer current.

A specializing generalist is one who is a generalist but has a strong specialization. I have always maintained you must be very strong in one area or more to become a generalist and succeed. No one can take away your specialized knowledge. You will always be able to rely on your specialization past to deal with other specialists, and to have a discipline of thinking. Be a specialist in your skills.

In our own field, we find most CX (Customer Experience) experts cannot see beyond experience and miss what Customer Value people can see more generically!

So, who creates more value? So, therefore, let us define value:

Creating Value is executing normal, conscious, inspired, and even imaginative actions that increase the overall good and wellbeing, and the worth of and for ideas, goods, services, people, or institutions including society, and all stakeholders (like employees, customers, partners, shareholders, and society), and value waiting to happen.

Value waiting to happen is ideas in front of us we do not notice, like porcupine quill design to suture wounds or using gecko-based adhesives to close surgical cuts. These were not discovered by experts but by generalists who thought cross functional. Many new entrepreneur unicorns are new to the subject and used lateral thinking.

There is no formula that can tell us whether it is the specialist who creates more value or the generalist. It depends on their way of looking at things, their breadth and interests, and their way of thinking. In the long run it appears generalists create more value than specialists.

Generalist–specialists or specialist–generalists may be the best at creating value.

What do you think?

Chapter 6

Businesses and Institutions

Value Creation Is Output/Input

Recently I was discussing setting up Value Creation Centres with Dr. Jagdish Sheth of Emory Institute.

We discussed Value Creation for companies. Dr. Sheth reminded me that Value was a term popularized by the investment community, where they talked about improving the value of the companies they bought. Generally, value was created by cutting costs and improving the bottom line.

Value Creation, as we define it, impacts the bottom line and the top line. By creating value for employees, customers, and partners, we reduce costs because we are more efficient, because we make fewer mistakes, decrease repeat and unnecessary work, and have better teamwork and focus. This improves the bottom line.

By focusing on customers, we are able to increase loyalty and market share by using customer value management techniques, and therefore, we improve the top line.

The improvement in top line and bottom line increases profits and the value of the company more dramatically than by "cost cutting" alone.

To see the impact on value creation, we should look at the effort, cost, and time in doing a particular activity and see what output we get. As the output/input ratio increases, value is created.

DOI: 10.4324/9781003381624-6

Thus, Indian companies can look at their CSR activities as being something essential because the government in India mandates CSR expenditure. It is viewed as a cost centre. But if designed and implemented properly, where your customers start to prefer you for your CSR activities, then increased value will be created. It is an output/input thing.

That is why we have terms such as return on marketing investment, return on assets, and return on investments; all can be viewed from an increasing value viewpoint.

Study after study has shown that increasing customer value increases the profits companies make. Part of this is a preference for the company; part is because of higher prices you can charge when you increase value.

If you are looking at transformation in your company, you can also look at it as an output/input system. You put in an investment of time, people, and energy and maybe money. What do you get? And if the output is greater than the input cost, then value is created.

Value is also created when you do things right for the customer. Generally, the cost of doing things right is minimal. So, returns are high and the value created is high.

Social media and public relations programs create value and, in some cases, generate demonstrable ROI. The two concepts are different in important ways. They are related like the ellipse and the circle. Remember those silly distinctions you learnt in elementary school? A circle is an ellipse, but an ellipse is not a circle. ROI is a form of value, but not all value takes the form of ROI.

Don Bartholomew, SVP of Digital and Social Media Research at Ketchum, warns, however, that ROI is a financial metric – the percentage of dollars returned for a given investment/cost. The dollars may be the revenue generated, dollars saved, or spending avoided. ROI is transactional. ROI lives on the income statement in business terms.

Value is created when people become aware of us, engage with our content or brand ambassadors, are influenced by this engagement, and take some action like recommending to a friend or buying our product. Value creation occurs over time, not at a point in time. Value lives on the balance sheet.

Don defines value as increasing the number of people who are likely to buy our products and services. Other programs may be designed to improve or protect the corporate reputation or to build and enhance brands. Much of this value is said to be intangible. It is goodwill that becomes tangible at the point in time a transaction occurs. When buying decisions happen, your investments in marketing, brand, and reputation work together. They become tangible. You can measure the ROI.

The point is that value can be created in many different ways and measured by different metrics. The best metric is Ray Kordupleski's Customer Value

Added; the value you add to your customers divided by the value your competition adds to its customers and is measured through customers' perceptions using market research.

* * *

Are Companies Loyal?

I came across a cartoon in *Economic Times*, which showed two executives speaking and one saying:

> It's no more about employee loyalty … try winning company's loyalty …

It got me thinking. Should a company be loyal? Can a company be loyal? To whom? I quickly googled, and there was hardly anything on a company's loyalty.

The first question is an easy one, a company can be loyal.

Should a company be loyal is more complex, till we answer the question to whom.

I guess we have to scroll through the stakeholders: employees, customers, partners, shareholders, and society. The easy answer is that a company should be loyal to all of these. If this is true, then we have to ask are most companies you know loyal, and to whom? Are companies you buy from loyal to you? I have found that whenever we as Customers have been good and fair to our suppliers, they tend to be more loyal to us than to other customers who are not as fair or good to them.

I would imagine most companies tend to be loyal to their major shareholders. They generally show their loyalty to the shareholder by offering him what he wants most: dividends, stock price, long-term growth, and market leadership. I suspect most shareholders want either dividends or stock price growth. Thus, loyal management works on these aspects.

Are companies loyal to employees? Is this loyalty secondary to the loyalty to shareholders? This makes us think of the Japanese lifetime employment system (only 8.8% of Japanese companies have this now). There were three models: Stationary (governed by a set of rigid rules, and the expectation that some non-performing employees would voluntarily leave), Growth (depends on organizational growth, and all grow with the organization), Stagnant (where the company when in bad shape lets employees go) … Assuming employees were given lifetime employment, what value was this loyalty? Apart from somewhat guaranteed employment, this system did not allow employees to easily switch and they became captive employees. Was company loyalty good for employees?

Outside of Japan, I am sure there are examples of companies being loyal to employees. I cannot think of many. We also notice that companies work on making employees loyal. One way is to make the employee feel indispensable. Or by giving golden handcuffs ... If you leave, you will be worse off or lose bonuses, or stock options.

The less said about true loyalty to customers. As long as the customer can be milked (can buy), he is worthwhile. In this instant gratification society, even this is short lived. Also, as I mentioned earlier, there is some loyalty to customers who are good to them.

I had written about company loyalty to suppliers, and that too is minimal and based on the benefit to the company (sometimes called mutual benefit). This loyalty is generally purchasing department led, though it is true mutual bonds between the supplier and the end user in the company do form.

The company's loyalty to society and sustainability has yet to be proven. There are examples of Unilever and others that are trying to be loyal to the environment and sustainability.

So, the company is loyal to the Owners ... in reality!

How can they change or be otherwise? Others have written that the company has to think of itself first. I think this is true for survival (first put the oxygen mask on yourself, and then on the kids ... but do not put the oxygen mask on yourself and abandon the kids). So instead of abandoning the other stakeholders, companies try to sustain them to the extent their loyalty to the owner (shareholder) will let them.

Many Customer consultants would want the company to be Customer-centric. Does that include company loyalty?

I think company loyalty and Customer-centricity is a thought process and requires enlightened owners, and enlightened managers and leaders, who look beyond profit being the strategy of a company.

* * *

The Real Sources of Value: Assets and Performance

Companies tend to focus on financial assets and financial performance. They measure every aspect of these, and in known periodicity. They report these internally and externally and are pleased that they are following the "really important factors" for the company's success and future wellbeing. These people are sometimes called bean counters aka finance people. They also track investor assets because they feel they have to compete in the marketplace for the investors' capital.

Because of this focus, the company loses track of other important assets and does not get the bean counters to track them well:

Employee Assets
Customer Assets
Partners as Assets
Social Assets
Intellectual Property, know-how, and innovation assets
Brand Assets
Value Creation Assets
Investors as Assets

Note you could use the word Capital instead of assets, although I prefer assets.

Just as an aside, traditional assets in a company have to be maintained. There is a maintenance and depreciation plan for them. Plant and machinery, mobile phones and laptops, furniture, and buildings all are maintained and all depreciate.

The other assets mentioned above are not always maintained well. In fact, many of them can appreciate in time (unlike physical assets that might depreciate), unless an employee leaves or a customer leaves. There are poor maintenance plans for them: just enough for them to stay on and perform. In fact, we are more interested in the performance than in the asset itself.

Non-financial assets are often shrugged away as intangible, difficult to measure (and therefore difficult to manage?) Or is our management and focus inadequate? Some will even say these intangible assets form 80% of the investor's focus on the company value. So, if we cared about our investors' assets, we would care about the non-financial or "soft" assets (and make them as important as "hard" assets).

I think most people understand the various intangible assets and broadly know how they are defined. Value Creation assets are less well understood and developed. Your value creation assets exist in:

Plant and machinery assets: you will certainly overhaul your manufacturing capabilities and watch, analyse, and revamp them to create more value
Product offering assets: you work on creating products that will create more value
Employee assets: you create value for employees in order for them to create more value and you invest in teaching your employees assets to create more value for the customers, the partners and society, and thereby for the company. You set up an environment conducive to and encouraging value creation (for example, value creation councils). The employee asset increases, thereby.
Customer assets: how do you create more value for the customer, thereby increasing loyalty, market share, prices, ambassadorship, and profit assets?

Social assets: where do you put funds that your customers perceive as adding value, thereby making them prefer your company more than competition? Do you understand how values create value for the company? Values include trust, honesty, loyalty (to customers), sustainability, safety etc. How do you get employees to create more value here? Also how environmentally friendly are you? Do you pay attention to ESG?

Brand assets: as value creation increases, brand assets increase. Value creating employees have brand equity that increases the brand assets of the company

Innovation, proprietary information, know-how, intellectual property assets: Value creation in the minds of the employee increases these assets, because they work consciously to create innovation and value

Do your investor assets really know about these intangible assets and the true value of these and how you are growing these, resulting in value for your company? Can shareholders really judge the true source of value creation? Are you giving them the tools to do so?

And are you putting the tools into place to create and measure value: the processes, structure, and organizational skills to do so? Are you creating value for the employees? Do you have a Chief Employee Value creator? And do you have Value Creation councils to bring to the fore value creation by employees for themselves, their colleagues, and other employees and their customers and society? And can you measure this value creation and the increase in assets and performance? Do we have the competencies to create more value, and to encourage value creation? So let us encourage Value Creation Councils. Let us report our intangible assets and their performance as much as we do the financial performance. A good way for leaders to differentiate themselves!

* * *

Value Creation and Destruction in Customer Value Constellations

I cannot help but use the word Customer Value Constellation for the Customer Value chain. I read the meaning further: in a Value Constellation, the focus does not lie on the company or the industry (as it previously did) but on the value creating system itself, within which different economic actors – suppliers, business partners, allies, customers – work together to co-produce value. We always said this in Value Co-Creation. Value co-creation implies creating value for the entire chain, the partners, the supply chain, the unions etc.

Now that we have definitions out of the way, I wanted to show how the delivery chain can add or destroy value for a Customer.

We worked with a company that had a three-tiered delivery system:

From the company to the dealer
From the dealer to the retailer
From the retailer to the Consumer (I use consumer as the final Customer)

Thus theoretically, the Customer has nothing to do with the company or the dealer. The retailer has little to do with the company on a day-to-day basis.

The company, through its products, dealers, and network, its marketing and service people wishes to deliver value to the Customer. Its points of contact with the Consumer and Customer are through the service people and their products and the retailers (who are serviced through the dealers).

The company treats the dealer as a Customer (they have a symbiotic relationship).

In a sense, they treat the retailer as a Customer but a more distant Customer.

In our first study, we found:

The loyalty of the dealer to the company was 50%
The loyalty of the retailer to the dealer was 20% (the retailer is the direct Customer of the dealer). The loyalty of the retailer to the company (secondary contact) is 50%
The loyalty of the Consumer to the retailer was 10% and to the company or product brand was 60%

Obviously, there is a deterioration (or destruction) of value in the chain or constellation.

After we worked with the company, dealers, and retailers, we were able to increase the loyalty of the dealer to the company to 60%, from the retailer to the dealer to 50%, and from the Customer to the retailer to 30%.

Thus, the value flow in the delivery chain must be examined. The value constellation includes the supply chain for packaging and raw materials to the company, the transport, and logistics companies from the company to the dealer, the warehousing system, and transportation to the retailer. The sustainability support by the value chain is also important.

All have to add value and improve value delivery to the consumer.

We put the constituents together in a Customer-centric Circle to work on increasing the value delivery to the consumer. Together they build a Customer's Bill of Rights and understand the significance of their role in delivering these rights, a promise to do their bit in honouring the rights. Then the value constellation works in unison and with a single mind purpose: to add value to the Customer. Much for leaders to think about.

* * *

Four Types of Companies: My Learnings from Value Creation

I have learnt from my experience with Creating Value and watching people and businesses around me, just as many of you have learnt from your experiences. Do relate what I write below to what you have noticed in your life. This reflection will help you look at businesses in a different light. First to the new Purpose of a Company.

For the last few years, I have been leading a campaign that the role of a company and an executive is to create value for customers, employees, partners, society, and investors on a long-term basis.

It is gratifying that on August 19, 2019, 181 CEO members of Business Roundtable, including Amazon's Jeff Bezos; American Airlines' Doug Parker; Apple's Tim Cook, Bank of America's Brian Moynihan; Coca-Cola's James Quincey; Eaton's Craig Arnold; Marriott's Arne Sorenson; Lockheed Martin's Marillyn Hewson; Morgan Stanley's James Gorman; Procter & Gamble's David Taylor; UPS's David Abney; and Walmart's Doug McMillon re-wrote the purpose of a company.

On top was Delivering Value for Customers and to all stakeholders.

Delivering value to our customers. We will further the tradition of American companies leading the way in meeting or exceeding customer expectations.

Investing in our employees. This starts with compensating them fairly and providing important benefits. It also includes supporting them through training and education that help develop new skills for a rapidly changing world. We foster diversity and inclusion, dignity, and respect.

Dealing fairly and ethically with our suppliers. We are dedicated to serving as good partners to the other companies, large and small, that help us meet our missions.

Supporting the communities in which we work. We respect the people in our communities and protect the environment by embracing sustainable practices across our businesses.

Generating long-term value for shareholders. [They] provide the capital that allows companies to invest, grow, and innovate. We are committed to transparency and effective engagement with shareholders.

Each of our stakeholders is essential. We commit to deliver value to all of them, for the future success of our companies, our communities, and our country.

Value Creation is executing proactive, conscious, inspired, or imaginative and even normal actions that increase the overall good and wellbeing, and the worth of ideas, goods, services, people, or institutions including society, and all stakeholders (like employees, customers, partners, shareholders, and society), and value waiting to happen.

That is why our parents teach us to be good kids and to do good. But this is soon overtaken by the goal of making a living, of being successful.

Lewis Hyde's book, *The Gift*, suggests that the most unbelievable gift is one with no expectations of a return and is truly unexpected. Value Creation is all about giving, not just taking. And delight occurs when you are given an unexpected experience!

The concept of Giving and just not taking is embedded in the Purpose of a Company.

I have learnt that there are four types of people and companies:

1. True Givers, Altruistic: people who give selflessly. They do so without any expectation of a return or what this will mean for them. I have been lucky in my journey to come across many such givers. You go to such people for help and they go out of their way to help, without asking unnecessary questions. They are true Value Creators. Many parents, teachers, and social workers give selflessly. I have true friends and acquaintances who fall into this category. Few companies fit into this category.

Examples of this are rich people like Azim Premji of Wipro, Narayanamurty of Infosys.

There are others like my friend's grandfather who did give and also taught his children to give 20% of their gross income to charity. He wanted them to physically give things to the poor. His children would go out to poor neighbourhoods and distribute blankets and food in the winter to the homeless. The next day when they went back, they noticed that one person whom they had given a blanket to did not have it. They complained to their father that he had probably sold the blanket in exchange for a drink. The father said, give him another. He is needy.

In companies, we find some that bend over backwards for their customers.

Companies I know will work with the community and poorer people to help the community become more self-reliant and the poorer people more self-sufficient. They will offer their executives time for charitable work.

Zappos and Amazon are companies that are willing to give back to a customer who is unhappy, a replacement or equivalent.

Truly Customer-centric companies fall into this category:

Galbraith (2005) describes Customer-centricity as a fundamental paradigm shift – away from the bias of the organization and its agents to operate on the side of the seller (i.e., itself) in any transaction, and towards operating "outside-in" – on meeting the needs of the users or purchasers of its products or services. This approach to organizing people and work embeds many HR and organizational development best practices – including self-management, direct and frank communication, individual change agency, and team-based decision-making – and places these qualities firmly in service of better outcomes for the end user, business, and employee engagement.

(Galbraith, J.R. [2005]. Designing the Customer-Centric Organization: A Guide to Strategy, Structure, and Process. New York: Wiley)

They fit into quadrant 1 of the chart below.

2. Balanced, Long-Term Thinking: people who give to get (in a generous way, not in a mean fashion). Others are also generous givers if they see how, it will help them, or give them a return in the future. Many people fall in this category. Most companies are in this category and balance Value Creation and the right amount of value extraction. Many business executives and companies fit this mode, as do many workers.

The company I worked for, Continental Can, fell into this category in a nice, generous, caring way. Our account manager for the company knew most people in the company, including the CEO, the CxOs, and even the third shift supervisor. He knew when someone was graduating or getting married and gave gifts. We all entertained lavishly. I myself entertained people some of whom I never met again. These people still remember the lunch or dinner with me because of the unexpected treat.

If one of our customers complained, we would have a team at his location to solve his problems, however small the problems were. In fact, the customer would get embarrassed and tell the salesperson of the problem asking him not to let me (the CEO of the division) know. We also had customer services people who could run our material (or product) on their machines like a charm when the customer's people had problems with it. Consequently, our product ran with the lowest spoilage than our competitors.

Why do I put them in the second category? Because the giver would always get something in return. For example, they would know about changes in the client company before competition did and forestall any negative impact.

I had a boss at Continental who taught me the art of reverse negotiation. He taught me to give more to a vendor or an employee than he was expecting, thus getting their loyalty in return.

I remember, I was negotiating polystyrene (PS) prices with a major supplier. The going rate was 31.5 cents per pound. I agreed to 32.5 cents a pound. My reasoning was that PS prices were going to double. It turned out that they went up to 67 cents a pound. Our supplier held their prices with us for a much longer time than our competitors who had bought at 31.5 cents per pound, giving us a great cost advantage for a period of time.

Another example was when we were to buy a second machine from a supplier. It was a custom-made machine. The first machine was sold to us at a throwaway price because the supplier was desperate to sell to us and to enter America from Europe. We also had a 10% penalty for late delivery. The machine was delivered late and we took the penalty. The supplier supported us magnificently flying people out from Germany to the USA to help us when needed.

We got ready to buy the second machine, and I negotiated a good price. When I chatted with my boss, he asked me if I was happy with the supplier. I said, very happy. He suggested I consider giving them the 10% penalty back. Would it really make a difference to our cost of manufacture, he asked? It really made a small difference and so I offered to give them the penalty money back. They were absolutely dazed by this. Even today, 30 years later they remember me as an unusual businessman! This is giving so that one gets loyalty in return.

You have had this experience, when an airline upgrades you free and unexpectedly, or does something really nice to you, like offering you the use of the lounge free.

The moment an Amazon re-seller says give me a good rating before I change your purchase to a working one, we know that he wants a quid pro quo and that puts him in the third category.

3. People who do not give because they do not see what is in it for them. Many people are in this category. You will notice some companies that are in this category and pretend to be customer conscious but are really company centric. They are sometimes givers and mostly takers.

Many companies also fall into this category. They are tough with customers. They will not take items back even if the problem was in the new phone.

In India, if you buy a cell phone from a vendor, and it does not work, they will not replace it. They will ask you to take it to the repair shop of the supplier, like Samsung or Apple. These people do not see what they will get by replacing the phone. They may lose a customer 2 years from now, but that is too far in the future.

They fall into the third category.

4. Takers or extractors: lastly, those who pretend to help or give and do nothing. They just don't have it in them to give. Sometimes our very good friends fall into this category. They are friends till tested. Many companies that focus on value extraction are in this category.

I am sure you can think of many examples of people and companies. Ask a company call centre or a telephone operator for the CEO's name. They will not give it, even though you can get it from the net. They just do not want to be helpful. These people lead to value starvation and value destruction.

That is why we are starting Creating Value centres, because we want more and more people to understand and contribute to creating value.

We also find some people who are close friends and they are not as helpful as we expect. Sometimes our outer circle is more helpful and unexpectedly. Such friends are important. Notice we spend more time and effort on our closest friends but not our casual friends. This networking is important as studies have shown more jobs and help come through acquaintances than from friends. Many casual friends are creating more value for us and never underestimate the power of networking. Remember there are altruistic givers and many who are not.

Below are some of the things that are happening (Figure 6.1):

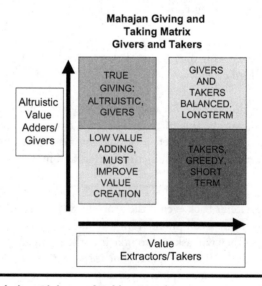

Figure 6.1   Mahajan Giving and Taking Matrix

Ask yourself in which quadrant you fall. Become givers and not just takers. Become a Value Creator.

* * *

Nine Reasons Why Your Company Isn't Creating Value

Value Creation is a distinctive mindset. It is a mentality driven by enhanced self-esteem, awareness, and pro-activeness. It goes beyond just doing your job, it is doing something extra.

Value Creation is executing proactive, imaginative, or inspired actions that increase the net worth of products, services, or an entire business to create better gains or value for Customers, stakeholders, and shareholders. Value Creation stimulates executives and business leaders to generate improved value for Customers, driving success for the organization and its stakeholders.

Value Creation creates Customer conscious companies that care about wellbeing.

If Value Creation is so good and basic a management technique, why is it not being adopted in a universal fashion? Which of these is holding your company from using it? (If you are using value creation techniques, you would be aware of this! Are you?) You will find that smart people like you will be able to create more value when you focus on doing so.

There are several reasons:

1. **You are captives of what you have been taught and what you have learnt.**

   a. You have been taught to be executives, and hard driving at that to create value for the company.
   b. You believe that Value Creation for the company means increased profits, typically by reducing costs, increasing efficiency, and trying to increase market share.
   c. You are taught to forget that you are Customers too. You therefore find it difficult to think like an executive and a customer at the same time. When you walk into the company, you take off your customer hat and wear the company hat!
   d. You have to take advantage of everything in your power to create value (profits) for the company. This could mean exploiting the employees, Customers, and partners, of society and ethics, if you have to. This concept

is undergoing a sea change, as executives now know the importance of employees, Customers, and partners and society and ethics (values). But it hasn't gone far enough.

All these prevent us from adopting Value Creation in the proper manner.

2. **In the last 20 years, CEO compensation has gone up much faster than profits and is based on short-term profits. The lifespan of CEOs has gone down, making them look for quick wins.**

   a. More and more executive bonuses are now being based on short-term profits. Stocks and options compensation has gone up sky high. Huge motivation to make more money now. Why worry about the long run? The CEO may not last that long.

See the two charts in figures (Figure 6.2), showing the lifespan of companies and executives is reducing and executive compensation is going up, especially through stocks and options.

Taken from James Montier* (Figure 6.3).

The short-term thinking is against Customer Value Creation and Value Creation in general, except for Value Creation for the shareholder.

3. **MBA and professional schools teach students to become executives and teach them that shareholder wealth is the real purpose of the firm, then that is what they will practice. They do not understand that shareholder wealth is a result and not the purpose of their existence.**

   a. Shareholder value is not necessarily shareholder wealth. It can mean much more than that. It could be a focus on employees and Customers or even societal value and the gains from them
   b. Shareholder Value (read Profits) grows by increasing Customer and Stakeholder Value Creation because it grows loyalty and market share

4. **There is an overemphasis on efficiency, systems, and processes. Not enough thought is given to mindset and attitudes, which are required to increase employee and Customer Value.**

---

* https://www.gmo.com/docs/default-source/research-and-commentary/strategies/asset-allocation/the-world's-dumbest-idea.pdf?sfvrsn=0

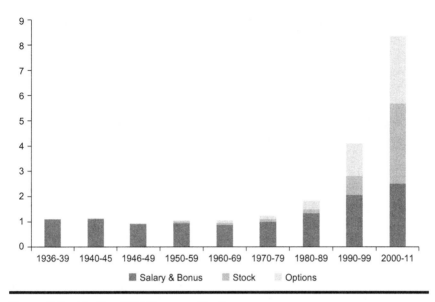

Figure 6.2   Median CEO Pay over the Years

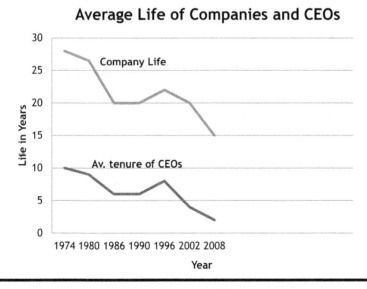

Figure 6.3   Average Life of Companies and CEOs over the Years

a. Mindset comes from education and awareness and wanting to create value rather than being forced to do so

b. Executives are taught to be functional and efficiency experts, and not value creators

5. **More time and emphasis are paid to correcting problems and settling complaints, rather than to get to Zero Complaints**

a. Every time there is a complaint, it takes away the value you are providing. What are you doing to prevent complaints from happening?

b. This requires a mindset that works systemically to avoid complaints, driving the business to a Zero Complaint state

c. There is a feeling that complaints give you the opportunity to interact with a customer. Surely, there are better ways to do so! Imagine, the waiter drops soup on you; a true cause for a complaint. Is this what you want as an interaction? Better to find more positive ways of interacting with customers

6. **Competition is doing the same thing, why change? Let's all make merry and get our bonuses.**

a. Why do we need to be different? Because we will gain competitive advantage and be ahead of competition, rather than be followers

b. Value creation is about differentiation and getting ahead

7. **Customer concepts apart from being executive led are also embedded by consultants who in a race to get ahead come up with niche phrases like CRM, CX, Customer Journey, Customer Effort etc., but all focused on processes.**

a. There is confusion on basic definitions. So work is done in bits and pieces instead of a real sea change as outlined in my book, *Total Customer Value Management: Transforming Business Thinking.*

b. You may not realize a customer journey requires an effort by the customer. You may not realize that the basic product and the service should provide the experience, and other journey experiences other than delightful ones are unnecessary. Thus, a good experience is when you are upgraded by an airline or are allowed to get free miles for lower accumulated points.

The reverse is having an experience such as cancelled flights. We do not want this experience. If it does happen, the Customer journey to get the problem solved should be minimal.

8. **Employees and departments such as HR and IT are not taught to create true value and remain staff functions.**

   a. Owners or managers or employees must realize that companies place a value on their (the employees) positions (what the company will get vs. what it costs them to have the employee). Value is created when employees do something extra and go beyond what is expected of them. Employees add value by doing things better than others. If their actions are worse than others', employees destroy value. Those who add value get promoted and get better raises.
   b. Employees destroy value sometimes. Why would one wish to destroy value, consciously? Most value gets destroyed, unconsciously
   c. Put your Customers at the centre of your business decisions on making organizational changes

Destruction of value happens unconsciously just as the creation of value. If you created value consciously and you understood this, you would work differently.

And companies, if they understood the true intent of shareholder value and that there is a strong connection between creating value for stakeholders and the value for the company and increasing profits, will embrace Value Creation.

9. **Value Extraction is more Important than Value Creation?**

Today's MBAs and managers are trained to extract value. Most executives work on administering, improving efficiency, making sure things are done effectively, and managing people to get the best out of them. How many are there to Create long-lasting value? How many are willing to change the rules of the game? How many are willing to ask why are we doing these things? Is there a better way?

You can extract value to a limited extent. Unless you create more value, you cannot extract more value.

MBAs have to be taught to create value. That in fact Value Creation is the top task of an executive. Not just value extraction.

Organization of the Future

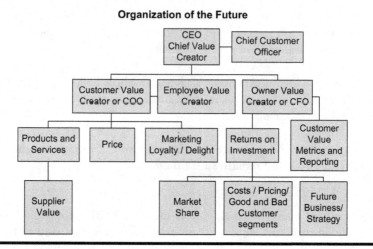

Figure 6.4 Organization of the Future

So we need Master's in Value Creation and Master's in Value Management and transform the company to create value for Employees, Customers, Partners, Distribution Channels, and thereby for the Shareholders.

Above is the organization chart of the company of the future (Figure 6.4), taken from my book, *Total Customer Value Management: Transforming Business Thinking*. Everyone has a value creation role.

* * *

Building Silos or Breaking Silos? Internal Customer Is a Flawed Concept!

I spent many years consulting on internal Customers. I helped companies look at internal Customers, and how they could get value from the other departments of the company. And keeping internal Customers happy. Companies would throw SLAs at me (Service Level Agreements) so that performance of departments and expectations of internal Customers were met.

But my work with external Customers showed that one very important reason for Customers to be unhappy was the various silos that are built in companies, and how departments are insulated from each other. Silos are promoted by the concept of internal customers. Departments tend to be independent of each other. This leads to a lack of internal cooperation (Figure 6.5). Even worse, everyone thinks the customer is taken care of because there is a customer department

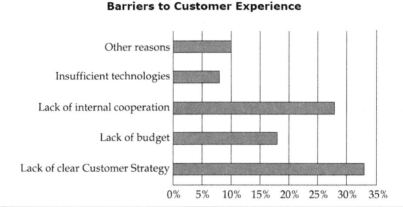

Figure 6.5   Barriers to Customer Experience

and they all wash their hands off the customer and think they have no customer role. The results of a survey with 400 CEOs show that the two major reasons for failure to provide a good Customer Experience are (1) lack of a clear Customer Strategy and (2) lack of Internal Cooperation.

Thus if you want to give your Customer a good experience, abandon the concept of internal Customers. Build internal teamwork and cooperation. We work with various departments in defining their Customer roles. We ask why departments such as HRD and IT are considered staff functions. The reason is they do not add value. They are really extractors of value not creators of value. When have you heard an HRD CxO ask: what value have I added to the employee? When did he ask whether the employee feels valued? Is it the HRD CxO's job or is it the department manager's job? Or is it everyone's or no one's job?

We improve internal cooperation and teamwork by starting a Courtesy System, so people are nice to each other and start smiling. This then shows in the way you handle your colleagues and your external Customers.

An external Customer could care less about internal silos. He wants a seamless experience. He does not care who is doing the work for him, and telling him this is the job of another department is most irksome for him (he doesn't want to hear: not my job!)

And we break silos by building a Customer strategy with tasks and leadership from various departments. We build the Customer's Bill of Rights, backed by a Circle of Promises from various departments so that the Customer realizes his rights are being honoured by the company.

This is the first step to creating Firms of Endearment, where all stakeholders feel endeared and the profitability increases.

Break silos soonest! Forget the concept of Internal Customers. Also look at the proposed corporate organogram in the previous article. In any event, learn to treat everyone as a desirable customer!

* * *

Management by Creating Value

Management by various thoughts has become the vogue, such as Management by Objectives, Management by Values, Management by Walking Around, and Management by Exception.

Now I am going to add Management by Creating Value to this list. This is not the same as Value Based Management which focuses on increasing share value alone. This is a concept that we all actually practice but unconsciously. We want to make Value Creation a conscious activity. People and companies that succeed do so because they create value.

Is there a need to do this in a serious fashion? Well, the Business Roundtable and the World Economic Forum at Davos both have announced the purpose of a company is to create value for all stakeholders. However, there is no mechanism in place at most companies to create value as an objective.

The first step is to formulate a strategy for the company by looking at Creating Value and avoiding value destruction. One has to shape such a strategy by first building a stakeholder strategy.

The next is to ground your decision-making on choosing options that create the most value or have the greatest value creation potential. Thus ask whether this option will create more value and destroy less value for you and others over competing options.

Take the example of driverless cars. There is value creation for some stakeholders (in light grey) and value destruction for others shown in dark grey (Figure 6.6).

Figure 6.6 shows where value creation is positive and where it is destroyed.

You will note value destruction for areas such as insurance and retail gasoline supply.

I wrote some time ago that we have to go to JIT (Just in Time), and towards local manufacturing, avoiding long inventory and building shorter delivery and supply chains. This will create value and here is a way to do so.

First, do not always think of economies of scale, especially when you want local manufacturing. Think of ways of making small quantities which can be sold economically to the local geography, maybe up to 1000 km away and not 10,000 km! This can work on exports also, with the last mile done in the host country. This is an example of Managing for Creating Value.

Also, when one thinks of cans, bottles, and toothpaste tubes, we are also shipping air ... and perhaps we can do some final manufacture on-site. For

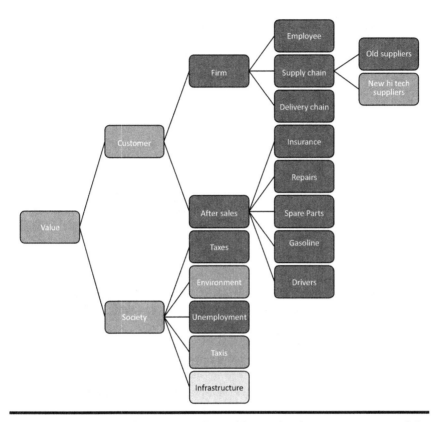

Figure 6.6 **Where Value Creation is Positive and Where It Is Destroyed for Driverless Cars**

example, instead of shipping toothpaste tubes, ship rolls of the sheet to the toothpaste tube manufacturer. Or, make bottles on the site of the bottling plant. Some of this is being done, but more is needed. Pet bottles are made in this way.

There could be special machines which are designed to be flexible such as in the manufacture of furniture. Machines can be programmed to make a table, and next a chair, and so on, rather than long runs of chairs, long runs of tables etc. This allows making furniture on demand, and not large-scale manufacturing which causes inventory build-up. Such machines exist today.

I remember in a study for SAIL (Steel Authority of India Ltd.), we found that manufacturing decided the runs, their lengths, the sequences, and the timing. This was to maximize manufacturing efficiency. Consequently, sales could not give exact dates of supply to the customer if the material was not in inventory. Customer projects were held up or delayed because sales could not give the customer delivery date. Sales lamented that manufacturing would let them know when the runs started and not well in advance.

Such steel items can sometimes be made on smaller scales in mini-mills.

Peter Diamandis quotes Christian Brecher, director of Germany's Fraunhofer Institute for Production Technology, who said the "internet of production," or industrial internet, is not as easy as the consumer internet because production is much more complex.

He noted that Europe, Japan, and some other parts of Asia have much knowledge about manufacturing, with which "we can create customer value." He said once data is merged with cutting-edge production technologies such as robotics, it will bring about a revolution in the manufacturing sector. Production knowledge exists but needs to be channelized, and soon there will be a knowledge explosion.

Peter Diamandis gives examples of 3D printing which is about to turn the entire retail industry on its head. The 3D printing market is already over $15 billion and growing fast.

Did you know that 3D printing can be used for clothes? Three accountants wanted not normal clothes but something exciting to wear.

Together, they formed a company called the Ministry of Supply, a clothing company with an intent on borrowing space suit technology from NASA for a line of dress shirts.

They designed the "Apollo" dress shirt, which uses NASA's "phase change materials" to control body heat and reduce perspiration and odour. It also adapts to the wearer's shape, and stays tucked in and wrinkle-free all day. Their company, Ministry of Supply, now makes high-performance smart clothing for both sexes, including a new line of intelligent jackets that respond to voice commands and learns to automatically heat to your desired temperature, says Diamandis.

And recently, they extended their high-tech approach to manufacturing. So now in less than 2 hours you can get customized dresses using a 4000-needle special machine with a dozen different yarns, the printer can create any combination of materials and colours desired, with zero waste.

Thanks to the smartphone, 3D-printed clothing can now be ordered from the ease of your living room.

Since fashion designer Danit Peleg's 2015 introduction of the first line of 3D-printed clothing available via the web, many designers are now offering 3D-printed clothes.

Even sports shoe manufacturers are using this technology.

Now retailers are following this and you can order drones, spectacles, jewellery, and deliver the like to their customers.

But fashion is only part of the story, as 3D printing is now showing up all over retail.

AI integration is making the design and manufacture seamless, easier, faster, and more available.

Can you imagine the end of traditional manufacturing, the end of traditional supply chains, the end of a large inventoried spare part market, and more customized and user-designed products with little or no waste?

And imagine a future with value creation, vehicles with fewer emissions, and reusable packaging. Use your creative thinking to design the future and be successful. Remember for value creation you need the 8As:

1. Awareness
2. Ability
3. Anticipation
4. Agility
5. Attitude
6. Adaptability
7. Ambidextrousness
8. Action

To bring the frontline people into the value creation loop, form Customer-centric Circles where value creation is described and frontline people can work together as a team to create more value.

Forbes, for example in an article on Value Creation, has suggested that executives and employees have to learn to create value. Rosa Vargas in Forbes asks would-be job applicants: what value did you deliver in each role? She suggests that if you are looking to hire, then you should start with reviewing Creating Value experiences. She says:

> Value your resume must highlight: Instead of leading with your job titles as evidence that you have done the job before and therefore can do it again, pin down three or four game-changing decisions and strategic plans that showcase your ability to thrive as a leader during challenging times. It doesn't mean that you cannot list achievements that were part of your mandate, but that you must lead with surprising triumphs versus what you were expected to deliver.

As we delve into this, we find that work is being redefined to create value. John Hagel, Jeff Schwartz, and Maggie Wooll wrote in MIT Sloan Management Review,

> The less familiar but more expansive approach is to redefine what work is all about: It shifts the primary objective of work from efficiency to broader value creation. When work is appropriately redefined, workers focus on identifying and addressing unseen problems

and opportunities instead of executing tasks. In contrast to the incremental and diminishing returns of job redesign, redefining work leads to increasing returns because of its significant potential for long-term value creation.

They go on to say integrating job redesign with work redefinition should expand both financial value for the company and create dynamic new sources of value and meaning for the customer.

Redesigning and thinking through the future of work is the potential – for expanding value and meaning. In a sense, one needs to get out of the efficiency trap. We have to redesign jobs and redefine work to mean the creation of value.

I used to think that useful work was what was desirable for the end user such as a customer. Now I feel useful work is what creates value for the end user or the customer.

At one company where I introduced this concept, employees and executives started to examine the work they were doing and see if this was Creating Value for whom and how. Was there a better way to create value? Could we prevent the destruction of value? Could we examine value destruction potential and convert it into a value creation potential? An example is when the employees discovered a change in the proposed plan would destroy value for some clients. They re-designed the offering to these clients so as to mitigate the destruction of value and add new value. The customers really appreciated the effort to take care of them.

These are examples of Management by Creating Value. One is that if the profit is focused on as a means and not a result, you spend time cutting costs. There might have been better ways of Creating Value, but you don't even think of it. Your strategy formulation can be led by Creating Value and converting potential value destruction into value creating ideas.

The Encyclopaedia of Management states that when broadly defined, value creation is increasingly being recognized as a better management goal than strict financial measures of performance, many of which tend to place cost cutting that produces short-term results ahead of investments that enhance long-term competitiveness and growth. As a result, some experts recommend making value creation the first priority for all employees and all company decisions. "If you put value creation first in the right way, your managers will know where and how to grow; they will deploy capital better than your competitors; and they will develop more talent than your competition," Ken Favaro[*] explained in Marakon Commentary. "This will give you an enormous

---

[*] https://www.favaro..net/publications/pvcf/ken pvcf.html#

advantage in building your company's ability to achieve profitable and long-lasting growth."

Finally, many companies look at environmental, sustainability, and governance issues (ESG) as items they have to do because they are mandated. They do not look at the potential to create value for themselves by pushing for improvements here. Results follow that create value for the company.

The first advantage is that companies, governments, or individuals you want to do business with will view your past record on ESG and how they perceive you as a company. We proved at Tata Power that values create value. That is to say, your values resonate with your customers. Your integrity and other ESG factors count.

You will be employee preferred and have happier employees working for a desirable company with values and a focus on the environment and sustainability and value creation. Firms that are viewed positively by employees tend to give a 2–4% higher return than those that are not.

Tata is a company that is considered desirable to work for over higher paying companies, because of their ESG, and their fairness. They are able to attract and keep employees even though the salaries might be lower.

There will be less governmental interference giving you a strategic advantage and more elbow room to manoeuvre. You will also be able to get subsidies from governments etc.

This can lead to top-line growth as you will beat out poorly perceived companies on their ESG stance. You will also have a better chance at other resources, apart from customer resources, to acquire other resources, like employees, natural resources, and overseas customers.

There is also the potential for cost reduction, by savings in energy, water usage, and other consumables. Unnecessary waste is reduced.

Next, you will make your investments also based on ESG getting a potential reduction in cost, productivity gains, and employee and customer value. You will avoid long-term environmental issues that might otherwise crop up.

Raj Sisodia, David Wolfe, and Jag Sheth in Firms of Endearment in 2007 proved from their research that firms that endeared themselves to their stakeholders, tended to give an eight-fold return over the broad market in 10 years, and the Good to Great companies (described by Jim Collins) by three times.

This then is your chance to overtake your competitors by managing by Creating Value. The CEO's message has to be one of Creating Value for this to succeed. Moreover, peg the CEO's compensation to ESG work. This will create value for all. Adopt Management by Creating Value!

* * *

Does Value Creation Need Financial Incentives?

When you wake up in the morning do you say I will Create Value today?

Before you can think of financial incentives for Value Creation, it is important that value be understood and recognized and also be measured. As you read further, you will relate to these important aspects of Value Creation.

Studies have shown that incentives do not improve the innovativeness of creative people. An experiment was conducted on two groups of creative people assigned to create a faster process. The first group was asked to increase the average speed. The second group was incentivized as individuals: the fastest two would get rewards. The first group members did better than the incentivized group. Further studies have shown that incentives work best for routine jobs. "More pay for laying more bricks" works.

Value Creation by employees has hitherto been an unconscious process. Few employees get up in the morning and say today I will create value. In fact, they do not know often know when they are creating or destroying value.

We are now suggesting to companies that the role of an executive and leader is to create value. We give examples of how value can be created or destroyed.

Now employees start to consciously think about creating value. What is this value and how is it perceived by others? How can it be measured? Intangibles are the most difficult to measure. Intangibles include corporate culture, brands, intellectual property, and employee assets. Value Creation impacts all of these. So, Creating Value in intangibles is even more difficult to measure unless one is using quantitative measures. Qualitative metrics ask recipients about value creation or whether they perceive value. Did they feel good, did they see a benefit? Were they happier with this? Would they do business again? What did they think of the employee? Were the errors reduced? Were systemic problems identified and corrected? Is the brand equity of the employee increasing?

Moshe Davidow of Carmel Academic Center in Haifa, Israel, and I had a delightful conversation on identifying and measuring value. Certain transactions, said Moshe, create value because the transaction ended in your buying something. I countered, if you had no choice but to buy, the transaction might have destroyed value (for example having to buy an expensive plane ticket on a route having little competition). We agreed value can be created or destroyed and this can be recognized by the receiver. We went on to discuss how value can be measured, and the value of a transaction.

Measurements change and improve, added Moshe, but we have to start somewhere. What gets measured gets done. The model he used to measure complaint handling when he was a manager is different (and less good) than the one he uses today. Rules change, and measurement changes (leading to managerial changes). In soccer, a tie was worth one point, and a win was worth two points, so there were a lot of tie games. When winning became worth three points, suddenly more teams started to go for the win instead of the tie. The game had changed....

Typically, said Moshe, satisfaction or service quality is expectation minus perceived performance and is measured soon after the transaction. Value is what it cost versus what benefits you got. Was it worthwhile? When you read this chapter, you are expending your time, and value is created for you if the time was spent in a worthwhile fashion or you got something worthwhile out of the chapter. Value therefore goes beyond satisfaction, and you can measure value of a transaction on a ten-point scale (and preferably against competing transactions). So how would you rate this chapter vs. the time you spent on a ten-point scale?

And you can see why I am against rating a lecture or a workshop at the end of the lecture. Do you rate based on what you learnt or on the quality of the lecture (was it fun?) or should you rate it on how you can use the learning? And if your boss sent you and he paid for you to attend the workshop, I would ask him a month later if it was worth his while to send Joe Blow to the workshop. He would rate the workshop based on how Joe used the learnings or how he had changed (versus the cost such as fees and travel and the loss of Joe's time at work), and not on whether Joe had a good time. That is why value goes beyond satisfaction on a transaction and can be measured on a ten-point scale. Moshe agreed.

So as value is being created and is being recognized, we can also measure value albeit in some kind of a personal, perceived fashion. This concept can be improved by smarter people than me (read you).

Take Jim Carras who worked with Phil Crosby. He told me that a potential customer, a current customer, and a past customer are the primary targets for Creating Value. Till a company or organization truly understands the customer's emotional feelings and traits (the key drivers that companies should impact), and what changes these emotions, they can never know what it takes to create value for the customer. Let's assume a company does have good data to support how customers really feel, and they also know what their company can do to increase "Customer Value," they have the bigger problem: how do they translate that down to their company employees so they can make a deliberate attempt to change what they do to impact Customer Value. You can't just tell employees to create Customer Value, because they need to know and then apply action based on factual information. While I agree with Jim on expected or suggested Value Creation, I believe as a start just going beyond your job requirements will create value or not doing your job will destroy value (being rude is an example of value destruction).

I believe (says Jim) the critical component of Value Creation is first, the ability of a company to truly understand the emotional drivers for what steers their customers' value, and then second, the ability to translate that into every employee in the company, the processes they follow, and the tools or technology they use.

And then we come to incentivizing Value Creation. As long as the activity is new and increases value to the stakeholders (including employees, customers, partners, unions, society, and the company), it requires some creativity and often conscious creativity. Can we or should we incentivize such creativity? And how do we differentiate between Value Creation and expected work or expected tasks? And then how do we measure these?

The easy answer is that Value Creation becomes obvious. We notice it, just as we would notice a smile on a normally frowning person or helpfulness of a generally unhelpful person (or company). But sometimes you Create Value in not-so-obvious ways, or in ways people do not notice. You replace 4 spoke revolving office chairs with 5 spoke ones which are much safer, but no one realizes safety has been improved and value has been created.

However, there are means to measure value as pointed out earlier, and slowly measurement methodologies can be implemented.

For these creative people, can we improve their value creation propensity by incentivizing them? Will they create more value? I have 18 patents, and incentivizing would not have made me more creative. Nor was I less creative because I received no incentives.

What is your take on this?

Moshe ended by saying, this is an exciting time to be working on Value Creation!

* * *

Companies Misunderstand Price

Most buyer and seller companies misunderstand price. Buyers, because they want the lowest price (price is all), and sellers because they do not understand the value of price. I am going to discuss Price as a business improvement tool and Price as an investment, for all companies. Companies are sometimes sellers and sometimes buyers.

Have you ever in your planning process thought of improving your business (read profits)? What do you think about first? You think about increasing market share or cutting costs. How many have your prime strategy of increasing price (a 1% increase in price can improve profits by over 10%)? How many think of adding value, differentiating, or telling a better story to skew the price in your favour? I'll warrant, very few!

And when buying or selling do you ever think of price as an investment rather than a cost? How do you talk about value and the value of your product as an investment? You will buy this suit and use it for 5 years, versus this one which is a throwaway? Or this car will cost me less because maintenance is less and the resale value is high? Or this car will be worthwhile because it enhances my image and self-esteem?

So, rethink and use price as a prime strategy for improving business and profits, and for thinking of what you are buying and selling as an investment.

If you do this, you can graduate to thinking beyond price as the only way to sell, and think Customer Value and value creation.

Most executives should know the impact of a 1% price increase on profits.

* * *

The Case for Value Creation Centres: Value Councils Go Beyond Pricing Councils and Innovation Councils

We have been working with companies to establish Value Creation Centres. We are in the process of setting some of these in MBA schools.

Recently I came across a blog by Paul Carpinella quoting Dr. Stephan Liozu who has set up pricing and innovation councils for several companies. This made me think.

Most companies I deal with work on pricing in an ad hoc fashion and have no real focused approach to pricing. They do not have pricing departments. They do not even have a pricing council.

Very often when I visited companies (and many were large companies), I would go past a meeting room and see marketing folks holding a discussion. I would ask, what are they discussing? Many times, they were discussing what action they should take because a competitor had reduced prices. Should they hold their price? Should they match comp?

I used to ask, how many times these people meet to discuss creating customer value or just creating value. And, generally the answer was never. Some brave managers said we do this when we discuss strategy. Give me a break, I would think, because strategy is generally about how we make more money.

After our Customer Value interventions, many of these companies stopped meeting competition's pricing and even ignored competitive moves. They concentrated on creating customer value and getting a price for it.

It is not easy. First you have to measure the value you are creating vs. the value your competition is creating. And you have to understand why people buy and what factors are truly important in the buying equation.

Thus, in buying a refrigerator is price (which is the actual price and non-price terms) 40% of the buying decision or is it 60%? Are the benefits 60% or 40%? And what are the relative importance of product, retailer, service, and performance? What is the relative importance of price and non-price terms? Are you better at these items? Often there is not much to choose between products (yet product-focused companies keep focusing on products, not customers).

And as you start to understand this, you start to create value. Some things in creating value are very simple. Doing your job better. Finding better ways to do your job and delivering happiness (as espoused by Tony Hsieh of Zappos) is value creation. Going beyond the requirements of your job leads to value creation. Doing things better is value creation. Touching customers better creates value.

And to do this well you must establish Value Creation Centres or Value Councils.

Many suggest that Value Councils should have a typical agenda of creating better prices or delivering a new product with innovative marketing, or value propositions, value drivers and messages, and value selling materials.

To me, this is an omigosh ... more of the same, an inside–outside look. Value Councils have to work on creating value for the customer.

Ken Favaro in his 1998 seminal article "Put Value Creation First" said that:

Value Creation tells You Where and How to Grow
Value Creation Gives You the Capital and Talent to Grow
Value Creation Increases Your Capacity to Grow

Remember, Ken wrote this in 1998. Value Creation by definition then was creating more profits and sustainable growth. But he was on the right path. Now you use this to figure out how you would create value for customers and employees. And suddenly, you are looking at work and the world in a different way by using the latest definition of Value Creation (for stakeholders, primarily customers).

Putting Value Creation first will happen with Value Councils. Value Creation will tell you where to grow because you focus on customers' needs and unmet needs, like an iPad that made even the most anti-tech or tech-allergic person participate in computing. And also got higher tech people to be happy to use simpler computing.

And talent and capital will chase you because people can see that your value creation will create value for them. Ken Favaro put it nicely: more importantly, though, companies that put value creation first will create over time a cadre of managers who have higher standards and better capabilities than the competition. In a world where nearly everyone faces abundant choices, the challenge for all businesses is to develop and sustain a uniquely attractive proposition for both customers and employees. But the hardest challenge is to do this in a way that also creates value. Holding your managers to this standard means continually asking, "What exactly do we do that's different from the competition, and how will this enable us to create value?" By instilling this discipline, you can make your people better managers and create an environment that attracts only people who adhere to the highest standards for business performance and personal achievement. In time this will give you more managerial talent than your competitors, enabling you to achieve higher levels of profitable and sustainable growth.

Disney is a great example of Value Creation. Steven Spielberg is another example. The shorter formats of cricket matches (one day, 20 overs etc.) are examples of value creation. And value creation happens when you leave your charger in a hotel, and the hotel says they will get it to you within 5 hours, instead of asking how you will pay for this. (This happened to me at Taj President Hotel in Mumbai and as I was catching a flight to Delhi I remembered about my charger and called the hotel.)

And finally, value creation gets you on a truly growth path. Leadership must believe in value creation and indeed put it first and set a culture and a process for value creation, and work with employees on value creation, whether it is to be world class or leaders. Short and long-term growth comes from value creation. Favaro goes on to say be better than your competitors at understanding where, how, and why value is created and destroyed within your markets and your company. This means by business unit, by product, by customer, by channel, by market, by technology, or by whatever "cut" will best reveal the truly distinctive capabilities and assets you have to drive profitable and sustainable growth.

If you put value creation first in the right way, your managers will know where and how to grow; they will deploy capital better than your competitors; and they will develop more talent than your competition. This will give you an enormous advantage in building your company's ability to achieve profitable and long-lasting growth. They will help with pricing and innovation.

Some small steps are being taken such as 360pi, the leader in retail price and product intelligence, announcing the appointment of Gregory Soussloff as Vice President of Customer Value. This is a start to building Value Councils.

* * *

Journey of a Customer Value Creation Evangelist: From Companystan to Customerstan

So many articles are written about the Customer and how to make him happier. These articles just tweak the same theme and play the same tune without understanding why true change is not happening. Talk to the customer, be nice to him, give him a good experience in journeys he may not want, and unleash CRM in different forms, but basically it is business as usual.

I just finished reading Dick Lee's in-depth and historical expose of companies in his book, "We Are Buyers. You Are Sellers. You're Busted." He talks about what companies have managed to get away with at the expense of the Customer and the country in the guise of growth and payers of tax and the supporter of big government (in the USA he states large companies pay only 17% tax). As the Russians said, the capitalist oligarchy controls these countries.

I believe we live in different spheres and thinking: Companystan (that is the country of Companies) and Customerstan (the country of Customers). The philosophy of the Company has been working with Profitstan in a world of Mediocristan (mediocrity). Few like Lee and me wish to visit Extremistan where change is wreaked on or legislated on companies to move towards Customerstan and report and use Customer data with the same passion as financial and profit data, just as a start. As companies move from Profitstan and Companystan to Customerstan, they will change and rename the operations department run by a COO to become the Customer Department (incorporating products and product development, employees brought in from Customerstan, all Customer focused work including accounts and finances to do with Customers, manufacturing, supply and delivery chain, technology and IT, the ethics department, the shareholder department, and teaching how to create value). Those left out would be routine accounting, tax and treasury, routine HR functions of policing, compliance and record keeping, routine maintenance, corporate social responsibility, government affairs etc. This routine department along with the Customer department will report to the CEO or could be outsourced.

So we also need some new definitions for words from Customerstan such as Customeric and Customer responsibility.

Customer responsibility: while this can mean many things, in this context it is the responsibility that the company takes for the Customer. So if the company has a bill of rights for the Customer, then it has a responsibility to uphold the rights. Or if they bring out a product, they have a responsibility the product will perform and be repaired if it does not. In an overall sense, the company must feel responsible to the Customer. The purpose of an executive is to care for customers. He has to understand he has a job because of customers.

Customeric is a word coined to show that a company has the Customer-in-Centre. The Customer is the centre of the company's strategy and its focus. The company is Customer-centric, takes Customer responsibility, measures Customer data, and lets Customer thought lead the business.

Then truly will companies migrate from Companystan to Customerstan, when they become customeric.

Do you think our Customer movement should force the move from Companystan to Customerstan? Should we concentrate on this than just get a process or system improvements for the Customer? Can Customerstan become a force to reckon with? I desperately need your comments even though you might decide to transport me to Companystan.

Chapter 7

Profits and Value

How the Pure Profit Motive Destroys Value

For years, we have been discussing value destruction. A prime example of this is given in Francesca Mari's brilliant article on the cover of *New York Times* magazine called "A $60 Billion Housing Grab by Wall Street." You can see it at:

https://www.nytimes.com/2020/03/04/magazine/wall-street-landlords.html

"Hundreds of thousands of single-family homes are now in the hands of giant companies – squeezing renters for revenue and putting the American dream even further out of reach," the article says.

Francesca describes a potential first home buyer.

> When Ellingwood began speaking to lenders, he realized he could easily get a loan, even two; this was the height of the bubble, when mortgage brokers were keen to generate mortgages, even risky ones, because the debt was being bundled together, securitized and spun into a dizzying array of bonds for a hefty profit. The house was $840,000. He put down $15,000 and sank the rest of his savings into a $250,000 bedroom addition and kitchen remodel, reasoning that this would increase the home's value.

For a variety of reasons including divorce, he was unable to make payments on the mortgage and had to sell the house. The buyer turned out to be a finance company (almost like a private equity company) who found this a lucrative market to invest in and squeeze higher profits from people who had meagre means.

Francesca writes,

Before 2010, institutional landlords didn't exist in the single-family-rental market; now there are 25 to 30 of them, according to Amherst Capital, a real estate investment firm. From 2007 to 2011, 4.7 million households lost homes to foreclosure, and a million more to short sale. Private-equity firms developed new ways to secure credit, enabling them to leverage their equity and acquire an astonishing number of homes.

You have to read the article to see the disregard for the customer in preference to make more money. The convenience of the company comes before the convenience of the customer. And sadly, this happens to a bunch of customers who mostly can barely afford to pay the mortgage and are not able to do any major (and often minor) repairs. The story is one of greed and making the purpose of a company to generate more money, and not worry about creating value for the stakeholder (the customers, the employees, partners, and society).

Thus a society meant to be one where people can get affordable housing could not exist for all because of such greed.

The private equity model that Francesca talks about, in general, prioritizes short-term earnings and harvesting as much money as possible even if it means destroying value rather than building a solid company that creates values and results in long-term earnings.

All this could be a repeat of the 2008 financial crisis, which damaged the economy and those who were marginal homeowners. Her article is a wake-up call for companies and governments to create value for people in the marginal category who have no choice but to rent.

This greed is how the economy collapsed in 2008. And this is being repeated. The problem emanates from a business strategy that tells the companies they can make more money by playing out the strategy. There is no customer strategy to ensure the customer is focused on and his wellbeing is important.

One solution is building and following a Customer and/or a Stakeholder Strategy.

For a long time, I have been advocating to CEOs that the starting point of a good business strategy is a customer strategy. The customer[1] strategy and the shareholder strategy should then be used to build a business strategy/business tactics. Today, we suggest the starting point is a stakeholder strategy to build a business strategy. And in today's age, both the business and the stakeholder strategy should be adaptive to the changing future.

To many, customer or a stakeholder strategy can appear to be redundant. But it isn't. It is crucial if organizations want to change and become truly

---

[1] What we say for Customer strategy in this section is true for stakeholder strategy.

Customer-centric. A survey of 400 CEOs showed that 33% felt that the number one issue in preventing Customer-centricity was a lack of a clear customer strategy. Twenty-eight percent felt it was internal silos. Customer strategy helps break silos and creates teamwork. This happens because CxOs are part of creating the strategy. They, therefore, become part of the customer strategy. They assign customer roles for themselves and their departments. They agree to lead certain customer-related strategies. They become part of the customer-focused team. And as KPIs include customer parameters, the customer strategy becomes a practical roadmap to build customer value and create value for the customer.

The customer (and even the stakeholder strategy) strategy should become an integral part of the business or corporate strategy led by the CEO. It will help him think about how to change the organizational structure to become customeric and drive the business with the customer in the centre. It will help the CEO implement the strategy and think through moving from selling to the customer to helping him buy to becoming an extension of the customer by building an inseparable and symbiotic relationship with him.

Much of this has also become more complex and intense in the fast-moving world and the customer focus is much more necessary for success and adaptability.

The company needs an inseparable and symbiotic relationship with the customer (some call this co-creation. I am going beyond this). What tasks will make this happen? To be successful, the company must be dynamic, understand its customers, and exercise its right to select the customers it wishes to serve. Often this is based on customer profitability (which includes margins, cost to serve etc.). Sometimes companies want customers who can recommend them or become brand ambassadors. But having selected the customers, companies must serve them also.

We helped several companies create customer strategies. There was a palpable change in these companies in terms of customer thinking and focus. Much value was created and many Customer-centric and customer-friendly programs were implemented. This resulted in reduced complaints, increased efficiency, higher sales, and higher business excellence scores (one company in the Tata Group went from being among the lowest in business excellence to the best in the group). Of course, proper implementation of the customer strategy is a necessity to get the benefits of the customer strategy.

Strategy must build a competitive advantage for the firm by creating compelling Value for Customers. Articulating why Customers will buy requires managers to examine strategy from the Customer's point of view. It encourages them to ask how the firm's activities deliver superior value to chosen Customers. The firm must choose the set of activities that serve target Customers better than competitors and shun other segments that demand incompatible activities. This is what a customer strategy will do for a company.

Many people ask me the difference between a customer strategy and a business strategy. They cannot see the difference since the business strategy is based on the marketplace. The customer strategy looks at the customer, his needs, and the customer opportunity. The difference can be seen from what happened in the recent meltdown of the financial markets, starting with the mortgage market crash.

The typical mortgage customer was looking for a product that would keep him safe if the prices of homes went down or interest rates went up. The mortgage company should pay attention to the customer's liquidity and ability to pay. A customer strategy would have revealed the customer's needs and also suggested what products needed to be created to make the mortgagee safer if prices of homes went down or interest rates went up.

The market opportunity that arose was to bundle mortgages and sell them to a bigger financial institution, thereby getting money back to give out more mortgages. These new mortgages were then bundled and re-sold from a bigger financial institution to an even larger one. The buyer of these bundled mortgages bundled more of them and sold them on to the next larger financial company. The mortgagee was no longer the real concern of the original mortgager. The paper was held somewhere else.

As you can see, the business strategy of bundling mortgages was a great idea to make money.

No one was concerned about the quality of the mortgagee and the loan. They were too busy fulfilling their business strategy of bundling mortgages and offloading them to the next person.

And what was the result? The mortgage market collapsed, because everyone took their eyes off the customer and did not have a clear-cut customer strategy, though they had a business (market-based) strategy. Often the customer was not worthy of a mortgage.

To end, we have people like iKnowtion Senior Partner, Don Ryan, and SunTrust Banks SVP and Director of Client Information, Greg Holzwarth, who are saying: Customers are changing. The recent financial crisis left many consumers soured on the state of the banking industry. They are now more empowered to demand better experiences and won't hesitate to switch banks if they aren't happy. In response, many banks are working to rebuild relationships by learning to speak their customers' language, act in the customers' interests, and improve their reputation and financial wellbeing in the process.

Customer strategy, specifically data intelligence, is at the forefront of one bank's effort to be Customer-centric:

- How can I stand out from competitors in a crowded and volatile industry?
- Who are customers? Who are my target customers?
- What do my customers value so I can provide them the value they seek?

- Are we creating more value than competition? If yes, then where and how? How do we improve?
- Should I concentrate on customer acquisition or focus on share of wallet?
- What can I promise customers and how do I keep promises?
- What additional value can I create for customers and other stakeholders, and those that serve them?
- How do I find actionable insights from internal and external data?
- How do I organize to focus on customers and other stakeholders?
- How do I implement customer programs?
- Who leads specific programs?
- What will the future be? How will our customers change, and how should we? Can we go beyond the pure profit motive?

Customer strategy also allocates customer tasks to various departments, breaking silos and making all departments have a responsibility for the customer. This builds teamwork and builds customer priority and focus in all departments. Key performance areas can then be customer-based and incentivized. This is an extremely important reason for the customer strategy being built.

The customer (or stakeholder strategy) strategy can then be a precursor to the business strategy.

You can see none of this was part of the corporate thinking in Francesca's article. And the state that was to monitor the wellbeing of the citizens abrogated their responsibility to greedy landlord companies.

Do you agree this is value destruction, and not value creation?

Companies and governments must have a stakeholder strategy to take care of their constituents. All this might sound like wishful thinking by companies, but customers are in their long-term interest and companies should avoid short-term money-making schemes.

* * *

The Great Balancing Act: You Can Tip the Balance! Increase Profits

Curt Fowler wrote in the Moultrie Observer on Driving Growth through Customer Excellence. He quoted HBR in Zero Defections stating that a 5% increase in Customer retention can increase profits up to 75%. In retail, they find a 1% increase in retained customers can increase revenue by 10%. Gartner estimated that 80% of your future revenues will come from just 20% of your existing customers.

Below is a chart (Figure 7.1) showing just this.

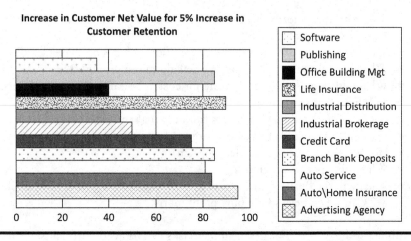

Increase in Customer Net Value for 5% Increase in Customer Retention

Software
Publishing
Office Building Mgt
Life Insurance
Industrial Distribution
Industrial Brokerage
Credit Card
Branch Bank Deposits
Auto Service
Auto\Home Insurance
Advertising Agency

Figure 7.1   Increase in Customer Net Value for 5% Increase in Retention

Very impressive, won't you say? And if you were the CEO of or on the Board of companies, wouldn't you want to retain more Customers? Wouldn't you make it your strategy? Wouldn't you want to tip the balance in your favour?

So we should be hearing great success stories, a great increase in profits. But we don't hear these stories. Why?

Start by answering these questions:

Are HBR, Customer Value Foundation, and Forrester and all the experts correct? Y/N

Does this data sound correct? Y/N

The CEOs and others don't believe these numbers Y/N

Or they do, but their training of focusing on shareholder returns, cutting costs, increasing efficiency and traditional ways of doing the done thing, prevents them from making a big change? Y/N

Or they do not know how to make the change? Y/N

They are happy with the status quo Y/N

They are balancing the focus on various stakeholders in favour of the owners Y/N

Or the change consultants are focusing on efficiency and systems while focusing on the Customer experience etc. and not the mindset and culture that need to be changed? Y/N

CEOs think culture is their baby Y/N

I truly would like to understand WHY? I'd like the reader to help. How many Yesses did you click? I bet there are fewer N (nay) answers.

So what really happens? In a given market, companies in the competitive mix are all losing and gaining customers. They report the customers they gain and not the customers they lose. The great balancing act: market share and retention remain static, and yet customers are gained. A wonderful game, as if all competitors are happy, and no one is tipping the balance.

As an example, in India prepaid cell phone Customers defect at an alarming rate of 30–50%. Yet market shares are static as those customers one company loses are made up as new customers coming in from competitor's customer losses.

Another example of companies not focusing on retention is Tata AIG. I tried to renew my home policy but could not do so online. I sent them an e-mail as suggested on their website. After 2 days, there was a response that someone would get back to me. After another 2 days, I got a message to pay within 3 hours on the payment portal they had sent in the mail with a link (this was at 6 pm). I had paid a week earlier, but there was no response from the company. Doesn't it appear that they are not interested in retention? (I always say retention is like farming, and acquiring new customers is akin to hunting. Hunting is more exciting, farming more boring. Learn to farm to retain customers. Make it interesting for yourself and your customers).

We need disruptors, and great CEOs to tackle this, to not only understand the opportunity but put into action the balance tipping strategies: build a customer strategy, change the mindset, and out strip competition.

I would choose Amazon, Airbnb, Costco, Wholefoods, and Zappos among others. Down the list would be United Air. You can see that some of the leaders are also disruptors and have built their businesses around the customer. United, on the other hand, does not seem to want to do so.

Brand Keys' 2015 Customer Loyalty Engagement Index® (CLEI) Ratings are based on a brand's ability to meet customers' ever-growing expectations better than the competition. That means a focus on the Customer by the company and the CEO. Leaders are:

Apple, AT&T, Hyundai, Ford, Avis, Domino's, Dunkin Donut Google, Konica Minolta, Discover, and the NFL maintained their #1 category positions. Brands that were rated #1 in their categories for the first time included Air Canada, Facebook, Kellogg's Nutri-Grain Breakfast Bars, Chipotle, Exxon Mobile, Nationwide, and Travelocity.

What does this tell us? Companies, that are on the top and want to keep retaining customers, work with a strategy and a culture to achieve just this. The CEO is motivated to retain customers. The newer companies on the list were able to reach the number one loyalty slot by focusing on the customer, giving him what he wanted and making him feel cared for.

Other companies improving retention did so by better customer engagement and better communications, and include High Ridge in packaged goods, Hilton, insurance companies such as Aetna, MetLife and Cigna, and brands like Nike. They focus on what customers want, how they want to be communicated with, convenience, personalization, a comfortable customer journey, and offering choices to customers.

So you can see that the winners learn to focus on the customer, retain more customers, and lose fewer customers. They tipped the balance in their favour.

Can you tip the balance today? Can you be the Value Creator for your Customer, and avoid value destruction? Can you make this a core task?

Come, let us win! Win the Customer and reap the benefits.

* * *

Death of Profit: Customer Power Requires a Mindset Change to Improve Customer Retention and Profits

In the previous chapter, I wrote about companies professing they had more important priorities than Customers. In more and more studies, we are finding that companies are losing existing Customers. The profit increase from retaining Customers is shown in Figure 7.1.

In a recent Business Line article quoting a global study, they stated that 80% of the Customers in India and globally who complained about poor service or product deficiencies had their complaints ignored. Companies lost at least 18% of their annual revenues because of poor complaint handling. In my opinion the number is higher but is masked. Companies cannot afford to lose Customers and allow profits to leak through the poor Customer experience sieve. They need to heed this. So, what are they doing?

Companies are planning to spend more in Customer support technology. They are thinking that technology will solve the poor Customer experience and retention problem. But what they need to do is to change the mindset starting at the top with CxOs and getting all departments to focus on the Customer and Customer issues. They need to break internal silos and build a circle of promises internally to make sure the Customer remains happy and stays with the company (and even attract new Customers by word of mouth). They also need to incorporate Customer Circles like the Quality Circles to start a Continuous Customer Improvement program. This will give them more mileage and will be cheaper than a mere technology intervention. Companies beware of Customer Power! Do not let your profits die!

* * *

Value Added Stories to Increase Price

If You Want to Raise Prices, Tell a Better Story

Ask a CEO if they want to spend a pile of money on an analysis of their company's story, and they'll probably throw you out of their office. But if you tell them that you have a powerful insight that can help them raise the prices of all of their products, they might ask you over to their house for dinner. Money talks, in other words. Unfortunately, in most companies, the power of story to affect pricing still remains unknown, or at least it's vastly under-utilized.

Pricing strategy usually follows one of four tracks. Bottom up: calculate the cost of everything that goes into making the product and add a fair margin on top. Sideways in: analyse and adopt the price of competitors' products. Top down: target a demographic or economic segment and engineer the product to meet that price. Or dynamic: use a complex, real-time calculation to gauge supply and demand, usually with the help of an algorithm.

What you almost never hear about is a fifth track, which I call story analysis: an analysis of a product's capabilities to fulfil a profound human need, to tell a story that gives your customers' lives richer meaning. In a world of abundance, what your product does for your customers is important, but not nearly as important as what your product means to them. And this second part – the story of your product – is what yields the greatest pricing power of all.

Not convinced? Consider this story.

Back in the summer of 2006, *New York Times* magazine columnist Rob Walker was mulling the question of what makes one object more valuable than another. What makes one pair of shoes more valuable than another pair if they both deliver on the functional basics of comfort, durability, and protection? Why does one piece of art cost $8,000,000 and another $100? What makes one toaster worth $20 and another worth nearly $400 if they both make toast? As Walker turned these questions over in his mind, he concluded that it is not the objects themselves, but the context, the provenance of the objects, that generates value. In other words, the value isn't contained in the objects themselves, but in the story or the meaning that the objects represent to the owner.

Walker decided to test this conclusion in a simple and direct way. With the help of a friend, he began buying random, worthless, or low-value objects at tag sales and thrift shops. The cost of the objects ranged from 1–4 dollars. An old wooden mallet. A lost hotel room key. A plastic banana. These were true castoffs with little or no intrinsic worth.

Next, Walker asked some unknown writers to each write a short story that contained one of the objects. The stories weren't about the objects, per se; but they helped to place them in a human context, to give them new meaning.

When Walker put the objects, along with their accompanying stories, up for sale on eBay, the results were astonishing. On average, the value of the objects rose 2,700%. That's not a typo: 2,700%. A miniature jar of mayonnaise he had purchased for less than a dollar sold for $51.00. A cracked ceramic horse head purchased for $1.29 sold for $46.00. The value of these formerly abandoned or forsaken objects suddenly and mysteriously skyrocketed when they were accompanied by a story.

The project was so successful (and so interesting) that they have now repeated it five times and put all the results up on the web. It is also a book.

Walker's experiment reminds us in a clear and extremely tangible way how the concept of value works in the human brain: a can opener is a can opener is a can opener until it is a can opener designed by Michael Graves and a part of the permanent collection of the Museum of Modern Art. A shoe is a shoe is a shoe until it is a pair of TOMS shoes. For every pair that I buy, a child who has never been able to afford shoes gets a free pair as well. Suddenly, these objects are part of an inspiring narrative – one that I can use to reveal something meaningful about myself to others. That's something I am willing to pay for.

That's where real pricing power comes from.

And as the number of products and brands in the world proliferates at an ever-accelerating pace, the power is only increasing. In 1997, there were 2.5 million brands in the world. Today? The number is approaching 10 million. So the trend is towards rapid commoditization of just about everything. In a world of almost overwhelming abundance, an authentic, meaning-rich story becomes the most important ingredient to drive a company's margins up.

* * *

How Economics Creates Value

Hunter Hastings,[1] General Partner, Bialla Venture Partners said that Economics is the study of value creation.

This might come as a surprise to businesspeople (even including some who studied economics at University or Business School) who view economics as irrelevant or unhelpful.

Carl Menger, a professor at the University of Vienna, published his Principles of Economics in 1871. This breakthrough book solved the problem of value in economics once and for all. Prior to the publication, economists had struggled with defining and understanding value. It had been thought that value was determined by the number of resources that were input to a good or service (and this thinking led to the destructive labour theory of value that propelled

---

[1] https://www.linkedin.com/pulse/new-economics-value-creation-hunter-hastings/

Marxism). Menger established that value is subjective – it is a perception of, and entirely determined by, the consumer or end user of the good or service.

Value is the importance allocated to a good or service by an individual in proportion to its perceived ability to meet a need of theirs. Value is a perception, an emotion, or a felt experience. It's not measurable in cardinal numbers. We can never determine that an apple is 2× or 3× or 4× as valuable to a person as a donut, or a CRM system is twice as valuable as a server farm.

People can, however, ordinally rank their needs: need A is more important to me (right now, in my current context, with my current knowledge) than need B, so with scarce resources, I'll attend to Need A first before I attend to Need B. This is revealed by behaviour (which good or service is chosen) rather than by stated intent (like answering a survey). Economics is a deductive science. Our data is human behaviour, from which we logically deduce value rankings, intent, and emotion.

(The value measurement also ranks the priority and level of importance of each attribute to the stakeholder.)

All economic phenomena and outcomes are determined by the individual actions of single human agents, interacting, and exchanging value in systems we call markets. This humanistic approach to the economics of value is the core of economics. It's a human science.

Economics was diverted from its human course in the 20th century. First, economics became a science of aggregates instead of people. Governments seized on economics to attempt to manage aggregate measures such as GDP and the total level of employment. Human economics became government economics. Partly as a consequence, and partly due to "physics envy," economics became mathematicized. Academic economics departments developed modelling: the representation of aggregates as mathematical symbols acting on each other in equations to generate predictions about the future state of the aggregates.

Business schools were infected by this redirection of economics to teach business in mathematical terms of prediction and control: strategy and planning as exercises in spreadsheet management and forecasting.

This diversion has redirected attention away from the humanism of economics, but it has not replaced it. Carl Menger's economics continues to inform business about how to create value.

- Value is realized by the customer; value is a feeling, and it can only be experienced by a customer.
- Value is a learning process. The customer first identifies potential value (will this offering be valuable to me or not?); then appraises relative value (in comparison to alternatives); then exchange value (how much money would I part with to acquire this offering?); then value-in-use (did the

offering keep its functional promise?); and ultimately assesses the value experience after-the-fact.

- The customer initiates the value process through the expression of dissatisfaction with the status quo. It is the singular drive of customers to always want better. No hierarchy of customer needs is ever completely fulfilled forever (otherwise no economic activity would take place).

- The co-creation force on the producer side is entrepreneurship. Menger identified entrepreneurship as the function of identifying customers' unmet needs through empathic diagnosis – an entrepreneur is like an economic doctor – and imagining future arrangements in which the need can be met. The entrepreneur combines and recombines available resources in new ways in order to make a new value proposition to the customer that they may or may not value. There is risk and uncertainty in entrepreneurship.

- Customers take the lead in determining value and the signal they send is through buying or not buying. Firms are successful when customers buy at a price that is greater than the all-in cost to produce, and they grow when more customers buy and repeat.

- Since value is a process and a mindset, customers are always learning what they want, and value is always changing. Since entrepreneurship is rivalrous, firms compete to serve customers in the best, most value-generating way, teaching them what they can want, and competition is a positive force for good.

The most successful firms are those that listen best, to pick up signals of dissatisfaction and trends in the market towards new value types; and those who adapt best and fastest to the rates of change and to the feedback loops from consumers as they assess their value experience in the final phase of the value learning cycle. Constant change in value is the norm.

Menger also demonstrated that the worth of any asset on the production side of the producer-consumer exchange is imputed from the subjective value of the final good to a customer. The land on which the factory is built, the buildings and machines, the trucks and transportation, and the people who work there, including the accountants and HR personnel, have economic value only as a reflection of the value attached to the final product by the end user. Firms can assess the economic worth of their supply chain, and every element in it, only in reference to customer value. In the famous example, Blockbuster's asset value shrank to virtually nothing once the customer's feelings about subjective value shifted from the in-store experience at Blockbuster to the in-home streaming experience of Netflix.

The economics of value is the ultimate guide to business success.

Leaders are advised to lead and lead from the front. However often this can be counterproductive and either destroy value or most certainly reduce value.

Let us give examples:

If you truly wish to have your people at the bottom of the pyramid or the frontline to really fire on all cylinders and take charge of the customer or their jobs, the leader should get out of the way and get these people to tell them what should be done and what they would like to do. Your role is to assure them of your support. True examples are the Customer-centric Circles, or Customer Circles for short (see my book *Customer Value Investment*). These Circles comprise of and are run by the frontline people to decide what to do for the customer. The leaders just supply support and listen. Listening and being supportive both create value.

These leaders just do not create a good business; they create other leaders who collectively build a better business.

Delegating makes you understand you cannot do everything yourself. We must overcome the feeling we can do things better than others! Not leading sometimes teaches you to create other leaders to support you. This is a way of developing and coaching others. It lets you empower and enable people while creating autonomy and value.

Examples at Godrej, Tatas, Coromandel etc. are shown in my books, *Total Customer Value Management*, and *Customer Value Investment*. Do look them up.

People can examine their purpose and the purpose of the organization. They learn to make connections to get the job done.

Sometimes people do not wish to lead and become leaders. This could be because they are afraid of losing interpersonal relations, or have an image risk. Also, some do not want to assume a blame risk. So, they prefer not to lead.

Leaders create value for such people by letting them lead under their guidance, and essentially by keeping them out of the way. Leaders, then, create value for these people.

Leaders should know when to lead from the front, and when to play second fiddle or be out of the way. Good leaders create value in many ways where they are not leading from the front.

Chapter 8

Value Destruction

The Ukraine War Showcases Value Destruction and Learning from It

Not one of us will disagree that there has been value destruction for countries, for people, for systems, and so on during the Russia–Ukraine war.

Most of us look at the actual value destruction during the war. Very few look at the value destruction that led up to the war and will continue after the war.

The value destruction was caused partly by:

The desire of two superpowers to become stronger
The positioning and posturing before the war
The lack of understanding of each other's thoughts, needs, and psyches.
    Above all, a real desire to avoid war did not exist.

To avoid these wars, we have to look at the defensive (value creation) rather than the offensive and such posturing.

The Desire of Two Superpowers to Become Stronger

The USA and Western Europe have been expanding into the hitherto Soviet territory or countries participating in the Warsaw pact (dissolved in 1991) and considered to be part of the Soviet Bloc. This included the Baltic states, Czechoslovak, Hungary, Poland, Romania, Bulgaria, Albania, and the Balkan states including Croatia and Montenegro, to name a few. Many, after the split

DOI: 10.4324/9781003381624-8

up of the Soviet Union in December 1991, were recognized by the USA such as Russia, Ukraine, Belarus, Kazakhstan, Armenia, and Kyrgyzstan. The Baltic states were the first to move away from Russia. Many have become members of NATO including Poland.

Wiki says: several disputed states with varying degrees of recognition exist within the territory of the former Soviet Union: Transnistria in eastern Moldova, Abkhazia, and South Ossetia in northern Georgia and Artsakh in southwestern Azerbaijan. Since 2014, the Donetsk People's Republic and Luhansk People's Republic in far eastern Ukraine have claimed independence. All of these unrecognized states except Artsakh depend on Russian armed support and financial aid. Artsakh is integrated into Armenia at a de facto level, which also maintains close cooperation with Russia. Prior to its annexation to Russia in March 2014, which is not recognized by most countries, Crimea briefly declared itself an independent state.

NATO had 12 founding countries. Today there are 30 countries as part of NATO. New entrants are Hungary (1999), the Czech Republic (1999), Poland (1999), Slovakia (2004), Romania (2004), Slovenia (2004), Bulgaria (2004), Estonia (2004), Latvia (2004), Lithuania (2004), Albania (2009), Croatia (2009), Montenegro (2017), and North Macedonia (2020). Turkey (1952) was an early entrant. The growth of NATO occurred majorly after the collapse of the Soviet Bloc.

You can see why Russia would become nervous. The Baltic states bordered Russia. Hungary, Poland, and Romania bordered Belarus or Ukraine. Ukraine could have become the next NATO country adding to the perceived threat to the Soviet Union.

Would the USA tolerate Mexico joining a Russian coalition? A communist Cuba was perceived as a major threat to the USA.

Russia has therefore been trying to control Ukraine, which was leaning towards the West and even conquer it as it did Crimea. It continues its bullying tactics, as it fights with Georgia, and postures against Finland.

In fact, short of annexing Ukraine, Russia wants to close Ukraine's access to seaports and have Eastern Ukraine move into Russia at the very least.

The Positioning and Posturing Before the War

Both the West and Russia tried to show their independence and that they could withstand non-war moves by the other. They flexed their muscles much like kids who say "my father is stronger than yours." Zelensky has proved to be a hero in spite of causing pain and countless tragedies for his country via Putin, who in his desire to have an ascendant Soviet state has put aside concern for human suffering and other damage he is causing. He has caused havoc with the global system.

The USA and the West challenged Putin to war while pretending to seek peace and threatened with a widening NATO and sanctions. Putin had also joined the peace wagon while openly threatening Ukraine and telling them not to join NATO. Today, Putin is putting his own sanctions, cutting off gas supply to Poland and Bulgaria!

All this will change the world's power balance and well-established precedents and systems in the world: the dollar, the trading system, the alignment and re-alignment of nations, a change in energy supply, and transportation, to name a few.

The Lack of Understanding of Each Other's Thoughts, Needs, and Psyche

This perhaps is the worst lapse. In spewing rhetoric, countries tend to believe their own words and beliefs (what I'd like to see) and even look at the other as they would like to think and ignore reality. Think tanks are most guilty of this. Honest assessments are parked as "never will happen" etc. I have seen this about China. Around 2000, I was at an Indo-US think tank conference. The Americans kept saying China will never be a superpower. They stated that China does not have their own technology and steals technology. It was so much wishful thinking. That is what they would have liked to see and therefore have started to believe.

The West, Ukraine, and Russia did not truly want to prevent escalation. It is almost like a proxy war between NATO and Russia. The USA has been planning something like this since 2014 when Hillary Clinton spent time in Ukraine (maybe all this emboldened Zelensky). Today, it appears that Ukraine may follow how Russia allowed Napoleon and Germany to enter but eventually weakened them and threw them out.

Do read *Never* by Ken Follett to see how the fallout of not understanding each other can cause catastrophic results.

Therefore, do not view everything like a chess game, moves, countermoves, obfuscation, deceit etc. As I said earlier, to avoid these wars we have to look at the defensive (value creation) rather than the offensive and posturing. We have to go out of the way to understand the others' psyche, pander to it, and build a relationship. Avoiding war is creating value, and so we have to do this.

India can start with China and build a broader understanding with it and of each other, each other's needs, the psyche, and the imponderables such as the path to internal power (pandering to voters or ensuring the military remains in your control etc.). Ensure more open dialogues and start Track II and other means to move forward so that reliable and credible channels are opened to prevent war. Simultaneously, true, unbiased intelligence is required. This is a tough job, but AI can help.

Value has been created for Russia by doubling its fossil fuel revenues. Value has been created for China as more Americans view it as a competitor and not an enemy. Nevertheless, Russia's war has destroyed value for all.

Can we prevent the primacy of greed, selfishness, power, and money? Do we want a bipolar or a unipolar world? Do we want to destroy value or create value?

* * *

Look at Value Destruction to Create More Value

> Every act of creation is at first an act of destruction.

> **Pablo Picasso**

Many companies analyse value destruction after the fact. Very few try to assess value destruction potential of a new strategy, a new product, a new technology, or even a new hire, when they are looking at these. In the literature, the bulk of the papers is on analyzing value destruction after the fact. The exception is Dunn et al. who discuss strategic risk to be studied up front. Furquhar suggests selective demarketing to get rid of non-attractive customers. Stokes and Mahajan discuss value creation and destruction in general terms. Were organizations and the managers within them do so, they would be able to avoid or reduce the value destruction potential and in fact create much more value. Many companies learn their lessons or become smarter from analyzing value destruction that has already happened. This is the normal way companies have viewed value destruction (Figure 8.1).

The aim is to carry out an in-depth analysis of possible value destruction. Understanding the causes of value destruction or possible value destruction, one would then analyse how one could avoid such value destruction and actually create more value. Looking at solutions that are generally accepted and asking how they might destroy value can help us figure out better and more value creating solutions. As an example, Sanghvi et al. (2017) suggest that just reducing value destructing waste is not enough.

An Example: Strategy

Shareholder value destruction over 10 years showed that strategic risks were a major cause of shareholder value destruction. This is because the strategic team does not look at risk and relegates this task to a risk evaluation team that does

Opposite thinking is a creative way to find
an alternative solution to a problem.

Figure 8.1 Opposite Thinking. With permission from Shep Hyken.

not have the "clout" to change thinking. We would like to expand this value destruction thinking beyond risk and shareholder loss, but also to other potential problems. The example of smart lighting highlights this and is discussed later.

Fabode shows how strategic digitization (his focus is on virtual energy companies) destroyed value for GE, as virtual companies reduced demand for GE's generating equipment.

Atasoy found that strategically designed digital goods get a lower price than physical goods, and warns about digitization.

Willigoose discusses Value Illness which prevents citizens from following the right things. Value starvation can also cause similar problems.

Liedtke states that value can be destroyed in mergers and acquisitions, even though moves are strategically thought through.

Along with pure strategic thinking, we have also to look at operational risk, compliance risk, political, operational, and regulatory risks. We are suggesting that this should not be done in a cursory fashion and just stating these risks have been looked at is not good enough, but to see what the company's leaders can do to mitigate these risks, reduce value destruction potential, and increase value creation potential. Chris Dann of Price Waterhouse uses strategic risk to reduce strategic value destruction and create better value.

The point is such value destruction should be foreseen and tackled in a serious manner.

One such thinking should be the impact of competitive disruptive moves. Companies should therefore embed value destruction and risk, operational, regulatory, and political risks in their thinking. How could these happen? What can we do to prevent these from happening? What moves can we make to alleviate the risk and foreclose competitive action? In what way should our strategy change to reduce value destruction? An example was when I was at Continental Can, we were getting ready to commercialize acrylonitrile bottles. Competition, not in acrylonitrile, was looking at PET bottles. We started a parallel program to develop PET bottles. The FDA (Food and Drug Administration) banned acrylonitrile for soft drink use, and we were able to move into PET seamlessly, thus alleviating risk.

As an example, in earlier decades, we had business development people who were rewarded for bringing in new businesses. Many of them never worked on the new business they brought in but were rewarded and moved on. I asked CEOs whether they rewarded business development executives for keeping them out of bad businesses. Most had not thought of this value destruction potential.

An Example: Smart Cities

1. Smart lighting: it is vastly understood and appreciated that smart lighting is the accepted approach for smart cities. While we agree, we also wish to examine what this means in terms of physical infrastructure:

The typical way of using smart lighting is to put poles on roads and have lights that turn on when needed. This is all value creating.

What is potentially value destructing is:

a. Physical infrastructure is used less than 10% of the time. The cost of poles and the space required can be high. This is value destruction. So if we assume there is potential value destruction, what can we do? We could think of replacing pole base lights by drones. Conceptually 50 poles could be replaced by a smaller number of drones.

The next thought is to look at using flying phones that can hover above the person walking, supplemented by fewer drones. Flying phones would belong to citizens, and therefore a smaller drain on the exchequer.

2. Physical transportation: smart cities imply improvement of wellbeing of (or creating value for) citizens. Just giving sensor-based information is not enough. Value is destroyed because people have to live sometimes far from their place of work or schools or airports (and other transport hubs). One common example is moving from point A to point B at normal times and at times when tourists arrive in large numbers. The normal ride could be 20 minutes, but in the tourist season it could take as long as 2 hours. Perhaps a system of driverless cars and networked transportation or a rope-way is the added value over just better information. For example, the use of tubular transport as suggested by Elon Musk is important.

3. People skilling: the next potential for value destruction in smart cities is that we do not have "smart" workers. Most current workers are untrained for this. This is a form of value destruction for the smart cities program and so these people should be skilled. For example drone handling skills, driverless car management skills etc. are needed. Next sensor handling and sensor troubleshooting may be needed. Therefore skilling academies are needed. Responsive urban governance should result in smarter value creation.

4. Self-healing and self-powering systems: sensors and other devices can detect cracks or defects in concrete structures or offices/homes. An analysis of this will reveal that this requires intervention by humans to repair these defects. Perhaps, if we could use bio-concrete to selfheal cracks in concrete, we could create even more value. Lastly, biomaterials have a great future. These include self-healing polymer building materials, graphene, and the like and buildings that can change with temperature, or self-adjusting buildings.

Further analysis may show that energy loss or where energy is not easily available, self-powering systems use could add more value and reduce value destruction due to power loss. For example solar power generation through solar layers on windows could add value.

There are other examples we can focus on:

Value destruction due to insolvency. The Indian Government brought in the Insolvency and Bankruptcy code 2016 to make insolvency easier. An example of possible value destruction is given below:

The potential for value destruction could occur if all the claimants were allowed to decide on the future of the company. Assured claimants would want their money fast and not worry about the value destruction to the company's net value. To avoid value destruction of this sort, strategically only those claimants who have a significant stake and risk in the wellbeing of the company should then be allowed to decide the fate of the company. Thus people who design the law from a value creation (or least value destruction point of view) would have designed the law differently (Datta, 2016).

Value destruction due to short-term focus: it is well known that short-term results and its reporting are a cause for value destruction in firms. A look at the value destruction potential would point out that companies must adopt a long-term view of their business, but the focus on stock prices and investor short-term gains obviates that. CFOs are encouraged to gain or manipulate numbers through accounting practices allowed under GAAP. Retail investors are more long-term investors and they are short-changed by this thinking (value is destroyed for them). A proper study of value destruction would reveal that this practice hasto be changed. It has resulted in shorter lives of companies, and shorter stays of people as CEOs in companies.

An example is what Paul Polman of Unilever did ... he told his shareholders he would only concentrate on long-term results and not short-term gains, and the result was spectacular for Unilever. Value is destroyed in yet another way by short-termism; lower returns mean lower investment which hits the entire society.

Value creation and destruction of society from technology and artificial intelligence (AI): while this is the topic of a conference with Kobe University and the Japan Advanced Institute of Science and Technology in Kobe, Japan, October 14–16, 2019, it is germane to point out that technology development outpaces its absorption by society. Society is unable to adjust to technology quickly enough, causing short-term value destruction. In the long run, the danger of technology overtaking and controlling society is very real. Such value destroying potential must be mitigated and reduced by strategic thinking by the owners and designers of technology, the designers of the recipient society, and all of us, in general.

Lastly, one value destruction potential of AI systems is when they do not respond to human commands. It might be possible to install a self-destruct system to circumvent such value destruction possibilities.

Value Creation/Destruction of plastic bottles: Continental Group introduced the one-piece plastic bottle as a source of large packaging (1 litre, 2 l) for beverages. When they started work on the smaller sizes (half a litre or less), the can-making part of the business complained of value destruction for cans because plastics could possibly take over some of the markets from cans.

The corporate strategy team examined this and found some minor cannibalization was possible, and a risk to the growth rate of cans. On the other hand, they found that the company could not stop the proliferation of bottles, because this would happen due to competition. Maximum corporate value creation would come from aggressive plastic bottle introduction by the company and also looking at upsizing cans to larger sizes and sealable metal bottles.

Unfortunately, no one looked at the value destruction of the environment due to plastic waste. The risk analysis revealed that the risk would be minimal (meaning legislative and environmental) in the short term and would not act aggressively enough early on, till the problem became unavoidable. This is a classic case of value destruction.

The computer in the cockpit: *The Economist* (2019) and the *Times of India* (2019) based on the Boeing crash in Ethiopia in March 2019 talk about aeroplanes flying on autopilot and with automated systems.

Humans struggle to cope when automation fails. What this means is that strategically and operationally we are working on automating transport systems and are training people in automation.

A study of this show there is value destruction potential. This can be reduced by thinking through:

What do pilots do when automation fails or plays up?

How do we train more manual controls in addition to the new training on computer control? Today pilots spend more time learning automated systems and less time on hands-on flying. Newer pilots who are more comfortable with automated systems cannot handle manual systems as effectively as older pilots.

What is the optimum manual–automated control? Which one should override the other and when?

The perils of the human–machine interface can then be reduced. Note that perhaps a cost–benefit analysis showed the current system is acceptable. Studying the value destruction aspect would cause better training and operating techniques to emerge.

Discussion and Conclusion

From a reading of the foregoing, and the examples shown, it becomes abundantly clear that the design and pursuit of a new strategy, process, product, or service looks predominantly at the positive value creation for the company or the people in control. Most do not pay heed to the value destruction potential or even ignore this, or in their minds minimize its impact. Much of this impact primarily third parties such as citizens, customers, employees (loss of jobs), and society.

However, from a corporate viewpoint, potential value destruction studies and analysis during the design process could have revealed better design, better processes, more effective service, and more pervasive products. This includes risk analysis, compliance studies, operational analysis, and environmental and societal thinking. This is a loss to the corporate entity and society. Companies can benefit themselves and their stakeholders including society from such analysis before the fact, rather than suffering after the fact or causing value loss to people and society and for the company itself.

In conclusion, this opens up the possibility of better value creating strategies. This means a different way of thinking and a more reasoned solution. This has to be taught and embraced by practitioners. This becomes a fertile area of research for companies and academics to analyse value destruction potential to create more value. We must get away from reactive and "after the fact" analysis to pro-active value creation and reducing value destruction, and learning from value destruction potential.

* * *

Co-Destruction

The only alternative to coexistence is co-destruction

Nehru

The author was judging PhD students' poster session at Leicester Castle Business School and the First Global Conference on Creating Value and was struck by one poster on co-destruction where the student went on to look at corruption as co-destruction.

Our difficulty was how two rational people would start a co-destruction process. While co-creation refers to the process whereby providers and customers collaboratively create value, co-destruction refers to the collaborative destruction, or diminishment, of value by providers and customers.

Can you think of any?

After reflection, we came up with two football teams willing to destroy each other or co-destruct, or openly start a war.

Ok, that is easy to understand. But do value co-creation and value co-destruction mean:

Prahalad and Ramaswamy define the co-creation of value thus: the consumer and the firm are intimately involved in jointly creating value that is unique to the individual consumer ... The interaction between consumers and firms becomes the new locus of co-creation of value."

When referring to one particular case, for instance, they infer that "not everyone enjoys such an interactive co-creation process ... Nor are all co-creation experiences positive."

According to S-D logic, value creation is then an interactive and collaborative process that occurs through the exchange of service between entities.

Plé and Ruben Chumpitaz Cáceres (2010) define value **co-destruction** as "an interactional process between service systems that results in a decline in at least one of the systems' wellbeing." Each person involved can thus be affected by or contribute to value **co-creation** or **co-destruction**.

Co-destruction can occur while two groups are working together to give value to each other ... a poor bus service can co-destroy value ... More specifically, the paper employs the notion of value co-destruction (cf. Plé and Chumpitaz Cáceres,[1] 2010), capturing the downside of interactive value formation.

You can see the definition is going from a collaborative process to an unplanned process. I think we need to be clear about whether co-destruction is:

1. Intentional and collaborative co-destruction,
2. Unintentional co-destruction,
3. Unintentional one-sided destruction, or
4. Intentional one-sided destruction.

Thus for any collaborative process, co-creation or co-destruction, companies and customers should align their mutual expectations. This means that firms should communicate precisely about the manner they expect their consumers to integrate and apply the resources needed for co-creating value. At eYeka, a co-creation platform, the brief always details what the brand expects from a call for entry, and the content is moderated appropriately. It might not unleash immoderate passion ... but it will also avoid negative side effects!

EYeka also states disappointing results of a co-innovation initiative, for instance, can be seen as co-destruction because time and money have been spent on something that merely leads to incremental innovation. Thus this is an unintentional result (which could also be a result of poor execution).

Thus, interactive value formation is clearly not only linked to positive outcomes and connotations. A framework that explains how interactive value formation takes place in practice needs to be informed by accounts of both the upside and the downside of the practice of interactive value formation. In line

---

[1] *Journal of Services Marketing*, ISSN: 0887-6045, Article publication date: September 14, 2010.

with Plé and Chumpitaz Cáceres (2010), we see reasons to suggest a distinction between the co-creation of value and the co-destruction of value during interactive value formation. While co-creation refers to the process whereby providers and customers collaboratively create value, co-destruction refers to the collaborative destruction, or diminishment of value by providers and customers. Thus, the co-destruction of value, like the co-creation of value, is likely to be an integral part of the interaction between sellers and users when the latter consumes the service. The paper specifies the notion of co-destruction of value and uses it as a basis for outlining the framework depicting how interactive value formation takes place in practice. Co-destruction can also happen when both parties do not look at risk of possible failure or external disruption.

Against this backdrop, we suggest defining value co-destruction as a relationship process between focal actors and their networks that results in a decline in at least one of the focal actors and/or their networks' wellbeing (Figure 8.2; http://www.naplesforumonservice.it/uploads//files/Lefebvre%2C%20Ple.pdf).

Before going any further, Plé suggests that value has a positive connotation. That is because it is based on the positive creation of good or improving wellbeing. The opposite, destruction of good or reduction of the wellbeing, is destructive value.

Peter Stokes suggested a financial services firm getting together with an ailing firm with pension liabilities and a large debt to co-destruct the company to

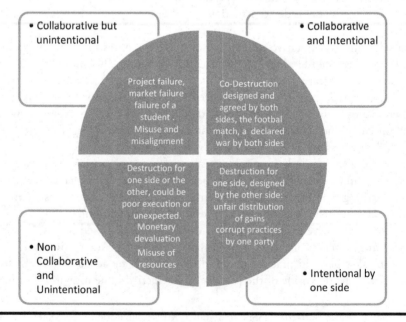

Figure 8.2   Co-Destruction in 4 Quadrants

gain a profit. According to S-D logic, value creation is then an interactive and collaborative process that occurs through the exchange of service between entities. Here we have collaborative and intentional co-destruction.

Non-collaborative and unintentional co-destruction is when I buy a new device such as a cell phone and it does not work. This can be a devaluation of your money or something in a network.

Intentional co-destruction is when someone goes out to cheat a partner, does not share the gains as agreed, or engages in corrupt practices.

Collaborative projects that fail include M&As that do not work or give the desired results or projects that do not sell or sell at a loss.

Misuse and misalignment, intentional vs. accidental.

Chief financial officers[1] often exercise discretion – even sacrifice economic value – to deliver earnings. Destruction of shareholder value through legal means is pervasive, perhaps even a routine way of doing business. Indeed, the amount of value destroyed by companies striving to hit earnings targets exceeds the value lost in recent high-profile fraud cases.

The same issue arises when looking at executive pay. Should we look at short-term results that may destroy long-term value or look at long-term value that may reduce short-term wealth? Value Creation and value extraction must be viewed in a continuum. We must have better metrics for long-term results, and perhaps better strategic long-term management, we should then have a strategic management system that allows managers to provide current results while driving towards long-term value. How do we look at potential growth and innovation? Strategic management performance metrics and incentive design are then also aligned with sustainability and value creation that benefits the eco-system: this may destroy short-term value, and this has to be taken into account.

Value can be created and destroyed in process improvement and service when we ignore other items such as waste created, and jobs destroyed.

Total Value created or seen is Value Created work minus non-value creating work minus value destructing activities.

Waste can include non-value-added work (this can be seen in the third and fourth quadrants in the chart in the next section).

When any resource is misused or badly used, value is destroyed. For example, providing a poor experience to a customer. There is a net value concept to customers where benefits and negative benefits/sacrifices are considered. This of course should be obvious from the definition of value, what you get for what you give or sacrifice.

So is destruction included in the value definition?

---

[1] https://www.cfapubs.org/doi/abs/10.2469/faj.v62.n6.4351

Value destruction can also occur when values are abrogated a la Enron … fraud, lack of integrity. Value can be destroyed in deceptive marketing; see Pfizer agreed to pay $2.3 billion to settle civil and criminal allegations that it violated federal rules governing drug sales. The pharmaceutical manufacturer was charged with illegally promoting its pain-killer Bextra and three other medications by offering doctors speaking fees and subsidized trips to resorts, among other benefits.

Value destruction happens when real estate values fall, which is yet another example.

* * *

Value Destruction: Non-Value-Added Tasks Destroy Value

Companies have many non-value-added tasks, processes, events, and wastage that are non-value adding. These include starting meetings late, wasting the time of many participants waiting for the meeting to start; reading unnecessary e-mails; correcting mistakes (especially for Customers and in production or in tax reporting); unnecessary travel which could be replaced by calls or video calls; 20 people picking up bosses at airports; not doing legal or moral work.

Non-value-added tasks are actually value destructing tasks. A whole discipline has been brought into play where value destroyed has become important. This in itself is an important discipline because it looks at net value which is value created minus value destroyed minus non-value-added activities.

Value co-destruction occurs mostly when there is a misuse of resources, either incorrectly, inaptly, or unpredictably. This happens when the available resources are used, say in an interaction. Companies can misuse their processes to create more value for themselves, thereby destroying value for others such as employees and customers. This is planned misuse. Accidental misuse can also be disastrous for customers and destroy value for them. The reader has examples of what has happened in his eco-system Corruption destroys value for some while adding value for others.

Or the value co-creation was one-sided.

And then there is the question of whether value can be co-destroyed. It can, as I explained earlier.

The definition of value is benefits minus cost. Others call this, benefits minus sacrifice. Whatever you sacrifice could be construed as value destruction … Ouch, this takes too much time or effort, or they make me feel like a fool.

However, very few researchers have looked into the possible downsides of value co-destruction. The risk of losing customers this way is highly likely, as 40% of customers who had a bad experience will discontinue doing business at the offending firm. To prevent nearly half of consumers from churning after a bad experience, it is therefore crucial that both parties communicate their expectations extensively towards one another so value can be co-created instead of destructed.

For **Customers,**

Necessary work is essential for, vital to, indispensable to, important to, crucial to, needed by, compulsory required by, or requisite for the Customer.

Relevant work is pertinent to, applicable, or germane to or appropriate to the Customer. This is work that can be eliminated without deterioration of the present service or product.

What work is the Customer willing to pay for?

Every business enterprise has at least eight stakeholder groups, whose concerns must be considered when analyzing business processes: customers, suppliers and partners, managers, employees, creditors, investors, governments, and community groups.

Customer Value added to task: (Value to Customer after the task) MINUS (Value to the Customer prior to the task)

Who is the Customer? Are some classes of work for internal customers necessary? If such work is free now, would someone pay for these services or work?

It is the final bill-paying Customer at the end of the entire value chain who determines if the work/task adds value.

Similarly, for **Businesses,**

Necessary work is essential for, vital to, indispensable to, important to, crucial to, needed by, compulsory required, or requisite for the Business.

Relevant work is pertinent to, applicable, or germane to or appropriate to the Business. This is work that can be eliminated without deterioration of the present service or product.

Let us list some of these tasks (Table 8.1).

The more companies can align their priorities with those of the Customers and make the tasks that are relevant and necessary for Customers, that is make their business priorities the ones important for the Customers, the more successful they will be. From my book, *Value Dominant Logic*

* * *

Table 8.1 Relevant and Necessary Tasks

		Relevant to	Necessary for	Relevant to	Necessary for
	Task	CUSTOMER		BUSINESS	
S	Sales and Marketing	Sometimes Yes	Sometimes Yes		Yes
A	Advertising	Sometimes Yes	Sometimes Yes		Yes
A/C	Accounting	Yes			Yes
T	Tax related	Yes			Yes
O	Offsite meetings				Yes
S	Strategy	Yes			Yes
B	Business Meetings			Yes	yes
T	Training			Yes	Yes
C	Customer Meetings	Sometimes Yes	Sometimes Yes	Sometimes Yes	Sometimes Yes
CT	Customer training	Yes			Yes
M	Manufacturing	Yes			Yes
R&D	R&D	Yes			Yes
SM	Social media	Yes			yes
IT	IT	Yes			Yes

PR	Public Relations	Yes			Yes
P	Profit making	Yes			Yes
PRICE	Pricing	Yes	Yes		Yes
CR	Customer Redressal		Yes	Sometimes Yes	Sometimes Yes
CS	Customer Service		Yes	Sometimes Yes	Sometimes Yes
CP	Company People		Yes		Yes
REL	Relationship with Customer		Yes		Yes
VALUES	Values of company		Yes		Yes
PR	Relationship with Partners	Yes			Yes
SCR	Supply chain relationship	Yes			Yes
DC	Delivery chain	Yes			Yes
O	Posh offices			Yes	
D	Data and data analysis				Yes
H	HR Department				Yes
CV	Customer Value		Yes	Yes	Yes
CE	Customer time and effort		Yes	Yes	

Will Value Destruction Ace Value Creation?
Big Brother: Google, Apple, and Microsoft

Recently, I had the opportunity to listen to Hal Varian, Chief Economist of Google on the economic impact of Google, and its futuristic thinking.

The Value Creation is immense. It includes social value creation, and things that are good for society. Countries like India are also working on connectivity and infrastructure that is good for society.

For the individual, there is a myriad of new apps such as Google Now. It gives you just the right information at just the right time. From knowing the weather before you start your day, to planning the best route to avoid traffic, or even checking your favourite team's score while they're playing, Google Now brings you the information you want, when you need it. You can also get assistance 24/7. It gives you relevant suggestions. There are Google books, and Google stores. However, they say You are in control.

But are you really in control, or is Google in control of you? They have so much information about you, and so they are in control, though they try to make you feel in control.

Then there are Google Offers. Google's Nexus phone, all tying you into Google, through the exclusion of others like Apple/Mac or Microsoft. Not that these are behind. They all want to tie you up and stick to their products and make it difficult for the non-savvy user to go from one system to another. Microsoft has free Xbox music online, a cloud storage system, and Infrastructure as a Service (IaaS); they have bought Nokia and have their own phone and mobile system. Apple is everywhere, from phones to pads, to laptops; from control centres to airdrops, to smarter multitasking and locational maps, information and storage of data, in stores, in music. All things that impact you on a daily basis. A form of Value Creation.

Microsoft forces you to join their Microsoft account. The other day I wanted to Skype, using Windows 8. I just could not get on till I registered on a Microsoft account even though I was already a Skype member. What right do they have to force me to join? This is how they destroy Value. Another example is when trying to save a Word document, Word forces you to choose OneDrive and you have to be cautious to save on "other" if you wish to save in a word document.

More than that, is big brother watching you? These big guys know your location, your preferences, when you like to work, and on what. The list is endless. Steven J. Vaughan-Nichols in "Big Apple, Big Google, Big Brother" says that one way to reduce the big brother data is to have short logs.

To me, the big brother syndrome and the fact they want me to be captive to them is a big Value Destroyer. We are so captivated by the Value Creation that we forget we are captives. And this Value destruction could cause the downfall of all the great value that is being created supposedly for us but in reality, for the companies!

It is frightening, the control they can exercise on me.

What is your take on it?

* * *

Power and Value

D. Sudarshan former Dean of and Prof Emeritus, at U of Kentucky, said to me that power creates value and is the ultimate value. He said the goal is also to empower stakeholders, and that of course includes customers. That empowering creates value is true.

Power assumes the right to control oneself, one's environment, and others. Personal **empowerment** assumes no such **power over others** but recognizes complete responsibility for self and the choices made by self. Those sound-like pretty clear definitions, but the urge to exert **power** over others might blur the lines between each. So, we need to clarify.

To me, power is one of the rewards people or companies look for beyond money or profits or instead of them (they feel the money will come to them because of power; or the reverse, power will come to them because of money). We have always said profits follow value creation, and so does power if sought: it follows from the creation of value. So, the more you create and the more you get, the richer you get and the more powerful.

Fame is yet another thing people seek (or being known for).

However, there are people who may achieve fame without seeking power. These are people creating value for others and not for themselves, and they create more value than power and fame-seeking people, who tend to destroy value also. Some college professors are examples of this.

Unfortunately, there is the possibility of pursuing and possessing too much power. Unbridled power, i,e,, power improperly used can and perhaps will destroy value just as will profit creation absent empowering customers. Some people feel only a tremendous amount of power can create value. This is a mistaken notion. For example, monopolies sooner or later get regulated or even broken up. Excessive power can be seen as a power imbalance and nature abhors imbalances, except in entropy – that too only as far as we know (who knows what black matter and black energy do for entropy!). Customers will form buying clubs or cooperatives either formal or informal in structure – neighbours helping neighbours.

The message is that power should not be misused. Such misuse causes value destruction for others.

The ultimate customer loyalty is when empowered customers choose a brand/firm over others because it serves them better and they see more value from them.

Empowerment creates value. Value is created when you empower someone, and empowered people create value.

Beware of powerful people and moneyed people who wish to wield their power and impose themselves on others. They are destroyers of value.

Today in COVID times in India, hoarders and black marketers exert their power over hapless citizens by controlling medicines and oxygen (and concentrators), hospital rooms, and so forth.

Big brother in the form of Google, Microsoft, and Apple hold power over me. May the curse be with them on their power.

* * *

Money and Power: Motivators of Conscious or Unconscious Value Destruction

A Case of the Blind Leading the Pack

Notice, I did not say a case of the blind leading the blind, because often the people being led are not so blind. Maybe they are intellectually honest or believe in their purpose. If purpose is just a set of words, with no or little honesty behind the words, then how can it work? In the minds of many, how can there be a higher purpose, other than money and profit and power? Fortunately, through the pronouncements of the Business Round Table and Davos, there is a higher purpose. Companies are starting to reshape their purpose.

An example is the textile company Patagonia based in the USA and as a benefit corporation has frequently supported social causes. The company often supported ideas from the social context in light of improving the living conditions of a society. It strives for being positive continues and also contrasts negative views; indeed, the CEO Gellert stated that the company decided to cut ties with a business owner who gave a platform to 'anti-democratic conspiracy theorists'. They state:

> Our Reason for Being

At Patagonia, we appreciate that all life on earth is under threat of extinction. We aim to use the resources we have – our business, our investments, our voice, and our imaginations – to do something about it (https://www.patagonia.com.au/pages/our-mission).

Indeed, someone from National Grid stated "that it's not good enough for the business to wear its values on its sleeve" and that "it's not about just saying it, it's about presenting the evidence to support it."

Earlier, I said that the main two motivators are money and power (or the pursuit of success to get power and money).

Destroying value with intellectual dishonesty

I do not mean to repeat myself but to give examples of intellectual dishonesty.

In a recent newspaper article in India, they said that 14 of the USA's most famous universities had formed a price cartel. Exactly what they are supposed to teach not to do! See Federal Lawsuit Alleges 16 Elite Universities Engaged in Price Fixing: https://www.forbes.com/sites/michaeltnietzel/2022/01/10/federal -lawsuit-alleges-16-elite-universities-engaged-in-price-fixing/?sh=745f209673ad.

Recently I came across someone who claims he is HBS approved for his process of creating value, and I found the process flawed and a poor understanding of the concept of value. How can HBS approve such things? Is it a lack of knowledge of the reviewer? Or are there other factors leading to such approval?

Another person came to me and asked us to get certified by someone who has no true knowledge of value. Such people will snarl unwitting people paying to get a stamp from such places to advance their customer value programs. Here the blind is truly leading the blind. And such people get the approval of HBS, NYT, and Forbes from editors with less knowledge but an eye for sellability, and readership. Another case of intellectual dishonesty.

Articles that are accurate, and do not mince words, but are not sellable are discarded by the press and they go their merry way instead of introspecting. They allow "false" news to seep in.

A very common example is companies measuring customer satisfaction. This is certainly a good starting point. But it is not good enough. When customer value measurements come along the managers while recognizing the superiority of customer value measurement do not go to their bosses and say, here is a better way, let's change. Instead, they hid behind having past data. They forget if customer satisfaction is not measured against competition, it becomes a case of measuring yourself against yourself and not your peers.

An example of intellectual dishonesty is to pass off lower-level people's voices as the CEO's voice in a survey, because the name of the game is getting more responses. The company doing the survey turns a blind eye to this, so as to show more responses.

Kids today are more aware of ecology and technology and often they can pull up their parents on things not being done right.

An example is that Diwali crackers which polluted were being stopped by kids getting awareness from schools and social media. Such a purposeful change did not start at home. For years, the Government or society was not able to prevent the use of crackers.

This happens in companies, where the Board members rubber stamp the management instead of saying what they truly believe in.

May I suggest, we speak out against intellectual dishonesty, maybe this will reduce it even marginally and thereby create value.

You need power only when you want to do something harmful.

Otherwise love is enough to get everything done.

Chapter 9

Leaders, Executives, and Value Creation

Value Creation and Leaders

This is partly taken from a keynote speech at the Kotler World Marketing Summit

I am the Founder Editor of the *Journal of Creating Value* and mentor the Creating Value Alliance. I help CEOs create value. This talk is about Creating Value and leaders.

Let me start with the definition of value. Value is a word used contextually and sometimes loosely. Value is not price; value does not mean quality.

Then there is a bunch of people who say Price for value meaning they are price conscious. But you also have heard people say Money for value meaning they are conscious about quality.

To put an end to all this, the *Journal of Creating Value* has a definition which is in use now:

Creating Value is executing proactive, conscious, inspired, or imaginative and even normal actions that increase the overall good and wellbeing, and the worth of ideas, goods, services, people, or institutions including society, and all stakeholders (like employees, customers, partners, shareholders, and society), and value waiting to happen. That is why our parents teach us to be good kids and to do good. But this is soon overtaken by the goal of making a living, of being successful.

I will discuss value waiting to happen later.

In a business sense, it is the worth or the value of your products that makes people buy. They buy your products over competitive ones if they perceive you create more value, better, better worth.

And you are creating value when you improve the wellbeing of people.

We have to keep this definition of value in mind.

Today I am going to discuss four different areas of Creating Value and Leadership. I have already defined Creating Value for you as a backdrop.

In this talk, I will focus on four points:

a. Phil Kotler on Value Creation and Marketing
b. Primary role of a leader is to create value
c. Leaders must have values
d. Leaders and the future

1. **Phil Kotler on Value Creation and Marketing**

Kotler wrote in the *Journal of Creating Value* that Marketing is Value Creation.

He says: leading marketers see modern marketing to be all about value creation. Marketing aims to meet human needs by creating value.

He goes on to say: "I do not know what you thought marketing was, but in my mind, marketing is intrinsically a value-creating discipline.

Outstanding marketing companies see marketing as intrinsically involved in value creation."

2. **Primary role of a leader is to create value**

Since this talk is about Creating Value and leaders, let me focus on this aspect. There are four areas I will touch on:

a. Leaders create value
b. Not taught to create value
c. Getting a value creation mindset
d. Value helps you strategize and innovate better
   i. You start to look at value destruction and at
   ii. Value waiting to happen includes innovation

Leaders Create Value

Let's talk about leaders. People are leaders not because they meet their performance goals, but because they create value, that is they go beyond the performance expectation. Notice all the leaders around you are there because they created value. Just meeting numbers and the performance expected is not good enough and not so in today's world.

Let me give you two examples:

Take the COVID crisis. Many companies hide behind the problems caused by the crisis. Some companies in India ignored the labour force in their factories because the factories were shut down due to the lockdown. The company I am speaking of (Parijat Industries) focused on these employees and the moment the lockdown was removed, they were ready with COVID protection measures and 100% of their workforce returned. Consequently, for a time period they were the only manufacturer and captured a higher market share, and even their collections (debts) improved by 70%. This happened because, first, they created value for their employees, and second, they created value for their dealers because they were able to supply to the dealers.

The second example is Bajaj Auto that 10 or 15 years ago started to feel that China might compete for motorcycles in the Indian market. They realized they had to start from scratch and hired fresh people to design, manage, and market world-class bikes. They wanted a value creation mindset. In a few years they had higher quality and higher technology bikes at reasonable prices. Result: Chinese bikes could not enter India.

Bajaj took these bikes into Africa, where China dominated. They took over the market leaving the very high end to the Japanese, and the very low end to the Chinese.

Today, unfortunately, leaders are influenced by the focus on the flavour of the month, CX, Customer Journey etc. These are old thoughts that are being recycled. They need to focus on Creating more value.

Many leaders believe the extraordinary is possible. They take advantage of the situation. Why not re-engineer our company for re-deployment and for not just coping with the COVID crisis? Why not start thinking long term not just short term and add true value?

Leaders not taught to create value

People who reach the top do so by creating value … No one has taught them how to do this. They do it because it is in their nature to do so.

Thus, they create value unconsciously and can also destroy value unconsciously.

And so, we have to teach them how to create value in a more effective manner.

Getting a value creation mindset

Value Creation for leaders is about you. You as a person and not just a leader.

You can only create functional value for yourself, like learning something, education, training, practice, and exercising.

But the most amount of value you create is when you create value for others ... so when you start to create value for your people, your employees, your customers, your partners, and society, they will come back and create value for you.

And they in turn create value for you ... they recognize you as a value creator.

Value helps you strategize and innovate better

Here we will look at:

a. You start to look at value destruction and at
b. Value waiting to happen includes innovation

You start to look at value destruction

First, gone are the days that the business strategy was all you needed to do. Till recently we advised companies to create a customer strategy which you used to make a business strategy. You as a leader must understand why a customer strategy is different from a business or market strategy. In the latter, we look at the market and business opportunities. The customer is secondary. The great market crash of 2008 teaches us the difference. Take the mortgage market. The customer strategy would have forced us to look at the customers better. Are they a good risk? And what will happen if prices of homes go down or interest rates go up? Do our products protect them?

The business strategy was a numbers game. Give as many mortgages as we can. Bundle them and sell them to the next larger bank or entity. You no longer carried the risk. And these folks bundled all their mortgages and sold them to the next buyer ... till a few companies were left holding the mortgages.

When the mortgagees started to default, the whole pyramid came crashing down causing unbelievable pain to the common man ... all because people took their eyes off the customer and there was no customer strategy.

Nowadays, we advise people to also create an employee strategy (for example what to do during a lockdown or replacing people with bots), and a stakeholder strategy, including one for customers, one for partners, and one for society and sustainability. These are then used to create the business strategy.

While preparing your strategy or while looking at projects, you must start to look at value destruction. What is the value destruction potential of what we are doing? For an electric autonomous car, there is value destruction for professional drivers, existing manufacturers and repair shops, insurance, and for taxes.

The number of accidents will reduce. The number of cars on the road will reduce as on-demand cars come into vogue.

New manufacturers and repair facilities will come in, creating value for these. The number of accidents will also reduce.

Another example is smart cities. Everyone will vote for smart lighting. I want you to look at the value destruction potential: street lights even smart ones require poles. Poles like other infrastructure are used less than 20% of the time, which is value destroying. They are expensive, and they take up land space. If we accept these to be value destroying, we are forced to look at alternatives. And what are these? You could use drones to light the street on an as-need basis. Or better still, our phones could be replaced by flying phones or drone phones and light the path for us as we walk. Elegant, simple solution.

Value Creation leaders have to look at the entire range and spectrum of stakeholders. They must have individual strategies for customers, employees, sustainability, and for shareholders. Using these strategies, they should build their business strategy. To do this, it is important to recognize that the customer pays for all of this and therefore find the relative importance of each of these, using Customer Value Added or measuring value.

Value waiting to happen includes innovation

Value waiting to happen is innovation potential all around us, that we do not notice. The autonomous car is an example all of us could have guessed but failed to do or even think about. A few people did notice and created value from value waiting to happen. Value often emerges for most of us.

Another example of value waiting to happen is learning from nature. Take seeds and their ability to absorb twice their volume of water can be used for sponge technology. MIT scientists wondered what energy was required to transport water and nutrition from the roots of trees to leaves 100 feet up. Using this technique, they have come up with an almost energy-less pump.

Medical people have seen the geckos have an adhesive system to cling to walls, and are using this to suture cuts during surgeries.

The list is long and full of innovation and value waiting to happen.

3. Leaders must have Values

Values are an important part of Creating Value. Values (value with an "s"). Value and values are distinct. Values form an important part of value creation and are our essential beliefs, ethics, and morals. Too many leaders and companies mistake corporate traits with values.

Traits include ambition, competency, individuality, equality, service, responsibility, accuracy, respect, dedication, diversity, improvement, enjoyment/fun, loyalty, innovativeness, excellence etc.

Items that fit into values are integrity and honesty. So, leadership training does not focus that highly on values.

But the culture must reflect basic values.

In business jargon, values are called ethics and traits are core values. In our definition core values are not traits but actually should be the ethical values.

In business jargon, values are called integrity, morals, ethics etc.

4. Leaders of the Future and Value Creation

More than ever before, our basic beliefs will be shaken, and our fears of lack of control as technology takes over will require business leaders who can create value and avoid value destruction. They will choose options that pollute the least, and that does not lead to losing control to technology, be it biotechnology or AI. This requires changing the entire old way of thinking that Value Creation means creating profit. Today in this period of COVID, low and declining growth is accompanied by an improved environment and reduced pollution and lower traffic, and a cleaner earth could lead to a healthier life and planet with more happiness. Leaders controlled by Creating Value for the stakeholders including society and sustainability will re-focus their businesses and even accept lower growth versus their non-value creating competitors who will vote for business as usual and that profit is king. Paul Polman of Unilever eschewed short-term profits and stopped suppliers who were not sustainability friendly.

In August 2019, the 181 CEOs of the largest US companies signed off on The Business Roundtable's new purpose of a company, to create value for all stakeholders: Employees, Customers, Suppliers/Partners, Community/Society, Environment, and Shareholders. Gone were the days when employees and partners were meant only to serve the company. Gone were the days when the environment and community were only talking points.

Davos in 2020 stated the same thing. So there is to be a supposed seriousness of purpose to create value. But the problem is our training and MBA schools have taught us to create shareholder wealth, and even well-meaning leaders do not know where to start.

So to start, you have to look at your Purpose. Ask:

What is your purpose for your family or your friends? A study has found people with purpose live 15% longer.
Is my Business purpose, to make money for stakeholders or to leave a happier world?

Since leaders can also be shareholders, should they look at creating happiness? Ninety-three percent of 2000 leaders surveyed could not state why their company is in business. This means that many purpose statements do not have a proper sense of purpose. Are yours one of them?

As a leader, you must have a purpose. What is a meaningful purpose you can express in terms of values, meaning ethics and morals etc. and in terms of what you want to achieve in life for yourself and your family? What will inspire those around you? Is it clean air, a happier environment, or a product with the lowest costs and highest quality? The last is practical, but it is expected of your job. Value Creation is going beyond your job and should be your purpose.

Do you know what your customers value, and what your stakeholder's value? How does your purpose reflect some of these aspirations and goals?

How can you inspire your people and family to create value and for whom and how? Granted it goes beyond the purpose, but it can help you formulate and articulate purpose better.

At the very least your purpose should go beyond making money and increasing shareholder wealth.

This purpose will help you revise your vision and then your mission. Working on a strategy for each of your stakeholders will get you to a great business strategy and reinforce your purpose.

The purpose to create value for stakeholders makes you ally with employees, customers, and partners in learning from them and co-creating value with them. They become part of your success.

Many of your employees prefer meaning to money. Should you too? Purpose improves employee participation and buy-in. It creates value for employees by improving their wellbeing.

Helping employees with creating value for themselves and having a purpose. It engenders thinking about themselves and deciding what matters in life. It builds on the self, a sense of freedom, and thinking about others.

Today, I have defined Value Creation. It is about doing good. I spoke about Phil Kotler's views on Marketing being Value Creation; you have learnt that the role of a leader is to create value. You are not taught to create value, and if you are doing this unconsciously, you could be destroying value unconsciously. Once you learn about value creation, you can get to a value creation mindset, which will help you strategize and innovate better, and you will start to look at value waiting to happen and learn to look at value destruction potential to create even more value. Your business purpose is to create value for all stakeholders.

We need value creating leaders for the future. Create more value.

Can Non-Owner Stakeholders Select CEOs to Create Value?

I was in a conversation with a friend deeply concerned about sustainability. He reminded me of the importance of sustainability for our happiness and good health, and for creating a planet that could continue to sustain human beings. He said that he did not think that any CEO would drive his business strategy through sustainability. After all, they are appointed by shareholders and their eye is squarely on quarterly profits and profits. The Business Roundtable is saying and that was Davos has stated that the purpose of a company is to create value for all stakeholders is a far cry from ground reality. He also suggested that maybe a non-shareholder selected CEO could work better at making the stakeholder role more cogent.

It is the norm that the CEO is chosen by the shareholders and remains at their pleasure.

Should this really be the case?

If both Davos and the Business Roundtable have suggested that the purpose of a company is to engage all its stakeholders in shared and sustained value creation. In creating such value, a company serves not only its shareholders but all its stakeholders – employees, customers, suppliers, local communities, and society at large. The best way to understand and harmonize the divergent interests of all stakeholders is through a shared commitment to policies and decisions that strengthen the long-term prosperity of a company.

So, what is the role of sustainability leaders or customer leaders? Customer leaders have typically belonged to marketing and do become CEOs, but do sustainability leaders or community development leaders in a company or outside become CEOs? Why? And why not?

For that matter, few HR people become CEOs. Why?

Probably because they are functional in style and thinking and do not really create value.

Employees, of course, become CEOs, but those who do from within the company, do they represent employees?

I think it is going to take time and serious thinking before any of the other stakeholders can become CEOs or select CEOs. This will require a serious effort to have a proper Purpose of the company.

Bold thinking purpose to improve the quality of life and happiness can bring great dividends. These improve the values of our company. We know from past work with power companies that over 60% of doing business with a company was their image and values. Values, we learnt from studies such as with Tata Power, create value.

Since leaders can also be shareholders, should they look at creating happiness?

Konagaya Akihiko wrote:

However, very recently, some investors notice the importance of the long-term sustainability of companies from the viewpoint of ESG (environment, social, and governance). They don't invest their funds in those companies which don't care about energy issues, that is, the companies which rely on oil energy, such as gasoline car manufacturing companies.

As for food and farming companies, organic farming becomes more popular. "Organic" becomes a brand to add more value to foods although organic farming needs more labour and careful observation than conventional chemical fertilizer-oriented farming.

If people noticed the importance of sustainability through the education and campaign of SDGs (Sustainable Development Goals), it would be better to choose wise CEOs who could understand the importance of "sustainability" of companies rather than short-term profits for the shareholders.

This makes our point.

* * *

To Create More Value, Leaders Should Not Always Lead

Leaders are advised to lead and lead from the front. However often this can be counterproductive and either destroy value or most certainly reduce value.

Let us give examples:

If you truly wish to have your people at the bottom of the pyramid or the frontline to really fire on all cylinders and take charge of the customer or their jobs, the leader should get out of the way and get these people to tell them what should be done and what they would like to do. Your role is to assure them of your support. True examples are the Customer-centric Circles, or Customer Circles for short (see my book *Customer Value Investment*). These Circles comprise of and are run by the frontline people to decide what to do for the customer. The leaders just supply support and listen. Listening and being supportive both create value.

These leaders just do not create a good business, they create other leaders who collectively build a better business.

Delegating makes you understand you cannot do everything yourself. We must overcome the feeling we can do things better than others! Not leading sometimes teaches you to create other leaders to support you. This is a way of developing and coaching others. It lets you empower and enable people while creating autonomy and value.

Consultants have to learn to do this. They cannot be seen as leaders but must effect the change they suggest and get people to buy-in. They have to remain on the side. They have to let others lead.

Examples at Godrej, Tatas, Coromandel etc. are shown in my books, *Total Customer Value Management* and *Customer Value Investment*. Do look them up.

The military is a classic example of when leaders do not lead. The military is a top-down organization where soldiers and juniors are taught to be disciplined, to follow orders, and not to question but to do.

During wars, often these troops are led by juniors, and not by the top and these people have to take charge and make things happen, not only to not being killed but to kill (to put it crudely). And they do this well and often come out with flying colours.

Thus, leaders must know when to let others run the show while not giving up control. They must learn to listen, to keep out of the way, but their presence remains in their support. They must learn when to speak and when to listen.

Good leaders don't lead; they let others lead. They can even become followers. And apart from being good followers, they learn to create better followers who can create value.

Those followers that have to lead under these circumstances go from being powerless and ineffective to becoming effective. Take the example of an executive in the administration who has got so used to following orders. He feels powerless. Sometimes, making him lead causes him to take charge and become effective. This is a great way to change the thinking that change can only happen from the leader. People soon learn that they can be change makers and suggest and incorporate a better way to do things. This is creating value, that is going beyond your expected performance and improving things. This means also going beyond functional thinking. People become leaders in their own sphere of influence and do not always wait to be told what to do.

People can examine their purpose and the purpose of the organization. They learn to make connections to get the job done.

We are finding that many membership organizations do not have elected or other leaders, and no hierarchy. Each member can choose to take a leadership role that interests him; otherwise, they remain followers. Taking up the leadership mantle for a specific task and doing the hard work makes people better leaders. The leadership of this sort starts from the heart.

Sometimes people do not wish to lead and become leaders. This could be because they are afraid of losing interpersonal relations, or have an image risk. Also, some do not want to assume a blame risk. So, they prefer not to lead.

Leaders create value for such people by letting them lead under their guidance, and essentially by keeping out of the way. Leaders, then, create value for these people.

Leaders should know when to lead from the front, and when to play second fiddle or be out of the way. Good leaders create value in many ways where they are not leading from the front.

Fear: Value Creator or Value Destroyer for Leaders

Fear is palpable, it is almost noticeable, and it is contagious.

Fear is an emotion we feel when we perceive danger or a threat. Fear can cause physiological changes and can lead to behavioural changes, such as fleeing, hiding, or freezing from perceived traumatic events .... An irrational fear becomes a phobia.

Fear starts with a perception of a threat or harm, real or imagined. This threat impacts our physical, emotional, or psychological wellbeing. Some activity or physical thing activates fear in most of us. We can learn to become afraid or not afraid of nearly anything.

Unfortunately, fear is used by parents and teachers to make students study … saying, study or you will fail. What will happen to you when you grow up?

Many people use fear as a motivator or to bully. Police fear, officialdom fear, and fear of one's boss or of losing a job are examples. There are many examples you can think of. Fear of failure is one major problem.

If fear is used gently, it can be a value creator, because you can see things rationally and the risk. If it goes to an extreme, it becomes a phobia and a value destroyer.

Fear of failure is a big value destroyer as it prevents creativity and working on new ideas in business and home life. It freezes action. One must remember that there are three ways of failing:

When we stop improving or we quit or we do not even try. Also making the mistake of equating failure to a person, not an event. Failure happens for a reason and not for you.

You must learn from failure and from value destruction, you will eventually reach value creation. Remember, failure is temporary and at a point in time. It is a learning experience.

Your ego gets bruised from a failure, you do not.

Leaders must remember failure is an integral part of business and their portfolio. So they must manage fear.

Also remember, lack of fear can result in reckless (I don't care, or I will win big) behaviour. Gamblers display this. Kids can often be fearless. So can some mercenaries and soldiers. This is to be avoided. Unfortunately, the evaluation of risk and fear is so subjective and somewhat controlled by our sub-conscious and not rational thinking. This is to be feared! Being fearless can make you risk-agnostic, and not look at things properly and rationally. This is a value destroyer.

Remember international politics thrives on fear, honour, and interest can also be the precursor to war.

When does fear add value?

Thus a leader must imbibe the value adding of fear and avoid the value destruction of fear, which translates into no decision or agonizing, or not making the right decision because of fear.

Fear also impacts your people. Generally executives are more risk averse than top people. Feeling the fear of the top man can make people even more risk averse, sometimes tantamounting to not taking decisions or sitting on things.

As a leader, a parent, or a teacher, use fear cautiously as a motivating tool. Do not let fear get the better of you and lead you into inaction. Fear of failure must be substituted by the joy of success for a leader.

Then you start creating value, new things, and new ideas!

* * *

Trust Creates Value

As we approach the Christmas season, it is very important to re-establish trust between friends and members of the family and to create value for each other. Remember the most value you can create for yourself is by giving and creating value for others. They will come back and create even more value for you.

This is the season to build trust. First by building and strengthening relationships and bonds with your friends and family. This relationship is important for creating value for stakeholders and especially for your customers and employees.

Relationship and trust are built on transparency and caring. Giving for the sake of giving is not good enough to build a relationship. Giving something well-chosen that the receiver will truly value is important. Giving so that we will receive is not what we are referring to.

Recently, in our attic we found a set of paintings I had bought from a famous painter, AW Hallet from Dharamsala. We could have sold them or given them away. We chose those that we thought would love and appreciate the paintings. Giving them a painting was most unexpected by them, with no ulterior motive. In return we got love and affection. The paintings made unforeseen gifts, and the thanks were genuine. Genuine giving creates trust and value.

Trust is based on truth, values, and established facts and not false information. Being truthful and factual increases transparency and trust and creates value for the receiver and therefore for the giver!

Just as important is to state that there is uncertainty in what you are saying and doing if that is the case. It is important for companies to use experts in resolving uncertainties. Creating value while living in uncertainty is an art and a science and must be cultivated. Take uncertainty seriously.

Communicating all this builds trust and therefore value. If you pretend there is no uncertainty, or if you pass off uncertainty as factual, you will diminish trust. Communication creates value.

Relationship and trust are further built by staying in your area of proficiency and skill. Pretending otherwise can make people say you are untrustworthy.

Relationship and trust are built on listening to all sides and trying to understand them.

Leaders and companies must imbibe these to build value and loyalty.

* * *

Should Creating Value Be Part of Leadership and Education

In HBR Ryan Gottfredson and Chris Reina wrote, and I quote,

> Organizations worldwide spend roughly $356 billion on leadership development efforts. Yet, the Brandon Hall Group, a human capital research and analyst firm that surveyed 329 organizations in 2013, found that 75% of the organizations rated their leadership development programs as not very effective. Why aren't companies getting more bang for their leadership development buck? Our latest research suggests it's likely because most leadership development efforts overlook a specific attribute that is foundational to how leaders think, learn, and behave: their mindsets.

That is why a focus on training and in particular education, and whether the MBA program truly creates leaders or just imparts knowledge, is necessary.

Leaders are born, often by circumstances, sometimes by opportunities, but most often by attitudes and mindsets.

MBAs are taught functional things. And they are great at these, and at playing what-ifs. But the focus on mindset is limited. No one has taught them value creation.

I say why not a mindset to get things done, to be liked, to believe in oneself, and in history and tradition.

My own experience is that mindset changes during times and situations and most leaders are a complex combination of all of these. In the good all days, we tried ego drive, social drives, tradition and learning drives, and the impatience to get things done.

Too much is taught about functional issues and traits but not about true mindset. One that is value creation is a thought process, a mindset that makes your training, your background, and your psychological needs focus on creating value. How do we teach this, which is not taught in MBA programs?

Mindsets are set from childhood experiences, likes and dislikes, events, and people. Mindset is influenced by books we read, our teachers, and our parents.

In later life, leadership coaches teach traits and functional changes we need.

Creating Value is a way of thinking. It, if part of the mindset, becomes a very powerful leadership tool by guiding the thinking towards positive leadership to do good and improve the wellbeing and worth of institutions. Because of Value Creation methodology's 8As (awareness, ability, attitude, agility, anticipation, adaptability, ambidextrousness, and action), it provides leaders tools to be pro-active. The earlier creating value is taught the better impact it has on mindset.

I am not saying a creating value mindset is the only requisite to being a good leader. It is not, but it is a very positive way of thinking and other traits can make a leader successful.

Executives and leaders are not taught to create value in MBA courses, and indeed in most education. Instead, the focus is on traits, values, and functional skills. All are necessary, but the creating value mindset makes you think of doing good, improving the wellbeing of, and increasing the worth of people and institutions, and the more refined, the more capable a leader becomes. He can then see things differently, he can weigh different options simultaneously, he is much more aware, he notices things that others might not, and he anticipates in a better way. He is much more adaptable in situations and has an attitude to see things differently and to win. Winning is not just for himself but for the best outcome for the team.

George Mason University cites core values (which are actually traits):

> Respect, as demonstrated by self-respect and respecting others regardless of differences; treating others with dignity, empathy and compassion; and the ability to earn the respect of others, making a difference are all traits. Integrity, authenticity, courage, service, humility, wisdom etc. are values.

Modesto A. Maidique and Nathan J. Hiller, Academic Director of the university's Centre for Leadership at MIT, divide core mindsets into Sociopath when you serve no one, the Egoist who serves the self, the Chameleon who is good to anyone, the Dynamo who serves goals, the Builder who serves the institution and the Transcender, who serves society. Everyone has a mix of these, and these mixes can change with circumstances. Thus, you may become a more of a Transcender when needed and so on.

That is why it is important for leaders to think of their purpose, and whom they serve.

This is the like the four basic traits we look at in people, their ego trait, a social trait, their drive (seen as impatience), and the traditional looking traits where your learning, your traditions, and history tend to drive you. The latter are good scholars. The relative importance of these four traits (and we can measure them) determines your personality.

The fact is we are not one self but a combination of many senses that must be impacted by a creating value attitude.

In her wonderful book, *Working Identity*, author and leadership expert Herminia Ibarra wrote: "We are not one true self but many selves and these identities exist not only in the past and present but also, and most importantly, in the future."

I quote Fiona of FPT (https://fptrainingltd.co.uk/why-focusing-on-a-leaders-mindset-makes-a-difference-to-a-leaders-performance/#:~:text=Mindsets%20are%20leaders'%20mental%20lenses,and%20influences%20their%20career%20choices):

> Mindsets are leaders' mental lenses that dictate what information they take in and use to make sense of and navigate the situations they encounter. Simply, mindsets drive what leaders do and why. For example, they explain why two different leaders might encounter the same situation (e.g., a subordinate disagreement) and process and respond to it very differently. One leader might see the situation as a threat that hinders his authority; another as an opportunity to learn and further develop. When leadership development efforts ignore mindsets, they ignore how leaders see and interpret problems and opportunities like this.

Lolly Daskal (LollyDaskal.com) thinks of leaders from a point of view of values and traits. Gleeson in Forbes' talks of traits like openness, ambition, desire for ROI, belief that it's important, fear of consequences of inaction, soul-searching, and commitment to self-Improvement.

This might seem obvious, but the best leaders see leadership as excellence and a constant journey as opposed to a destination. They are never truly satisfied with the status quo always asking, "How can I improve?" They are life-long learners and always ripe for growth, she adds.

I feel that we are more comfortable talking about functional things and not the mindset so necessary in a crisis, in a situation requiring change, fast action (or even inaction if necessary).

Bob Dunham of the Institute of Generative Leadership talks about a value creation culture:

If we are going to grow a value creating culture, we need to see that organizations exist to create value, not just to get things done. If what we are doing isn't valuable, then it likely is a waste. As leaders, we want to help our teams, organizations, and communities go from cultures that focus only on excellence in execution to cultures of value creation.

He calls it a field of action that has structure, process, and skills. It's something that can be learned and grown over time, and it is becoming more of a competitive necessity in a changing world.

We need to make value creation a practice and a skill.

He emphasizes that value is as seen by the customer or the beholder.

Yes, creating value is an essential part of leadership and education and must be embedded in both, through mindset and thinking.

* * *

Why Leadership Development Programs Fail: A Contrarian View

In a recent article, Pierre Gurdjian, Thomas Halbeisen, and Kevin Lane of Mckinsey outlined the reasons why leadership development programs fail. Some salient aspects: much money is spent on such programs. Sixty-seven percent of companies rank leadership development as the first three human capital priorities. Thirty percent of CEOs believe they lost international business opportunities because of poor leadership. Only 7% of the companies say their programs are effective.

Top business schools charge about $150,000 per person for such programs. Training of leaders is a big business, and the trainers are often profit led.

Wow, 93% of such leadership development programs fail and yet companies still continue with such programs. With such appalling results, why do people try to look at seemingly obvious reasons for failure and are unable to reduce the failure rate?

If you couple this appalling training failure with the American Customer Satisfaction Index or ACSI score which has not improved in the last 20 years, from 1995 (score 74) to 2014 (score 76). What does it tell you? What does your leadership training do? It is failing in getting our leaders to be customer focused? The customer is the real reason for a company being successful or not.

The companies' consultant advisers keep pushing them into new leadership development programs, with new ideas like let's have programs that focus on companies needs and teach potential leaders how to manage two or three needs.

Other reasons for failure had to do with reflection vs. hands-on training. The next was measuring the result of the programs, and perhaps the most important was underestimating the mindset.

Unfortunately, it is not the mindset of the leader trainees but the trainers. (Ask yourself, if there is only 7% success, either selection of potential leaders is a problem or the trainer is a problem: he is teaching the wrong thing or the wrong way?)

As a contrarian, I am against training. I am for education and self-learning through reflection, catalyzed by the teacher, to help leaders understand how to create value, and for whom.

Obviously, value is to be created for the employees (not mentioned in the article other than to call leaders employees) and the customer. The customer is mentioned tangentially as "hunting for customers" or for joint ventures in the article.

The mindset is most important, but again they are looking for a "leadership" mindset not for a "customer" mindset. The current leadership development mindset is an inside point of view and not an external focus.

I think our current trainers have to unlearn before they can teach new things. The leadership candidates also have to unlearn all the gibberish on the day-to-day stuff they have learnt, such as the leader's role is to administer and to bring in efficiency, and profits (these are the minimum the leader has to do, but he has to go beyond to create value).

They need to concentrate on becoming Customeric and creators of value and not silent destroyers of value.

Potential leaders must develop a customer mindset.

And as they reflect on this in their leadership self-development, they will soon come to the conclusion that they are in a people business, and they need to work with both internal people (partners and employees and unions) and external people (customers whom they need to internalize).

Such people businesses understand changing social needs and social media, and the changing world.

They understand the value of creating employee value. And they then develop or find specialists to aid them in tasks such as acquisitions of companies (for customer-related needs), or to develop or innovate new products that customers can relate to, or services that wow customers, and to find joint venture partners or new markets that are useful to customers.

This then is the mindset we want to inculcate. Forget whether we should make the leader aggressive (and if his mindset is mild, to change that) or make his mindset innovative (even if he is a person that focuses on efficiency or stability) or make him an internationalist.

Get the potential leaders to focus on people, particularly customers and to find specialists who can help them with processes and systems, acquisitions, cost cutting, increasing prices etc., entering more lucrative markets, finding talent etc. Do not make him the one who does this but one who can lead and create value for the benefit of the customer, the employee, and the company. This is true leadership creation.

* * *

Why Training Does Not Create Great Leaders?

One of the greatest pains to human nature is the pain of a new idea.

— *Walter Bagehot*

Unfortunately dated ideas still control the industry. One is training, another is CRM. Yet another is that satisfaction by itself Creates Value, and NPS is a great predictor of market share. Few want to let go and unlearn and create the next practices. Others want to be followers by seeking best practices.

For years, I have been flinching when introduced as a trainer. Training is for dogs, and education is "for human beings." I do not teach "Sit," "Stand," or "Bark." I teach people to transform themselves to create value and the next practices. I want them to build their self-esteem, awareness, and proactiveness.

So what is wrong with training has been enunciated so well by Mike Myatt, and he discusses the difference between training and development (and what I call education).

Quoting Mike, the following 20 items point out some of the main differences between training and development:[1]

1. Training blends to a norm – Development occurs beyond the norm.
2. Training focuses on technique/content/curriculum – Development focuses on people.
3. Training tests patience – Development tests courage.
4. Training focuses on the present – Development focuses on the future.
5. Training adheres to standards – Development focuses on maximizing potential.
6. Training is transactional – Development is transformational.
7. Training focuses on maintenance – Development focuses on growth.
8. Training focuses on the role – Development focuses on the person.
9. Training indoctrinates – Development educates.
10. Training maintains the status quo – Development catalyzes innovation.
11. Training stifles culture – Development enriches culture.
12. Training encourages compliance – Development emphasizes performance.

---

[1] https://www.growthandprofit.coach/difference-leadership-training-vs-leadership-development/

13. Training focuses on efficiency – Development focuses on effectiveness.
14. Training focuses on problems – Development focuses on solutions.
15. Training focuses on reporting lines – Development expands influence.
16. Training places people in a box – Development frees them from the box.
17. Training is mechanical – Development is intellectual.
18. Training focuses on the knowns – Development explores the unknowns.
19. Training places people in a comfort zone – Development moves people beyond their comfort zones.
20. Training is finite – Development is infinite.

If what you desire is a robotic, static thinker – train them. If you're seeking innovative, critical thinkers – develop them. Unquote.

* * *

The Leadership Skill of Being Able to Unlearn: Create Value through Unlearning

> There are assumptions you hold, and assumptions that have a hold on you
>
> *Prof Robert Kegan of Harvard*

"The illiterate of the 21st century will not be those who cannot read and write, but those who cannot learn, unlearn, and relearn." This is a famous quote by American futurist Alvin Toffler.

As adults, too many of us are still puppets to the past, doing what was taught to us 40 years during our "indoctrination!" The essential leadership quality of tenacity sometimes hinders success. There is a saying that old ideas only die when the people holding them die. Irwing Corey said if we do not change the direction, we will end up where we are going (sometimes nowhere!).

In today's world, change is happening so fast that for us to keep up, we must change, and to do that we must unlearn. Unlearning is a prerequisite for problem solving, innovation, and creativity. If leaders wish to be progressive and have lateral thinking, they have to learn to unlearn. Leaders who imbibe unlearning avoid strategic mistakes and avoid missing the bus. They are more adept on capitalizing on the winds of change. Unlearning is harder than learning. Unlearning is exactly what it says: intending to let go of what we have already learnt or acquired. It is not about right or wrong. It is about being open to and exploring something that lies underneath the judgement, underneath the right and the wrong.

Unlearning could be also described as stripping the existing paint off a wall so that new paint sticks. As you know stripping is 70% of the job and repainting is 30%.

Unlearning can also help you innovate and think differently. What if your soap does not exist? Can you unlearn the soap and think of using a cleansing alcohol?

Examine a case in the field of medicine. For years doctor's felt ulcers were caused by stress and spicy food. In 1985, a young Australian doctor, Barry Marshall, had the audacity to suggest that ulcers were caused by bacteria. When he first proposed his theory at a medical conference, he was booed off the stage! Twenty years later, he was awarded the Nobel Prize for Medicine. Just imagine how many more people could have been better served if only hundreds of arrogant doctors were willing to unlearn!

The future is in how fast you are at unlearning. Yes, we're under pressure to learn more and to learn quickly, but the future goes to those who can unlearn faster than the rest, because you can't always learn something new until you first let go of something else. And learning to let go of rules is one of the first things we (and our managers) have to learn to be quicker at.

Sometimes that means letting go of something that served you well for a long time. And that's the toughest thing. Think of all the things you might have to unlearn, even in the course of a year: for middle and senior managers,

Sometimes you unlearn too much and forget things you could do with your past learning. Relearn.

Remember, unlearning can help you think about the future. Think of things you are used to. What if they were not there, what would you do? Very often people have learnt to send messages by email. What if the message bounces? You try again and then tell your boss you cannot send the email and stop. You have unlearnt of using the postal service, courier, or phone to contact the person. Unlearn your unlearning.

You have learnt to write letters in a classical way. You have unlearnt this to learn how to use emails.

You have learnt that to work you must come to an office. Unlearn and work from the home, and think of better ways to do this and yet be part of the culture.

These are simple examples. You can think of others more complex. (Taken from various souces on internet.)

- Unlearn what your target market is (because it just changed)
- Unlearn that you work for your company (because you work for your customers)
- Unlearn short-term thinking (because you will get long-term success)
- Unlearn that your product will last forever and competition will not catch up
- Unlearn you will remain market leaders (because Mahindra Motors just overtook Tata Motors)

- Unlearn old policies and procedures (because the new generation requires different rules)
- Unlearn the way you advertise and market (because your market just got a lot smarter)
- Unlearn the way you approach your brand (because it's no longer within your control)
- Unlearn the way you teach (because learners need to unlearn and learn simultaneously)
- Unlearn the way you treat your employees (because before you know it, that "meets expectations" review might come back to haunt you on a blog)
- Unlearn the technology you use (self-explanatory ... we're all living this one)
- Unlearn plain vanilla business excellence (because you need Customer Excellence)
- Unlearn that processes and systems solve everything (because you must have Customer-centric attitudes)
- Unlearn that success leads to success (because Bill Gates says it is a lousy teacher; it makes smart people feel they can't lose)
- Unlearn your role is just to lead and be a good administrator (because your role is to create value)

You can add to this unlearn list!

Now leaders have to learn that their role is to create value for all stakeholders and unlearn that old paradigm that profit is the purpose of a business. Unlearning will help you create value faster.

Some information has been taken from a blog quoting Kathy Sierra

* * *

No Time for Customers? Conduct a Task Audit

I discuss the importance of Customers, Customer Value, and Creating Value with CEOs and CxOs of companies of all sizes. We discuss how increasing Customer Value leads to increased profits. Many CxOs end the conversation by saying, "What you are suggesting is important and certainly the Customer is crucial for us. However, we have too many other programs in place." Customer priority is generally low in these companies.

At first, I used to be mystified that the Customer was not that important to these companies and that they had no time for the Customer. So, I asked myself, what is more important? What tasks are they carrying out that is more significant? I then started to work with companies on a Task Audit (and these included India's largest companies). We looked at Figure 9.1):

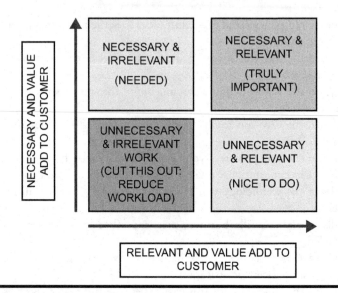

Figure 9.1 Mahajan Task Matrix

Necessary and Relevant work for the Customer

Necessary and Irrelevant work

Unnecessary and Relevant work

Unnecessary and Irrelevant work

AS DEFINITIONS, **Necessary work** is essential for, vital to, indispensable to, important to, crucial to, needed by, compulsory required by, or requisite for the Customer.

Relevant work is pertinent to, applicable or germane to, or appropriate to the Customer. This is work that can be eliminated without deterioration of present service or product.

What work is the Customer willing to pay for? That would be termed as **Necessary and Relevant**.

We conducted research on tasks done by executives through questionnaires. Half of the executives answered the questions themselves and the other half with the researchers. Not surprisingly, the ones who answered the questions themselves found that 70% of their work was useful (either necessary or relevant to the Customer). The executives who filled the questions with the help of researchers found only 50% of their work was useful. The rest was useless (this makes sense, because people have difficulty in admitting that what they do is useless)

Examples of useless tasks are redoing reports, unnecessary meetings, waiting for meetings to start and most important of all, reading useless emails. If you spend two hours on emails at least 30 minutes plus are useless. And if you are a department of 16 people you are losing one man's day on useless emails. Start thinking of this and eliminate useless work and start useful work for the Customer.

In the *Times of India*, March 8, 2013, there is an article called "E-fatigue setting in? Firms may kill emails."

Mckinsey is quoted as saying employees spend 28% of their time reading, sorting, and sending emails every day.

CxOs, you have a choice of hiding behind the excuse of not having time or doing something about it and helping Customers get more value. Act now!

This section is relevant for leaders to deal with and find time for all stakeholders.

* * *

Are You a Value Creator or a Value Taker?

I am writing this, because I want readers to think about the future, and not be like me, when I was in middle and senior management to think only about the wellbeing of the company rather than the wellbeing of those we were impacting, the world at large, ecology and sustainability. While many might think this is meant for CEOs, this is the right time for all of us to start thinking about serious issues like ecology, corruption, value destruction or being one-sided (my company uber alles, the company must win, right or wrong).

In my book *Value Dominant Logic*, I tell the story of my heading a team to bring out and commercialize the one-piece PET beverage bottle. We were led by the desire to win, to be ahead technically, and to see our product dominate. We never entered the debate of whether what we were producing could damage the environment, or not be good or sustainable. Why were we like that?

Were we driven by our customers' needs, or for us to disrupt glass packaging? Or for helping our company make profits *for its shareholders*? Or for the larger ecosystem?

Readers must start to think truly about the Customer (for most, it is what we can get out of the Customer). The Customer just not as a buyer, but the Customer representing us as a user, as part of society, as one who needs to improve the wellbeing of those around us.

In this article, I wish to debate Customer Value creation (and value creation in general) versus value extraction. Too many people believe they are creating value, whereas they are extracting value. The global financial crisis of 2008 makes us rethink the modern capitalist system which is far too speculative: it rewards takers over true makers or wealth creators. It allows the growth of finance and greater rewards for the speculative exchange of financial assets versus investment that leads to new physical assets and job creation.

In the recently completed First Global Conference on Creating Value at Leicester, UK, organized by DMU and me, Ashok Ashta, an attendee wrote:

I personally enjoyed the blend with the practical as instantiated by the Fujitsu presentations. The three speakers I found the most thought provocative were: Chris Baker, Scott Sampson, and Michael Shafer. If there is one line that will remain embedded in thought, and that I will perhaps reuse is, "students looking to work in financial institutions such as Goldman Sachs etc. are aspiring to work in criminal organizations!".

Debates about unsustainable growth are increasing calling for reforms and rethinking of the financial system. We need the financial system to re-focus on the long-term, and sustainable development rather than quarterly returns, and gaining exorbitant executive pay. This includes proper governance and thinking about the future of us and our planet.

Mariana Mazzucato in her book *The Value of Everything* argues that critics of the current financial system remain powerless – in their ability to bring about real reform of the economic system – until they become firmly grounded in a discussion about the processes by which economic value is created. It is not enough to argue for less value extraction and more value creation. First, "value," a term that once lay at the heart of economic thinking, must be revived and better understood.

> Value has gone from being at the core of economic theory, tied to the dynamics of production (the division of labour, changing costs of production), to a subjective category tied to the "preferences" of economic agents. Many ills, such as stagnant real wages, are interpreted in terms of the "choices" that particular agents in the system make, for example unemployment is seen as related to the choice that workers make between working and leisure.

By losing our ability to recognize the difference between value creation and value extraction, Mariana argues, we have made it easier for some to call themselves value creators and in the process extract value, like the financial services companies.

Thus GDP and corporate annual reports must reflect the quality-of-life indicators, happiness, caring etc. versus just financial gains.

Value extractors in finance and other sectors of the economy get more emboldened. Here, the crucial questions – which kinds of activities add value to the economy and which simply extract value for the sellers – are never asked. In the current way of thinking, financial trading, rapacious lending, and funding property price bubbles are all value added by definition.

When price determines value, and if there is a deal to be done, then there is value. Therefore, a pharma company can sell a drug at a hundred or a thousand times more than it costs to produce, and there is no problem: the market has determined the value.

The same goes for chief executives who earn 340 times more than the average worker (the actual ratio in 2015 for companies in the S&P 500). The market has decided the value of their services – there is nothing more to be said.

Second, Mariana continues the conventional discourse devalues and frightens actual and would-be value creators outside the private business sector. It's not easy to feel good about yourself when you are constantly being told you're rubbish and/or part of the problem. That's often the situation for people working in the public sector, whether these are nurses, civil servants, or teachers.

Mazzucato adds that when Apple or whichever private company makes billions of dollars for shareholders and many millions for top executives, you probably won't think that these gains actually come largely from leveraging the work done by others – whether these be government agencies, not-for-profit institutions, or achievements fought for by civil society organizations including trade unions that have been critical for fighting for workers' training programs.

All of which serve only to subtract value from the economy and make for a less attractive future for almost everyone. Not having a clear view of the collective value creation process, the public sector is thus "captured" – entranced by stories about wealth creation which have led to regressive tax policies that increase inequality.

This is not only true for the environment where picking up the mess of pollution will definitely increase GDP (due to the cleaning services paid for), while a cleaner environment won't necessarily (indeed if it leads to less "things" produced it could decrease GDP), but also as we saw to the world of finance where the distinction between financial services that feed industry's need for long-term credit versus those financial services that simply feed other parts of the financial sector are not distinguished. You can think of other examples: poor road construction leading to increased repairs builds GDP. M&A fees add to GDP. The middleman making more than the producer.

So think of becoming a value maker, a value creator, and not just a value extractor, the role of many when they are in management. Maybe this is the time for you to think of your role. Are you going to be a blind follower? Can you do some things at your level? Examples of what you can do at your level are to be transparent, caring for your employees and society, and not accepting dishonesty from above. You can start to provide an island of "goodness" in your department, and if many do this, the message will be heard at the top. We call this the bottom-up approach, versus the top-down system we live in. The power is with you.

* * *

The Chief Creating Value Officer

In my books, *Total Customer Value Management* and *Value Creation*, and in my 2010 article, I called the CFO the chief shareholder value creator.

A few years ago, I suggested that the CFO take an additional role to align the finance function with all stakeholders and act as a stakeholder business adviser for all CxOs, adding strategic value by enabling creating value methodology and enterprise transformation. The CFO has to be able to measure and balance Customer Capital and Returns, Employee Capital and Returns, Partner Capital and Returns, Societal Capital and Returns, and Environmental Capital and Returns and balance them with Shareholder Capital and Returns. He should help the company answer:

What is the value the Customer, Employee, Partners, Society, Environment, and shareholders (or owners) create for the company?

What value does the company create for the Customer, Employee, Partners, Society, Environment, and shareholders (or owners)?

Does the company gain net value (that is they get more than they give) from the Customer, Employee, Partners, Society, Environment, and shareholders (or owners) or do they lose value (spend more on and get less benefits from) to each of the stakeholders?

Does the company destroy value for each of the stakeholders?

Do any of the stakeholders destroy value for the company? For example a shareholder may demand more from the company to the detriment of its long-term success. How do we create more value for each of the stakeholders and thereby create more value for our company, and how much more?

Sadly, many CEOs and most CxOs have never thought this way, and a new beginning is needed with the new purpose of a company.

In August 2019, the CEOs of 181 of the 188 companies who are members signed off on the purpose of a company: Creating Value for all stakeholders. These included Jamie Dimon of JP Morgan Chase, Tim Cook of Apple, and Jeff Bezos of Amazon. Notable exceptions were Larry Culp of GE and Stephen Schwarzman of Blackstone.

The Purpose Statement contains the following statements:

> We share a fundamental commitment to all of our stakeholders. We commit to

- Delivering value to our customers.
- Investing in our employees.
- Dealing fairly and ethically with our suppliers.
- Supporting the community in which we work.
- Generating long-term value for our shareholders.

This is supposedly different from the 1997 enunciated purpose of a company to increase shareholder wealth. (Business Roundtable, 1997). Many articles recently written wonder if this new goal will happen. Many suspect not, unless the CEOs, CxOs, and especially the CFOs understand the purpose of a company and understand how to measure stakeholder capital and returns.

In 2010, I wrote the role of a CFO was to help other CxOs (like CMOs CFOs etc.) align better with Customers. This was because in 2010, I was more focused on customer value. Today I would replace Customers with stakeholders.

For example, I suggested:

For CFOs, measuring Customer Capital, Customer Assets, the correlation between value and share price, pricing techniques based on the Customer and perceived value, segmenting Customers from shareholder value viewpoint, reporting CVA scores with financial data, looking at financial systems and billing/credit from the convenience of Customer etc. CFOs should become the Chief Shareholder Value Creators measuring ROC (Return on Customers), Value of Customer, customer equity, and customer capital.

The CFO cannot do any of this without understanding Customer Value and his role in building it. The CFO should be focused on the future, new businesses, new products/creations for Customers and the finances, and shareholder value. He is more than just a Chief Financial Officer. He has to look at future strategy, mergers and acquisitions, and growth. He has to look at your scarcest resources: Customers, capital, and investors. Today, the CFO measures return on capital and return on investment, but not Return on Customers.

The CFO should correlate Customer Value and its increase to ROI, shareholder value, and indeed, share price or company book value and look at the investment in Customers and their return on investment (Return on Customer) and to the company.

He should report all this to the Board along with his financial results. The Board can then notice if the non-financial scores are improving or not.

The CFO or the shareholder value creator:

Understands and quantifies the increase of shareholder value with value and satisfaction increase
Segments Customers by profitability
Measures Customer Lifetime Value
Recommends how to grow Customer Lifetime Value
Measures and finds ways to increase and maintain Customer assets and Customer Value
Ensures Customer focus and Customer tasks are part of his department
Institutes Customer friendly billing, financial terms, and payment receipts
Establishes simple enquiry systems on bills, payments etc.

Ensures executive understand that Customer Value impacts pricing and urges
them to grow Customer Value to impact pricing
Teaches executives how to do price negotiations
Helps companies institutionalize price justification
Keeps in contact with the Customers
Balances convenience of the company with the convenience of Customer

Or for HRD heads, assessing Customer needs, and providing education based
on this, hiring based on Customer value, measuring and adding employee value
added, correlating employee value to shareholder and Customer value, and
reducing employee churn.

The COO becomes the Chief Customer Value Creator. Generally, the role of
the employee is crucial to the Customer and the Chief Customer Value Creator
becomes also the de facto Chief Employee Value Creator.

If one accepts value creation as a company's goal for the shareholder and
the Customer, then the organizations have to be structured to deliver value by
having the CEO become the Chief Value Creator and have a Customer Value
creator and a shareholder value creator. The CEO has to balance and maximize
the value creation between the shareholder and the Customer.

The CEO becomes the Chief Creating Value Officer, balancing the Customer
Value Creator or COO with the Chief Shareholder Value Creator.

This is shown in my organogram, where the CFO or shareholder value
Creator is called the owner value creator (Figure 9.2):

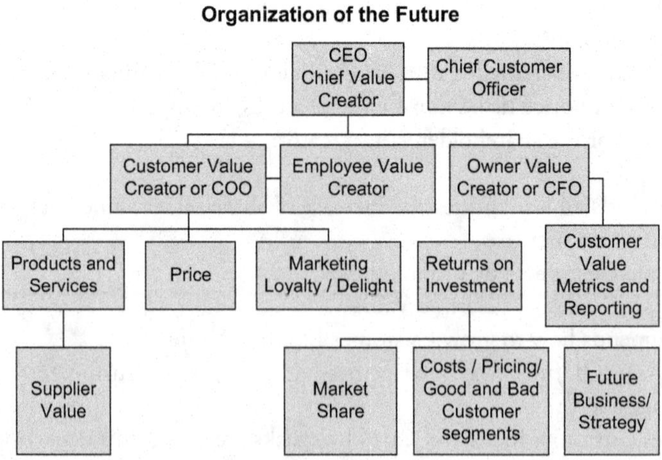

Organization of the Future

Figure 9.2   The Organization of the Future

In 2010 and my later *Value Creation* book, I suggest CFOs and indeed CxOs go from functional to strategic to value creation for all stakeholders, the precursor to the Business Round Table Purpose of a company. The CEO still remains the Chief Creating Value Officer.

Will companies change? I think shareholder thinking has to change as Paul Polman of Unilever worked on. Then CEOs and CFOs have to view their roles differently and transform business or company thinking to Create Value for all stakeholders. This requires much work and thought.

One way of making a start is to network with like-minded people at the Creating Value Alliance, www.creatingvalue.co and read and write for the *Journal of Creating Value*, http://jcv.sagepub.com.

* * *

Value Creation Implementation Ideas. Avoid Value Destruction

We have talked about many ways of Value Creation, and why Value creation is important.

How do executives create value for themselves and their organizations?

By differentiating themselves.

Being on time, reliable, timely.

Become knowledgeable about the company and the customers so that others seek them for help, or for government rules and regulations. In short become the acknowledged resident expert in something the customers want.

Be accessible to your colleagues and to your customers.

Do things right.

Keep promises.

The above may sound like motherhood statements, but they are made because executives do not always follow these. They are often casual, lackadaisical, not willing to take the extra step, and not willing to keep customers informed.

Examples of extra steps executives can take (of course, this depends on your role in the organization).

Get to know your customer and his needs better. Become the preferred source of contact in your company for the customer. Have you noticed how you often want to deal with a particular salesperson in a store, retailer, or a customer service person? This is generally because you have more faith in them, believe them a little bit more, find them reliable, and think they will give you good and genuine information and advice

If you do something special for a customer, ask yourself if this problem is genuine or germane to other customers. How can you flag it for systemic changes? For example if a customer calls and says your website does not give proper information on your branches, don't just give the customer the information, but see how you can initiate the program for making a permanent change. Or if you find a customer cannot get options available in the company on the net, let the right people know. Or if you are told by a customer he cannot input his passport number because it does not fit in the required field

Your boss asks you set a meeting for 10 days from now. You do it. On the day of the meeting confirm with the person your boss is to meet that the meeting is on at the right location. This adds value to your boss.

If you are taking an address take it carefully. And if you are sending someone for a service call, make sure he gets the address and directions

Examples of value destruction that can be avoided.

A major company advertises their addresses on the net. Some of the offices have moved location, but the net information is not updated. Value is destroyed for the customer who goes there. If you are told about this, do not just apologize, get the information updated. Even more, make a check on other locations

If you are a car dealer, and your customer wants a test drive, and the information has been taken (like customer name and address, type of car he wants to test drive, and at what time), do not re-ask these questions when you call to check if the test drive had been done and you are told No.

A customer calls and wants to know your CEO's name. Do not ask why, who are you? Etc. His name is public information, and you will just get the customer to do extra work to get the name, and also get him irked.

Do not answer a question with a question.

I get so irked when a courier company calls to say am I sure my address is right. Where is your office? Don't courier services have means to find address information?

The car dealer service people call you for an appointment two days after you got the car serviced.

Notice many value creation ideas are doing things right. Notice when people add value to you and when they destroy value.

Try answering these:

1. Someone calls your extension asking for someone
   a)   Should you hang up
   b)   Tell him this is the wrong number
   c)   Or tell him it is the wrong number and I will transfer it
2. You walk into your coffee room and see it is messy
   a)   Walk out
   b)   Get your coffee and leave
   c)   Either get the responsible person to clean up or do it yourself

3. You send an email and it bounces
   a) Do nothing
   b) Call the party and say the email is bouncing
   c) If you cannot call do you send this by mail

You can be a value creator today!

Your comments are welcome. Part of this section has been used in an earlier chapter.

Chapter 10

Transformation and Value Creation

Value Creation for Transformational Growth of an Organization

This section is about Creating Value and Transformation. We have two Value Schools in Japan, a Value Research Centre in Kyoto and a centre in Denmark and the USA. Value Wheel Lab from Nova School of Business has joined our consortium. Our Fifth Global Conference on Creating Value was held in Japan on September 2–4, 2022, all focusing on mindset transformation.

Transformation is change and the process of changing. Value Creation helps you transform in the right way and by doing good. Leaders have to create value to transform effectively. And transformation managers too have to create value.

I will not discuss the process but examine your purpose, how to create value, how to get a value creation mindset, and how to create a truly lasting transformation.

Companies like people keep undergoing transformation routinely, and we notice some of it. McDonald's making a vegetarian burger is a transformation. Many during COVID have tried to become more nimble, agile, and fast. Companies are learning that Customer-centricity is real and a need.

Many companies keep transforming themselves over the years. Many are transforming with technology and digital technology and data.

But some go through major transformations:

DOI: 10.4324/9781003381624-10

Amazon was an online retailer of physical books in 1995 selling for others in 2000. In 2006, started cloud computing and is one of the biggest in the world

American Express started in 1850 as express mail delivery and transformed into credit cards in 1950 or so.

Corning converted from glass bulbs, to speciality items, Pyrex and gorilla glass

IBM decided in 1993 to abandon hardware and moved into soft services

Netflix changed from renting DVDs to streaming content and owning content

YouTube, a dating site in 2005, was bought by Google in 2006 to become a video site

Apple went from desktop to mobility when Steve Jobs returned

Management must learn to transform effectively.

Leaders know a great deal about transformation and can get more ideas from the net, and much is process driven. Steps include:

1. Evaluate your existing business situation
2. Get executive buy-in
3. Get employees' buy-in
4. Engage all employees in daily conversations
5. Focus on your communication strategy
6. Build an efficient change management process
7. Set clear short and long-term goals
8. Foster a sense of urgency
9. Eliminate fear in the workplace
10. Enable cross-departmental collaboration
11. Choose carefully the communication channels you're about to implement
12. Be agile and encourage new ideas
13. Close the skill gap in your organization
14. Measure your employees' engagement
15. Talk to customers and other stakeholders

Most people fail and companies fail because they do not focus on mindset.

Value Creation and Leaders

Let me start with the definition of value. Value is a word used contextually and sometimes loosely. Value is not price; value does not mean quality.

Then there is a bunch of people who say Price for Value meaning they are price conscious. But you also have heard people say Money for Value, meaning they are conscious about quality.

To put an end to all this, the *Journal of Creating Value* has a definition which is in use now:

Creating Value is increasing good and wellbeing.

In a business sense, value is the worth or the value of your products that makes people buy. They buy your products over competitive ones if they perceive you create more value, better, better worth.

And you are creating value when you improve the wellbeing of people. So, transformation must have an ultimate goal of improving the wellbeing of people, (employees, customers, partners, society, and of course shareholders).

We have to keep this definition of value in mind.

Leaders of the Future Must Transform through Value Creation

This section has to be read along with the section on Value Creation and Leaders.

We need value creating leaders for the future to create more value.

Transformation must have an ultimate goal of improving the wellbeing of people and stakeholders (employees, customers, partners, and society).

How to Transform

Start with purpose
Work on mindset change
Avoid value destruction
Culture Transformation must be based on values
Figure out how to add value
Remember there is no one formula
Generically create Value in your life and thinking

Leaders, if they adhere to the Value Creation tasks and the learnings from the chapter on Value Creation, will become great at the transformation.

* * *

Transforming companies through Value Creation, Not Value Destruction: The Balancing Act

Understandably, no one will want to change unless he sees value in the change. And the value has to be tangible and worthwhile.

Value Creation is obviously a good idea for companies. Sometimes, evangelists like me forget that for most people the current situation is comfortable (they derive value from comfort). Many have bosses or Boards or company owners who demand profitability albeit short term. And if they do not deliver, they run the risk of being fired (a value destruction situation for them). So there are many reasons for following the road well-travelled. My friend Jim Carras said to me:

> You seem to make a big point of shareholder value not being a good objective for companies and I fully understand your concept. I believe you will need to accentuate the positive and not be too strong in changing what others believe to be important. I know it has a shock value for people to hear that shareholders should not be the focus but rather customers. It makes for good press. My first boss was Phil Crosby (ITT) and I can still hear him today preaching about customer satisfaction. You should take caution in how you sell the idea.

Talk about putting me in my place, Jim! But Jim is absolutely right, and if companies do even bits and pieces of value creation like some innovation, like some social work, like some customer value creation they will be ahead of the game. The CEO has a balancing act on being accepted by the customers and by the investors!

So, maybe we should start with what not to do. **Avoid destroying value.** Keep looking over your shoulder and keep ahead of competition. Avoid becoming complacent, and continue to add value to your employees, customers, and partners.

It is easy to be destroying value even when you are creating profits. You can be running your company into the ground, by not renewing assets.

For example, the 16 oz. plastishield glass bottle, selling 10 billion units for soft drinks, suddenly disappeared. You could, like Enron, destroy value for millions of shareholders. You could be like Blockbusters and Borders (my favourite bookstore), like Blackberry, letting go. Ambassador and Fiat India, RCA, Paine Webber, Drexel Burnham Lambert Beatrice foods, General Foods, Eastern Airlines, TWA and my old favourite Pan Am, Burger Chef, Compaq, Arthur Andersen, Standard Oil, American Motors etc. are examples that were successful but eventually died. Complacency, irrelevance, not reading the signs, destroying value to some stakeholders.

And don't ignore countries that ruled the world or tried to, the British Empire, the French territories, the German war losses, and Japan's downhill ride. Ask what caused this.

So what do we learn? Nothing is forever; you can't take the future for granted.

Failure and success do not happen overnight. More often we fail to see the signs of failure.

Failure does not mean extinction; you can bounce back by adding value.

Never ignore anything that is negative, like customer complaints or a poor response to a product.

Add Customer Value, first by measuring it and understanding why customers but and by adding value. Karl Slym, President of Tata Motors, got 357 ideas just by talking to TCS (Tata Consulting Services) employees, many of whom were his customers. So innovation is what you must do and it adds value. And talking of TCS, they were named among the most innovative companies, the most green company, the best CEO of the year, the best mobile learning program etc. ... all indicators of value creation.

On the other hand, Stock Guru wrote:

In the name of Power (a power company) one man made a sucker of the entire Indian population. A case study for future generations. He collected record amount of money from the public and the stock has become worthless. Marketing professionals and a greedy promoter made a sucker of the entire investor community. Destroyed value!

Today the rules are changing, the customer economy is taking over and so should you.

So what do we do? Gregg Gordon in "The CEO's Balancing Act" wrote:

The CEO, however, has the objective of achieving two goals. The first is success in their customer markets. The second is success in capital markets.

Two Goals

What makes these two goals particularly difficult is that to be judged successful CEOs must achieve both goals simultaneously. To achieve the first goal, the CEO must deliver more customer value than their competitors through better products, services, and effective use of their channels. As a measuring stick, most of us would gauge success in the customer market by a company's revenue or profit. The capital market, on the other hand, comprises investors that make up hedge funds, pension funds, mutual funds, private equity, and banks. These investors are only interested in determining the correct valuation of a company to ensure they make a wise investment.

For the capital market, absolute profits are very important, but that's not enough. Investors want to understand how a company earned that profit. That's because the size of the profit doesn't provide any indication of how much effort it took to earn. For example, two companies may be generating the same amount of profit at the end of the year on the same revenue but are valued very differently. The reason for this may be that one is competing through low-cost production and has high levels of debt due to automated factories. The second may be competing on high levels of service. It may have no debt but high labour costs. Even though the revenues and profits are the same, investors will value these companies differently, which in turn influences the behaviour of their respective CEOs.

What's surprising, though, is that with all the metrics a company puts in place to measure the fiscal and operational health, very few are able to overtly measure and improve their employees' innovative ability, and the true customer value they are creating and whether they are improving the wellbeing of all stakeholders.

Chapter 11

Purpose and Value Creation

Our Purpose in Life

Much has been written about the Purpose of a company. I have written about purpose in some earlier sections.

There is a need to enunciate our purpose in life (at least to ourselves). Individuals should have their own purpose in life or their own mission, but having a purpose is a universal need.

I would say that our Purpose in Life is to Create Value all around us, for others and ourselves. That means we should actively create value for others, like our families, our society and nation, and our firms. We will thereby create more value for ourselves.

Leaders must have a purpose for their lives, as much as a purpose for their companies.

A purpose deals with why you exist while the mission focus on what you wish to achieve. It is more strategic and gives a vision and road map for you to follow.

Purpose and mission will help you make the choices you choose in your life. This includes the values you follow and the rules you wish to live by.

To make this effective, you need to enunciate it in writing, having derived the mission from your purpose. You even might wish to share this with others. Now and then reflect on the purpose and mission and see how you can improve performance.

You will be ahead of the game.

Remember, purpose and value creation come with values, which are integral aspects of a person's life. Values are the rules that guide our decisions in life and help define our goals. They are what tell us when we're on the right path or wrong path and help us find and connect with others who share our way of viewing the world.

Remember also that life's purpose can become a driving force, even causing you to get out of bed! Your purpose in life is not only to create value for yourself but for others also. You influence people around you and so you have the ability to create value for them.

You need meaning with purpose, and you get the best meaning by following your passion and what you are good at. Meaning helps you answer the question of why you are living and what gives you meaning, and therefore a purpose in life.

If you know your purpose, you tend to lead a more meaningful life, living each day to fulfil your purpose and living life to its fullest, because you have thought through who you are, what you are trying to do, and how to get there. Your life has clarity. You are highly motivated and focused and passionate. You feel fulfilled and you also live by your values. Life can be more fun! You will avoid value destruction because you are also driven by your values, and you will create more value, more trust, and more respect all around.

The purpose helps us take care of ourselves and those around us with spiritual, mental, and physical meaning.

Purpose and value creation help you guide your life and make better decisions. If purpose is connected to what you do, you tend to perform better and become more valuable. Very often when you retire or lose your job, you can lose your sense of purpose and can start to drift living from day to day. If you are comfortable with this, it is ok. If not, you have to find a new purpose, a new cause. Many people turn to doing charitable and helping others work. This then helps decide what you would do if you left the job or your house. Purpose can also help you manage your time.

* * *

The Purpose of a Company Defined by the World Economic Forum

The World Economic Forum on its 50th Anniversary at Davos Updates the Purpose of a Company.

Madeleine Carlisle of Time reported on the purpose of a business. "Is it to generate wealth? To further social good? To deliver for shareholders? That question seemed to echo throughout 2019."

The World Economic Forum issued a new "Davos Manifesto," titled "The Universal Purpose of a Company in the Fourth Industrial Revolution."

> The purpose of a company is to engage all its stakeholders in shared and sustained value creation In creating such value, a company serves not only its shareholders, but all its stakeholders – employees, customers, suppliers, local communities and society at large.

The Manifesto declares that companies should pay their share of taxes, fight corruption, support human rights, push for fair market competition as well as be stakeholders themselves in the future of the globe.

Now on its 50th anniversary, World Economic Forum has updated its guiding document to address the realities of our time – climate change, automation, and globalization – while reaffirming its support for a "stakeholder" focused model of capitalism. The new Manifesto will guide the next Forum on January 21–24, 2020.

> Others are finally coming to the 'stakeholder' table. The US Business Roundtable, America's most influential business lobby group, *announced* in 2019 that it would formally embrace stakeholder capitalism. And so-called impact investing is rising to prominence as more investors look for ways to link environmental and societal benefits to financial returns, we should seize this moment to ensure that stakeholder capitalism remains the new dominant model.

Read the full Manifesto below.

The Universal Purpose of a Company in the Fourth Industrial Revolution

The purpose of a company is to engage all its stakeholders in shared and sustained value creation. In creating such value, a company serves not only its shareholders but all its stakeholders – employees, customers, suppliers, local communities, and society at large. The best way to understand and harmonize the divergent interests of all stakeholders is through a shared commitment to policies and decisions that strengthen the long-term prosperity of a company.

A company serves its customers by providing a value proposition that best meets their needs. It accepts and supports fair competition and a level playing field. It has zero tolerance for corruption. It keeps the digital ecosystem in which it operates reliable and trustworthy. It makes customers fully aware of the functionality of its products and services, including adverse implications or negative externalities.

A company treats its people with dignity and respect. It honours diversity and strives for continuous improvements in working conditions and employee wellbeing. In a world of rapid change, a company fosters continued employability through ongoing upskilling and reskilling.

A company considers its suppliers as true partners in value creation. It provides a fair chance for new market entrants. It integrates respect for human rights into the entire supply chain.

A company serves society at large through its activities, supports the communities in which it works, and pays its fair share of taxes. It ensures the safe, ethical, and efficient use of data. It acts as a steward of the environmental and material universe for future generations. It consciously protects our biosphere and champions a circular, shared, and regenerative economy. It continuously expands the frontiers of knowledge, innovation, and technology to improve people's wellbeing.

A company provides its shareholders with a return on investment that takes into account the incurred entrepreneurial risks and the need for continuous innovation and sustained investments. It responsibly manages near-term, medium-term, and long-term value creation in pursuit of sustainable shareholder returns that do not sacrifice the future for the present.

A company is more than an economic unit generating wealth. It fulfils human and societal aspirations as part of the broader social system. Performance must be measured not only on the return to shareholders but also on how it achieves its environmental, social, and good governance objectives. Executive remuneration should reflect stakeholder responsibility.

A company that has a multinational scope of activities not only serves all those stakeholders who are directly engaged but acts itself as a stakeholder – together with governments and civil society – of our global future. Corporate global citizenship requires a company to harness its core competencies, entrepreneurship, skills, and relevant resources in collaborative efforts with other companies and stakeholders to improve the state of the world.

A company serves its customers by providing a value proposition that best meets their needs. It accepts and supports fair competition and a level playing field. It has zero tolerance for corruption. It keeps the digital ecosystem in which it operates reliable and trustworthy. It makes customers fully aware of the functionality of its products and services, including adverse implications or negative externalities.

A company treats its people with dignity and respect. It honours diversity and strives for continuous improvements in working conditions and employee wellbeing. In a world of rapid change, a company fosters continued employability through ongoing upskilling and reskilling.

A company considers its suppliers as true partners in value creation. It provides a fair chance for new market entrants. It integrates respect for human rights into the entire supply chain.

A company serves society at large through its activities, supports the communities in which it works, and pays its fair share of taxes. It ensures the safe, ethical, and efficient use of data. It acts as a steward of the environmental and material universe for future generations. It consciously protects our biosphere and champions a circular, shared, and regenerative economy. It continuously expands the frontiers of knowledge, innovation, and technology to improve people's wellbeing.

A company provides its shareholders with a return on investment that takes into account the incurred entrepreneurial risks and the need for continuous innovation and sustained investments. It responsibly manages near-term, medium-term, and long-term value creation in pursuit of sustainable shareholder returns that do not sacrifice the future for the present.

Leaders can create more value by understanding these principles and create a purpose for their companies.

* * *

Why Purpose Creates Value

The purpose of a company is not used much by businesses. For that matter, it is not used much by people for themselves.

Companies are satisfied by having a vision and a mission statement. These normally outline the business vision and mission. How are they going to create profit and be advantaged in the marketplace?

But they normally do not start with a purpose. Many of us humans and many businesses do not have a purpose in life other than to have a comfortable one with enough money. One is reminded of Alice in Wonderland asking the Cheshire Cat, which way she should go. To which, the Cat asked where do you want to go, and Alice replied she really didn't care. The Cheshire Cat answered it does not matter which way you go.

I am not suggesting meandering is all bad. Most of us meandered into what came our way. And managed to do well. Had we had a purpose, would we have done things differently? Would we have taken a different path? Would we have pursued other goals? Would we have been more successful, and happier?

Purpose helps you answer who you are, what you want to be, how you belong, and how you can feel whole and get a sense of accomplishment.

An Uncle who always wanted to paint was forced into the family business and did well. When he retired, he started to paint again, and was so much happier, because he was doing what he had always wanted to do.

This is true of companies. Yes, they strategize. But their strategies must emanate from their purpose.

The purpose keeps you focused on why the company exists beyond the financial reason, if any. The purpose is about the company and the outside world and what the company stands for and what it will do for others. The vision and mission are more for internal guidance, though we try to use them externally, also. The purpose gives you an identity and tells everyone who and what you are and what you stand for and believe.

Vision aligns you with the goals, and the mission tells you how to accomplish them. Vision tells you what the future will look like for the company and where you will land.

Mission answers the question of how you will achieve the vision. Mission also guides your strategy,

Purpose Is in a Sense Why, Vision Is What, and Mission Is How

Note, for employees and different stakeholders, purpose comes from three sources, the organization, the work and type of work, and from the outside environment, from their family, friends, and society.

Investors or a group of people starting something must ask the purpose or why they are establishing this new venture. They then answer what is the venture meant to be in the future and then how they get there.

So, for an entrepreneur, the purpose may be to prove that my ideas are better than others, that I can shake up the world, or that I can do something different. Or people will get convenience from what I do. The idea may be to do service to the people or to make the world a happier place. This idea becomes the basis of the business vision and mission.

What the business idea *is* is the vision and how to achieve it is the mission.

The purpose is there to inspire the stakeholders, why you and your company matter, what your company stands for, what it believes in, why your company is important, and why what you do has a meaning. This then links you to your values, and how you can create value for the stakeholders. This outlines your culture, and why your company should matter to the followers or stakeholders.

Purpose tells people what they are to do. It influences decisions and culture and behaviour.

Thus, the purpose of a food company could be to make food available to the poor or to add nourishment. Another company may wish to reduce poverty among its stakeholders.

Or for another company, confronting climate risk may be the purpose.

Let us take easier examples:

An author may write: the purpose of this paper is to advance the knowledge (in this field). Or to show you the results of my research.

The purpose of my visit (to this country) is to have a good time. Or to learn about the people. Or to understand business etc.

What you do during the visit and how you do it follows.

Ted Talk's purpose is to spread ideas. What they will do and how follows.

Therefore, combine your passion and ambitions to make a purpose.

The Business Roundtable and Davos have stated that the purpose of a company is to create value for all stakeholders. This is a good starting point but is a catch all and has to be distilled down a little more. Sustainability, the environment, and society have taken a legitimate place in the purpose.

You can see a good purpose in life, in a business, and in a family, which gives you direction and a long-term goal, keeping you always focused. All this creates value for you and for your business. Businesses that have a commitment to purpose tend to get more loyal customers and better employees, have a competitive advantage, and increase their chances of success while focusing on the environment and society. Purpose guides life as it did for McArthur and Tiger Woods, has an impact on behaviour, gives a focus on direction and goals, and makes life meaningful and full of value.

A great purpose is 'Work as a professional and live as a human being.'

Purpose creates value all around.

Happy to hear your comments.

* * *

What Is Value Creation and the New Purpose of a Company?

My friend, Dr. Eddie Pinto, who is one of the best medical doctors I know, knowledgeable, up-to-date, caring, and concerned about patients wrote to me:

Value creation has been happening for 15 years in medicine. It screws the doctor and patient and limits care, makes it more expensive and enriches only the large pharma groups and insurance companies. We need to thank the globalist Obama!!!

He sent me an article on how Medical providers should create value, in the blog: https://www.kevinmd.com/blog/2019/03/how-big-medicine-is-hurting-patients-and-putting-small-practices-out-of-business.html.

I wrote back:

"Eddie, Value Creation is a good thing. But whom are we creating value for ...? if for Big Medicine, Insurers and suppliers, then we are in the old world of value creation, which means increasing shareholder wealth. Our definition of value creation is creating value for the customer, the employee, and the independent doctor, maybe all doctors and for society. There is a big difference, and we can make a difference if we follow value creation in the way mentioned above, that is focusing on customers and employees and society."

Recently the Business Roundtable, the association of the largest companies in the US signed on to the new purpose of a company: To create value for all stakeholders, starting with customers, employees, partners, and society. 181 leaders from Amazon, Google, and Microsoft, among others signed off on this purpose, outdating the 1997 purpose Eddie was bemoaning (creating shareholder wealth). The number 1 purpose is creating customer value!

There are three real dangers that prevent this from happening:

First, companies and their leaders are just mouthing something nice. Why was this not done before? Why were we spewing shareholder wealth as the focus of a business?

Second, there is so much pressure from the stock market and the shareholders, forcing quarterly results to be more important than long-term wealth, and not understanding that creating value for all stakeholders creates greater shareholder wealth.

And third, companies have the mistaken view that creating value for other stakeholders is costly. Doing the right things and preventing poor information and communication is value starvation and should be avoided (take, for example, most companies allow one-way communication; the company can communicate with you. But try communicating with someone of responsibility in the company. Even his name is a guarded secret). We have great ways of teaching how to create value, from a customer strategy to Customer-centric circles, from measuring Customer value and understanding why customers buy to using existing resources in the company like quality control to focus on creating value. And of course the CEO must become the Chief Value Creator!

The biggest danger is those consultants who will jump onto the value creation bandwagon without understanding the meaning of value creation. Watch out for these people.

This is what caused Eddie to worry about value creation.

In the *Sunday Times of India* (29 September 2019), Namrata Singh wrote in "Purpose + Profit: Capitalism Is Getting a Makeover." This is one of the first articles in India after the Business Roundtable declaration of August 19, 2019, on the new purpose of the company. The article talks about Conscious Capitalism but does not mention two giants, Raj Sisodia and John Mackey the former owner of Whole Foods. Conscious Capitalism started over a decade ago.

Nick Gillespie in Capitalism in 2018 wrote in his article called 'John Mackey and Conscious Capitalism Have Won the Battle of Ideas with Everyone but Libertarians':

> Thirteen years ago in the pages of Reason, John Mackey, co-founder and CEO of Whole Foods Market, debated Milton Friedman, the Nobel-winning economist famous for declaring that "the social responsibility of business is to increase its profits," and T.J. Rodgers, the CEO of Cypress Semiconductor who was (rightly!) famous for publicly telling activist-investor nuns that they had no understanding of how to create jobs.
>
> Mackey argued an early version of a business philosophy that he would later codify in a 2013 book, Conscious Capitalism, and a non-profit organization of the same name. Contrary to Freidman's Ahab-like focus on shareholder value, Mackey said.
> The enlightened corporation should try to create value for all of its constituencies. From an investor's perspective, the purpose of the business is to maximize profits. But that's not the purpose for other stakeholders – for customers, employees, suppliers, and the community. Each of those groups will define the purpose of the business in terms of its own needs and desires, and each perspective is valid and legitimate.

Value Creation can only be understood when one sees the definition:

Value Creation is executing pro-active, conscious, inspired, or imaginative and even normal actions that increase the overall good and wellbeing, and the worth of ideas, goods, services, people, or institutions including society, and all stakeholders (like employees, customers, partners, shareholders, and society), and value waiting to happen. This leads to better gains or benefits for Customers and all stakeholders, including enhanced returns on investment.

That is why our parents teach us to be good kids and to do good. But this is soon overtaken by the goal of making a living, of being successful.

The role of an executive is to create value, and not just be a good administrator and an efficiency expert. The executive has to go beyond being a functional manager to being a Value Creator and avoid destroying value. To teach this role, the MBA program has to shift from bringing out good efficiency experts and administrators to bringing out value creators, to shift from an MBA to Master of Value Creation.

This is the start of making the Purpose of a company really to create value.

Chapter 12

Sustainability and Value Creation

Creating Value through Sustainability

Sustainability is a mindset, and to become sustainable you need to have that type of mindset or you have to change your mindset. The first thing is to believe you can create value through sustainability. What we say holds for ESG (Environment, Social, and Governance) because they are closely related.

The connection between corporate sustainability initiatives and long-term value creation is becoming more and more obvious. Hence companies must use sustainability at strategic and operational levels to gain long-term business advantage and value.

Through studies, E&Y showed that better sustainability companies had 20% higher returns than those with poor practices.[*]

In this section, I will make it easy to understand value and how it can replace economic value as a valid measurement for sustainability. More importantly, that measuring value is a two-way street, value that a firm creates for sustainability and value it gains from sustainability efforts. Can sustainability become a profit centre? Everyone is talking about value, but only a few know how to measure it.

---

[*] https://www.ey.com/en_vn/sustainability/how-to-enhance-long-term-business-value
-through-sustainability

DOI: 10.4324/9781003381624-12

While I will show that you can create value through sustainability, I also want to show the connection between marketing and creating value in the words of Phil Kotler:

> He said the role of marketing is to create value for all stakeholders in his article in the Journal of Creating Value.[*]
> To create value through and for sustainability, you must:
> Know what value is
> Know how to measure value
> Your mindset has to change to make sustainability a profit centre and to extract value
> Make sustainability a marketing tool using the value it creates
> To do this, you must know the value you create in sustainability and the environment, and the value the environment (sustainability) can create for you.
> The difference is the net value created for you.

As an example, Mumbai, India, has three power companies namely BSES, BEST, and Tata Power supplying power to commercial, industrial, and residential customers. Till over a decade ago, the three companies had to sell in territories allotted to them. The Government then de-regulated and allowed all three to sell anywhere in Mumbai. Tata had been mostly selling bulk power to its competitors, though it had some residential, industrial, and commercial customers. Tata decided to expand in the commercial, industrial, and residential markets. They decided they needed to understand the value they created for each of the segments.

Tata Power conducted a Customer Value study through Customer Value Foundation (CVF). They discovered that the electricity supplied by all three companies was about the same according to consumers and therefore the power itself was not an important reason to choose one company over the other. Customers chose Tata Power because of the image of and trust in Tata Power. The image was:

Image = Brand + Sustainability efforts + effort to keep tariffs low

---

[*] Kotler, P. (2020). Marketing and Value Creation. *Journal of Creating Value*, 6(1), 10–11.

In the buying equation, the benefits of using Tata Power were 65% due to image, and in the image, sustainability efforts were 60%. Hence people chose Tata Power because of its image and sustainability efforts.

Value includes both economic and non-economic factors. This is very important to understand. For example, a firm may donate 100,000 USD to an environmental firm and believe it is creating value for the environment. Society may not perceive this as value for the environment, and hence the money the company spent does not add value to the environment from society's perspective.

Having said this, we find most managers including marketing managers say, we have to spend time, money, energy, and other resources on sustainability. What good does it do for my company? It's just a waste of time and money for us. So, a half-hearted effort is put into sustainability. Platitudes and PR are out in full force to say we support sustainability and that we are sustainable. This is greenwashing or value washing.

We have to change all this.

So let us start with the definition of sustainability. I find these two good definitions:

Avoidance of the depletion of natural resources in order to maintain an ecological balance

Meeting our own needs without compromising the ability of future generations to meet their own needs

Thus, sustainability occurs when natural resources are preserved.

I find many definitions defensive. Don't hurt the environment. I do not see a proactive move to improve the environment, work on the environment, work on areas where our company is hurting the environment, reduce waste, and reduce the usage of natural resources rather than just taking steps to improve damage to the environment. Work is needed on:

What can I do to improve the environment and impact my profits?

Make the environment a profit centre rather than a cost centre.

Suddenly, you start to see things differently. I can increase profits by using renewable resources, wasting less, recycling, substituting more environmentally friendly products, and more importantly, winning the hearts of customers. This causes us to be innovative.

Paul Polman of Unilever supported the environment by stopping buying non-sustainable palm oil. When he did this, product costs went up. But customers were willing to pay for this.

Let us start with value.

Know What Value Is

The first step is to know what value is. It can mean many things. But its definition in the *Journal of Creating Value* is:

Creating Value is executing normal, conscious, inspired, and even imaginative actions that increase the overall good and wellbeing, and the worth of and for ideas, goods, services, people, or institutions including society, and all stakeholders (like employees, customers, partners, shareholders, environment, and society), and value waiting to happen.

That means we have to improve the wellbeing of the environment and sustainability and wellbeing of the people in the firm and the society. We have to be innovative and look for value waiting to happen (value is possible to create if we look for it and put our minds to it).

For example, now we believe electric cars can protect the environment. Before we became aware of it and its potential, it was value waiting to happen. In smart cities, smart lighting is an example of how value can be created.

Know How to Measure Value

You also have to learn how to measure value. Value is both economic and non-economic. Value is a perception. It is contextual and changes over time as the giver and receiver of value change their offerings and perceptions.

Thus, value is benefits and cost, and if benefits–cost is positive value is created. Or you could say benefits minus sacrifice.

Remember, the perception of the giver of value (the firm in this case) is different than the value perceived by the receiver of the value (in this case the environment).

The environment (or people responsible for it) has a perception of the value they are creating for the firm, and this perception is different from the perception of the firm on what it receives as value from the environment.

Remember value is a two-way street: you create and you receive value.

It is very important to remember value is not just about creating, it is also about receiving value. This value received can be extracted. In a crude sense if you receive more value than you create, then you are making a profit. Take customers. You create value for them. They perceive this value in their own way, and if they find your value worthwhile, competitive, and better than other offers, they buy from you. In return, they create value for you, partly through payment, future service charges and maintenance charges, re-purchase, loyalty, advocacy, influence, keeping your factories filled with orders etc.

In all of these companies must divest "bad assets," bad for the environment.

Does sustainability add value?

Ninety-eight percent of businesses that used sustainability standards reported sales and marketing related benefits. These include an improved reputation (60%), improved profitability (53%), lower costs (30%), and increased production (30%).* This report from Rainforest that works on sustainable farming and therefore related issues such as community and human development.†

Your mindset has to change to make sustainability.

A profit centre

A marketing tool using the value it creates

This is perhaps the most difficult thing to do. Most firms believe their purpose is to create profit, something instilled in the firm's business jargon for a long time and reinforced by Milton Friedman. This mindset comes from a belief the most important stakeholder is the shareholder. And what is best for the firm is best for the other stakeholders. This is drilled into management and marketing's minds as being of utmost importance.

Profits come from reduced costs, better market acceptance, higher revenues from sustainability, and other benefits that increase enterprise value.

You can become more profitable by making your business more sustainable. Reduced business costs, more innovative strategies, an improved reputation, and more new customers who value sustainability all work to increase the amount of money sustainable businesses earn.

Now this profit mindset has to change, but it is not easy to change mindsets.

First the managers and marketing have to come to grips with what is the purpose of the company. This purpose must go beyond profit to value creation for all stakeholders, as prescribed by the Business Roundtable in 2019, and WEF, Davos in 2020.‡

Next you can help employees and frontline people to become more aware and incorporate the 8As in their work. Especially for promoting sustainability. The 8As are Awareness, Attitude, Ability, Agility, Adaptability, Anticipation, Ambidextrousness, and Action:

Awareness: leaders and executives and frontline people must be aware of things around them, they must be curious, they must want to know more, and they should notice more, notice the damage to the environment.

---

* https://www.rainforest-alliance.org/business/marketing-sustainability/what-is-the-business-value-of-sustainability/

† https://www.rainforest-alliance.org/resource-item/2019-annual-report-our-alliance-in-action/

‡ World Economic Forum's Davos Manifesto 2020 (Schwab, 2019).

If executives do not notice such damage, how can they change the situation?

Attitude: your people must have a super attitude, positive, forward thinking, and multi-dimensional. Able to be strategic and innovative to practical. Some executives are functional in thinking, and this needs to change. Mindset plays a major role.

If you promise, your attitude must make sure you follow through.

If you do not try to get things rectified, such as improving the environment, then problems get larger. If you do not notice (awareness) or do not care (attitude), how can things be rectified?

We have run Customer-centric circles to get frontline people and staff to take charge and talk about what they see as environmental problems and solutions. Attitudes change as people become aware of what they are doing wrong and what they should be doing; Customer Circles have worked at Tata's, Birla's, L&T, Godrej etc.

Ability: much of this is innate, but some come from learning and experience.

A great mindset helps here.

Ability is important to be caring, for wanting to help customers.

Agility: this comes from a mindset and mental make-up to get things done.

Adaptability: being able to change with circumstances.

Anticipation: being able to be ahead of others by forward thinking and view.

Part of this comes from a sixth sense which is developed in your mind.

Ambidextrousness: capability of doing more than one thing at a time; capacity to think of different things. Sustainability along with other jobs you are doing.

Action: convert into action.

You will be on your path to reducing Customer Value Starvation and improving the environment.

8As help us get opportunity awareness and steps to help the environment and sustainability.

Opportunities in Sustainability

1. Investments and new projects, making sure one minimizes sustainability risks and maximizes potential to receive value from sustainability
2. Invest in poor sustainability companies that can be turned around into good sustainability companies. Work on converting grey to green assets. Become transformation leaders rather than merely disinvesting
3. Look at advising on sustainability and making sustainability a business. Teach people due diligence for ESG

4. Converting potential value destruction into value creation

Earlier I gave the example of smart lighting. If you look at light poles as being potentially value destroying, because they are used for around 10% of the time, they are expensive, and they have a large footprint. Then you start to think of alternatives. One alternative is to have a couple of drones to light the path as needed. Or better still, help people use flying phones to light the path. You become much more sustainable. This is also an example of value waiting to happen.

Then you can start actions to obtain direct sustainability benefits and quantify them. In essence you can protect or improve profits, enhance revenue, and reduce costs while minimizing sustainability risks.

Many examples exist of manufacturing companies that are reducing greenhouse gases, putting in high return renewal energy resources, through low energy using gadgets like LED lighting.

Simultaneously work with partners, both suppliers and distributors, to reduce energy costs and become environmentally friendly.

All this increases the firm's worth in the marketplace and stock market.

Despite these drivers of value, remember there are just as many hindrances and destroyers of value. These include improper purpose, inertia, lack of knowledge which prevents new looks, cultural and team thinking to do this. Lack of expertise and an inability to measure results and share good work news is a problem.

Thus, one has to learn to look for value and to capture it. To do so, ensure the **purpose** and culture flow through the organization and to all stakeholders including employees:

Look for investors and shareholders who believe in sustainability

Have committed leaders

Have a sustainability and ESG strategy, and make it part of key leaders' objectives

You have to search for champions, train them, and enable them

Integrate sustainability into KPIs etc., key performance indicators, board room, and investor reporting and quarterly reports

Improve communication and value understanding of sustainability

Learn and strengthen measurements

Start and reward innovation and experimentation, and look at value waiting to happen

Look at value destruction points and make them value creating

Measure value created by sustainability.

Even investor teams are becoming sustainability conscious and scan the portfolio to identify immediate win–win potential, sustainability-related cost-saving, and risk-mitigation opportunities.

1. **To do this, you must know the value you create in sustainability and the environment, and the value the environment (sustainability) can create for you.**

The steps are (Figure 12.1):

Value the firm perceives it is creating for the environment.
Value the environment or society perceives it is receiving.
Value the society or environment perceives it is creating.
Value the firm perceives it is receiving.[*]
Note these are all perceptions.
Remember value is Benefits minus Cost.
Remember also value is both economic and non-economic.

So, environmentalists want to know what we have done for the environment and the cost to the environment for our presence and our extraction of resources and damage to the environment. This is the value we destroy for the environment.

Environmentalists and we have to determine the value the environment creates for us (a clean and healthy place to live, natural resources, the beauty of nature and leisure and picnic spots, open areas etc.). The value is all these benefits minus taxes for such benefits, cost of maintenance, and cost of improvement. Likewise, what value are we creating for the environment?

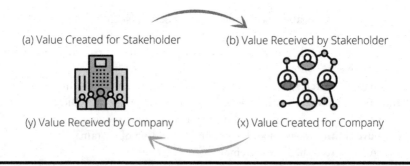

Figure 12.1 **Value Created by and to Company, and by and to the Stakeholder**

---

[*] From an upcoming paper by Philip Sugai and Gautam Mahajan.

Sugai and Mahajan's forthcoming paper shows how to conduct a two-way measurement of value.

As I said earlier, Sugai and Mahajan in their forthcoming paper have shown how value can be measured. Till now value measurements for sustainability have been economic. Value is both economic and non-economic.

2. The difference is the net value created for you.

If you perceive you create value for the environment or sustainability and also know you receive value from the environment, you can get a perception of whether you are giving more value than you receive, or you receive less value than you give to the environment. This is the net value created for you, and if positive, it is a kind of profit or value bank you have created.

This last point can help you create profit centres out of sustainability rather than consider them cost centres.

* * *

Conclusion

We have shown how value can be created by the firm for the environment and how the environment can create value for the firm. We have shown the meaning of value, to do good and improve the wellbeing of people or the firm or the environment, and how value can be measured. We have shown that value is a two-way street, for and by the firm; by or for the environment, and that they all have different perceptions.

By understanding all this, firms can create more value and destroy less value. Having a purpose, culture, and strategy can make sustainability a value creator.

Partly taken from my talk:

Marketing Changes to meet the Sustainability Goals, *World Marketing Summit 2022*

* * *

Value Washing

Try googling Value Washing. You get washing machines. This is not what we mean by Value Washing a term first used by Prof. Philip Sugai of Doshisha University in Japan in his *2019 article* for Campaign magazine.

The unfortunate reality is that we have gotten used to value washing. Many companies make statements they do not follow such as we are customer friendly, we are Customer-centric, the customer comes first, we are environmentally friendly. These words are meant to give a warm fuzzy feeling but fail to actually improve the situation for their customers.

Value washing is a form of fluffy (and often meaningless) statements companies make when describing their work in value creation. This is more common for societal and environmental value creation. However, as one digs deeper, washing is present in all forms of stakeholder value creation whether for customers, employees, or partners. Value washing can happen by using jargon, vague terms, outright lying, irrelevant claims, and often with no proof something is really happening or that there is a change in thinking or action actually being set in place.

Often this is just plain whitewashing and often brainwashing.

This happens because:

Many companies have mastered the art of washing by giving meaningless statements and platitudes to customers for years. They keep saying we are Customer-centric etc., but they are not. They in turn may actually believe what they are saying but never put in place actual metrics to measure their results nor transparently disclose these so that an outside authority can judge whether or not they are indeed doing what they say.

This also happens when companies begin to write about issues that are currently trending, in order to improve traffic to their websites or social media accounts without actually offering anything concrete. Value creation for stakeholders has become fashionable, and companies feel they have to show they are doing something. Therefore, the fluff and meaninglessness of the words that they use relative to their actions.

To do so, let us explore what value is and how it is washed for each of the following stakeholders, whether customer, employee, partner, society, or nature. We start with a well-known term, greenwashing.

Greenwashing is the process of conveying a false impression or providing misleading information about how a company is environmentally friendly or the company's products are more environmentally sound. Greenwashing is considered an unsubstantiated claim to deceive consumers into believing that a company's products are environmentally friendly (taken from Investopedia).

An **example of greenwashing** is the multinational oil and gas corporation ExxonMobil indicating they were reducing greenhouse gas emissions while they were actually increasing these (*January 20, 2021, article*[*]).

"Greenwashing" refers, for example, to fashion companies claiming that their products are environmentally friendly, when often they are not. Examples of greenwashing from companies today include the fast-fashion brands Uniqlo, H&M, and Lululemon – which are popular with college students (March 3, 2020).

---

[*] https://www.feedough.com/what-is-greenwashing-types-examples/

Let's contrast this definition with the meaning of value creation:

Creating Value is executing normal, conscious, inspired, and even imaginative actions that increase the overall good and wellbeing, and the worth of and for ideas, goods, services, people, or institutions including society, and all stakeholders (like employees, customers, partners, shareholders, and society), and value waiting to happen.

Based on this definition, we want to improve the overall good for or improve the wellbeing or worth of people, companies, goods and services, and stakeholders including the society and the environment.

Thus, companies have to do good for or improve the worth or wellbeing of these various stakeholders. Taken by itself, it may appear to be one sided. After all there is no question that companies exist to create value for themselves and to make a profit. They are not meant to be purely charitable organizations. This was the point that Milton Friedman clearly made in his infamous 1970 *New York Times* magazine editorial,

> In the present climate of opinion, with its widespread aversion to "capitalism," "profits," the "soulless corporation" and so on, this is one way for a corporation to generate goodwill as a by-product of expenditures that are entirely justified in its own self-interest.

Thus, companies have to extract value from stakeholders to be profitable, and if in the process they need to say something to generate goodwill, so be it. This, crudely, was the profit motive. However, if the purpose is also to create value for stakeholders, who in turn create value for the company, then this becomes meaningful. Such value created by stakeholders for the company can be extracted. Of course, it is important the stakeholder feels value is being created for them. This becomes a win–win situation (Figure 12.2).

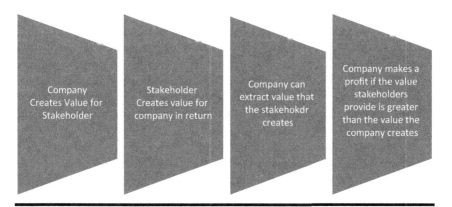

Figure 12.2   The Route to Profit, Starting with the Value the Company Creates

What is important is that the company must realize they are the first movers within the value creation process. They have to create value for the customer, who in turn decides to buy from the company based on the value the company has created for him or her and other stakeholders. In making this decision to buy, the customer most likely is looking at whether the company is adding or destroying value for society and the environment and other stakeholders.

When the customer buys, they hopefully give the company value which is partially profit, partially long-term loyalty etc.

Creating value for society can mean good governance, can mean helping employees to benefit, and directly serving society through social responsibility actions, through adding to the tax base, through consuming from other companies in the society mix, by hiring people, by adding infrastructure, etc. Companies can add value by using their expertise to help solve societal problems, taking up humanitarian causes, or having products or services that can do that.

Society creates value for companies through good governance, by being a source for people, services such as sewers and power, by being a marketplace for the company by providing roads and infrastructure, a justice system, and so on.

Creating value for the environment means being environmentally friendly, not destroying the environment, replenishing the environment, using recyclable materials and products, creating environmental awareness within employees and to society at large and managing such efforts, not wasting power and other resources, and even trying to reduce their usage. Protecting the environment creates important value for the company as does the prevention of natural calamities caused by human error and design like pipe bursts, oil spills, forest fires, etc. Deforestation, over-mining, over-fishing, and dumping waste into nature are examples of destroying the environment which companies should not do, and efforts are underway globally, through the Capitals Coalition and other organizations to make companies accountable for such value destroying activities.

Value created by nature for the company could be realized as a good environment to work in (assuming they have not polluted the environment), natural parks and wilderness to enjoy, giving renewable resources to the company such as rainwater harvesting (which is an example of co-creating); nature is a primary source for raw materials and energy, a source for food and good air, and diversity of flora and fauna. A good environment reduces stress and increases pleasant feelings. The destruction of nature will eventually lead to a future where our planet itself can no longer sustain us.

We can think of value created for employees to include such things as a good place to work, giving meaning and sustenance (financial and non-financial) to people. Employees in turn create value for companies by making the company more human, earning profits through their good work, and working on and helping society and the environment.

For partners, it is to be fair and honest and help them make a good profit and in turn partners create a supply and delivery chain that makes a profit for the company.

The shareholder profits from the company by sharing in the profits while in turn supplying capital and other support to the company. It is well known that the cost of this money has to be less than the profits generated or extracted from this investment.

To do this, a company must have a purpose, and not a wishy-washy value creation statement but a true value creation objective.

They then have to have a vision and mission that includes value creation. This then becomes a culture to perform. Lastly the company has to believe that they are human and not an inanimate entity and that profit is a result of creating profit, which can be intangible and tangible.

You can see a good purpose in life, a business and a family, which gives you direction and a long-term goal, keeping you always focused. All this creates value for you and your business. Businesses that have a commitment to purpose tend to get more loyal customers and better employees, have a competitive advantage, and increase their chances of success while focusing on the environment and society. Purpose guides life as it did for Gandhi and Eichi Shibusawah and sports people like Tiger Woods. Purpose has an impact on behaviour, gives a focus on direction and goals, and makes life meaningful and full of value.

The purpose has to be good for the company and the stakeholders and must therefore be good for people, and society. These concepts are called Blended Value by Jed Emerson.

Sadly, there has been the destruction of the environment, of people, and of society under the guise that the company is good for the people. Carelessness and bad management have led to damage to the environment and forest fires, or oil spills, whose impact is disguised through the use of value washing. Getting companies to think they are human and not inanimate is a good starting point. Getting them to commit to a clear set of objective goals with clear and transparent reporting on their efforts to achieve them is the next step and one that many organizations globally are working to help us achieve.

We would like to have your views.

Chapter by Mahajan and Sugai.

Chapter 13

Disruption and Creating Value

Creating Value in a Disrupted Marketplace

Adapted from Speech at Fore International Marketing Conference – 2021, November 26–27, 2021.

The purpose of my talk is to make marketers go back to creating value and have less focus on functional subjects like promotion, brand, and communications. These are all things they have to do. You have to go beyond these. Creating Value will disrupt your marketing thinking and help you be a disruptor in the marketplace.

This section will discuss creating disruption using a value creation mindset, and also how you can win in a disrupted marketplace, using Mahajan's 8As of Value Creation, which I will discuss later.

The modern marketing orientation or the marketing concept emerged in the 1950s. Characteristics of the marketing orientation were meant to be: thorough understanding of the customer's needs, wants, and behaviours should be the focal point of all marketing decisions.

Unfortunately, marketing has evolved to a "better" selling opportunity, and so branding, product management etc. have taken over. The eye on Customer Value is not the big focus.

Phil Kotler has been saying, and I quote from the *Journal of Creating Value*:

> I think that too many marketers have too narrow a view of marketing. Many see their primary job as advertising and promotion. They

are called in after the product has been created. Their job is to help sell the product rather than to participate in making a great product with the right price, features and distribution.

Outstanding marketing companies see marketing as intrinsically involved in **value creation**.

(https://journals.sagepub.com/doi/full/10.1177/2394964320903559)

I would add marketers have to be disruptors and innovators and manage in a disrupted marketplace. All disruption is not huge. You can disrupt marketing thinking in your disrupted marketplace in small ways. Can we sell this product where no one else has thought of? To different people? Can I bring new products in?

Having said this, what is value creation (which is the role of marketing)?

Creating Value is executing normal, conscious, inspired, and even imaginative actions that increase the overall good and wellbeing, and the worth of and for ideas, goods, services, people, or institutions including society, and all stakeholders (like employees, customers, partners, shareholders, and society), and value waiting to happen.

An example of value waiting to happen is looking at nature and coming up with something new. We call this value waiting to happen. By studying how geckos stick to walls, scientists were able to come up with a tape to close wounds during surgeries!

In 1948, Swiss engineer and amateur mountaineer George de Mestral went hiking in the woods with his dog. Upon arriving back at his home, he took note of the burrs that clung to his clothes and he wondered if such an idea could be useful in a commercial application. He studied a burr under a microscope only to discover that they were covered in tiny hooks, which allowed them to grab onto clothes and fur that brushed in passing. And he developed this into Velcro.

We call this type of thinking value waiting to happen.

Max Bazerman of Harvard Business School said:

> We'll use the word "ethics" similarly to how utilitarian philosophers use the term: to achieve the greatest good by creating as much value as possible for all sentient beings in the world.
>
> By creating more value, you will be better and do better. Our goal will be to identify concrete steps to access our capacity to create more value and reach what I'll refer to as our maximum sustainable level of goodness.
>
> (from Max Bazerman book, *Better, Not Perfect*)

So as value creators, we have to imagine the new normal and get ourselves ready for it through baby steps, where we adjust to the changing present normal and disruption and become ready for the coming normals (note the use of the plural). Doing this requires our becoming more aware of value waiting to happen, that is what new happenings are possible. Will there be flying phones and devices, will we be wired, can we teleport ourselves, will we be able to decide when to die? Can we open up our products to new markets and users?

Some background realities have to be noted:

Money and power will remain the number one motivator and normal
People want to belong and conform

We seek to go back to the old ways of thinking, though some changes could become permanent.

We will forget the pandemic forced a disruption and a new future, which did not become a new normal. We started to put less stress on the environment, and we stopped rushing around, which was for the greater good, but we have gone back to our older ways and older normal, without disrupting our lifestyle for good of the environment.

What it tells us is that **all** new and big changes do not become disruptors and the new normal. They may be temporary. We seek to go back to the old ways.

Yet we know the new normal creeps up on us, and we have to start accepting them … telephone, cell phone, data, and its ubiquity.

Some new normals happen fast, like the change in length of women's dresses, below the knee, above the knee. Slower was the acceptance of Western dress in Korea, Japan, and elsewhere where it has become the new normal, because people want to belong and conform.

How can we create better ways in this environment?

I had written about the short-term new normal:

Corona Virus or COVID-19. Such disruptive events happen often. In public life, it is like a world war or the financial meltdown in 2008. In private life, the loss of a Job can be disruptive. Someone's death may be disruptive for the survivors. For companies, such as Boeing, the 737 Max tragedy was disruptive. They all destroyed value.

I would like to introduce my 8As' thinking which are Awareness, Ability, Agility, Attitude, Anticipation, Adaptability, Ambidextrousness, and Action. We will use this in the disrupted marketplace to create value.

What are the lessons we can learn? Often these disruptive occurrences can be destroyers of value, but they are also an opportunity, to create value. How do we do this? For example, the driverless car can cause destruction for some (drivers, car repair shops) and creation of value for others such as insurance companies.

Let us take examples:

Will studying at home and on the net make more people more robotic and increase the influence of AI and technology and less on human thinking?

All these will lead to disruptive opportunities. First, are we aware of these, and how can we take advantage of them? For example, chatbots make it convenient for people to get information.

Our idea of management and work has to change. Why is it necessary for office workers to concentrate in an office? For better communication? Efficiency? Our ability to manage and ensure people are working? Are on time? Are disciplined, are following the rules?

Changing this thinking may bring the same level of efficiency with lower stress. Commute time will be reduced. Infrastructure stress on roads, on mass transport crowds, will reduce. People will learn to do things remotely and probably become more self-reliant.

How do we become aware of opportunities and use them? For example, at-home delivery of food and goods, home offices, and supplies.

This is an opportunity to bring in new apps, services, and ideas.

Internet payment and services will increase, because people would prefer less personal contact.

Thus, we have e-challans and e-payment systems. Does your system have this? Are your IT and marketing coordinated?

The idea of globalization modified by glocalization may not be the path for the future. Globalization is more for suppliers and manufacturers. By and large, the consumers are local, although they are made to feel global because they buy goods made globally, in China, India, Mexico etc. Does it matter if a local product gave the same value?

How do we make that happen?

Maybe our concept of manufacturing of scale is outmoded. This requires huge manufacturing facilities and even larger distribution and supply chains. Movements such as eat local, grow local; closer to home trade are starting.

What are the products we can make through distributed manufacturing? We may have to use technology such as 3D printing or innovative manufacturing and assembly techniques. An example is machines that can manufacture furniture on demand. They are programmed to manufacture different furniture, a table, and a chair with select raw materials. Inventory and distribution costs are reduced. Scale is no longer important, and Just in Time will increase by putting up local satellite plants, giving us a local advantage. Even today, computers made in China are branded to make people feel they are buying a local product and can get local service.

How can we change our thinking?

Everything will need a hard re-look:

    a. In design and architecture, should homes be designed for social distancing, for ease of sterilization, and also how to allow homes to work well for people working from home, and make them energy efficient and self-healing and self-repairing?

    b. Infrastructure. A great time for us to rebuild and redesign and better transportation, not more rails but aerial transport or single-on-demand transport using the rail system.

    c. Sharing economy, hotels (which sold rooms) moving to Airbnb, Uber etc. which shared services.

An example of something that will disrupt marketing is the prevention of customer value starvation. Stop long waits on the phone, prevent irritation to customers, create value for them, and you will disrupt your competition.

We will all have more leisure time and less hectic activity. Is this a wake-up sign that the rat race may not be necessary? A slower economic growth may not be a bad thing. Can we re-invent ourselves and our lives? Can we find more time for each other? Can we become more caring? Make it fun for people to do business with you, and to enjoy life.

Will this lead to a happier, more balanced society?

How can we create value in this sector? How can we market in this disrupted marketplace?

Reduce economic inequality which can happen to less educated/less trained as technology eliminates jobs. This means more racial and social justice is needed, including a new definition of capitalism, which now is thinking of creating value for all stakeholders.

Can you build a new elite?

What are the lessons we can learn?

Often these disruptive occurrences can be destroyers of value, but they are also an opportunity to create value. How do we do this? First and foremost, our thinking has to change from bemoaning the disruptive event to seeing how we can convert it to our advantage, without impacting our values (that is doing bad things like charging more for masks or hand sanitizers).

Ask yourself, what I can do differently for the future. What is my purpose or what is the purpose of my company? How can I succeed in the future by creating value, and turning value destruction and disruption into an opportunity? Re-examine what my purpose is or what the purpose of my company is.

This is our global opportunity to re-invent ourselves and move from value destruction to value creation.

To do all of this, we need to use my 8As of Value Creation: curiosity and Awareness. Without this, we cannot look beyond the obvious; we have to use our Ability to see, change, and win in a disrupted marketplace; we need the speed or

Agility to make changes and grab opportunities; and we must have an Attitude to make things happen, Anticipation of what to do and what competition might do, an anticipation of the future, Adaptability to circumstances and to change is necessary, and we may have to sell our ideas to others; and Ambidextrousness to handle the present and the future and convert into Action. Use these 8As to change the future and win in a disrupted marketplace.

This is our global opportunity to re-invent ourselves and move from value destruction to value creation as marketers in a disrupted marketplace. Become winners!

* * *

Marketing and Disruption

Most people write about high-tech marketing. My article is very basic because I want you to get back to basics. Most projects fail because the basics and fundamentals are ignored.

What is marketing?

Marketing used to be all about the four Ps and then five Ps.

Kotler has been saying since the early 2000s that Marketing is creating and delivering value. Today's marketing is all about creating customer value and building profitable customer relationships.

The American Marketing Association agrees with this definition.

How many of you concentrate on creating value?

What is value? Value is about doing good and about worth. We define Value Creation as:

Executing proactive, conscious, inspired or imaginative, and even normal actions that increase the overall good and wellbeing, and the worth of ideas, goods, services, people, or institutions including society, and all stakeholders (like employees, customers, partners, shareholders, and society), and ideas and value waiting to happen.

What Kotler is saying is to stick to fundamentals. Ensure whatever you do, you create value, especially customer value. Figuring out why Customer Value is important and what creates value for the customer. Never stop creating more value (Figure 13.1).

The Vodafone Managing Director for Australia, David Maher said that the Customer Value Added scores predicted market share to within 1% accuracy and that it predicted Customer churn accurately. Maher's Financial Director stated that the Customer Value score was more accurate than the financial scores.

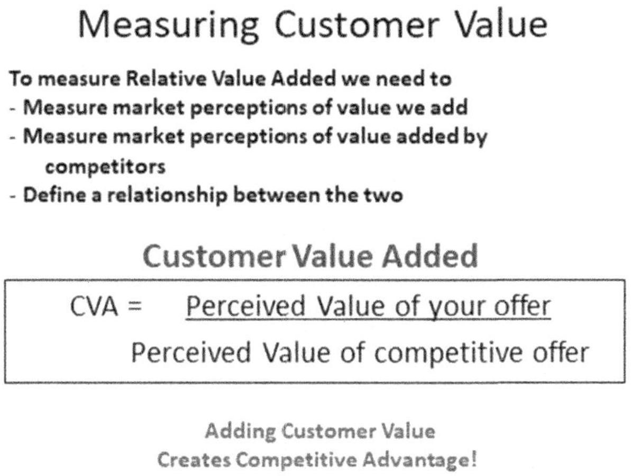

Measuring Customer Value

To measure Relative Value Added we need to
- Measure market perceptions of value we add
- Measure market perceptions of value added by
  competitors
- Define a relationship between the two

Customer Value Added

$$CVA = \frac{\text{Perceived Value of your offer}}{\text{Perceived Value of competitive offer}}$$

Adding Customer Value
Creates Competitive Advantage!

Figure 13.1   Measuring Customer Value

Customer Value Added is a leading indicator of market share and consumer thinking. Most people measure transactional data such as satisfaction and experience and these are lagging indicators.

Sadly too few companies put customer value scores in their balance sheets.

Disruption is an offshoot of value thinking: the idea of disruption is to create value for customers in a different way. If you stop creating value over the disruptor, you will get disrupted.

Technology by itself is not the disruptor; destroying value or not creating new Customer Value is the disruptor.

Netflix did not kill Blockbuster: Ridiculous fees did
Uber did not kill the Taxi Business: Limited access and fare control did
Apple did not kill the Music Business: Forcing people to buy full-length
   albums did
Amazon did not kill Retailers: Poor customer service and experience did
Airbnb did not kill the Hotel Business: Limited availability and pricing
   options did

So destroying value or your competition creating more value causes disruption.

Lesson: you can be a disruptor by creating value with something different or new.

So if you want to be a disruptor, look outside your business boundary:

Retailers think of other retailers as competition, not virtual selling

Hotels think of hotels as competition not homes
Taxis as other taxis, not of every one of us with cars or driverless cars
New things are outside the business boundary ...
So go beyond the business boundary

Be aware, curious, and look outside the business boundary ... the driverless car, so obvious now, and so 8As, Awareness and curiosity, Ability, Attitude, Agility, Anticipation, Adaptability, Ambidextrousness, and Action. Learn to dream, and make your dream a disruptor.

Look at creating customer value, which is the art and science of marketing, and Become a Value Creator.

Many of you have created value. But you did so unconsciously. Imagine if you created value consciously, how much more you would create, and you would destroy less value.

Moreover you have gone beyond functional thinking. Functional thinking inhibits value creation. So stop thinking like a manufacturing man, a finance person, or a marketing woman. Think like a Value Creator.

A small example: two accountants do a super-functional job. You are happy with their performance. One, however, sends you a note on what to do with Brexit on the horizon, and the new tariffs Trump might impose. He creates more value for you than the other accountant.

Look for value waiting to happen.

Uber, driverless cars, Airbnb, and Amazon were ideas waiting to happen. Very few of us in this room thought about the driverless car 10 years ago. Those who did discarded the idea as wishful thinking. A few picked up the idea and ran with it. They were the Value Creators. We need real value creators and thinkers to emerge.

Let me give you examples of value waiting to happen ... I want business leaders to think.

Plants: leaves and how nutrition reaches them, and MIT has produced a microchip pump based on this principle.

Plants, and their ability to tell what is in the soil. Danish scientists have used this for mine detection in the soil.

After observing roses, IIT Guwahati has come up with a super-hydrophobic polymer coating that behaves like rose petals, the water just runs off or forms a drop, and they can change the properties as they like.

Plastic bottles instead of glass: a dream that required massive thinking to make plastics to hold pressure and become low in permeability and creep.

The ability of seeds to absorb more water than their size
Porcupine quills and gecko adhesives to suture surgical incisions

Plant fuel cells based on plants and microorganisms

There was a news item titled: "New lung-inspired device turns water into fuel." Scientists at Stanford have used the principle. Air moving into the lungs has moisture in it. It eventually moves into small sacs called alveoli, which have a micron-thick membrane that repels water molecules. This process is used to get micro-catalysts for clean energy.

Or changing the 144-year-old QWERTY keyboard, not by a better keyboard but typing by moving hands in the air and tapping signs for letters, or by using sensors on your head to read what your brain is thinking and translate into typed letters, like Neurable is trying.

Or flying phones to take 360-degree selfies, light your path in the dark, or on command will fly into your hand. Or phones with shock absorbers like airbags to prevent damage.

Marketing is getting organizations to generate high growth and profits by creating value for customers in uncontested market spaces ("blue oceans"), rather than by competing head-to-head with other suppliers in the bloody shark-infested waters with known customers in an existing sector ("red oceans"). A different "Value Creation playbook" is needed to accomplish it.

I add that marketing is more about Value Creation and giving than value extraction. Too many people want to extract value rather than give more of it away. Look at the great success of Google Search and Facebook which gave you useful items to use free of charge. Value extraction came much later. Remember value is about doing good and improving the wellbeing around you.

And tomorrow nanobots will put nutrition into our body cells, and we will not need the digestive system. If oxygen is also put into the cells, we will not need blood as a transport system, or the lungs.

So our bodies will become mere skeletons with nothing in them but muscles and cells.

What will happen to our food needs? Our cosmetic needs; our effluent needs?

So what are the lessons for building a better business boundary and disrupting by creating value?

Lesson 1: have a Value Creation mindset. Stop being functional in thinking.

Lesson 2: go beyond the business boundary, be aware, curious, and look outside the business boundary ... such as the driverless car, so obvious now. Look at the 8As (Awareness, Attitude, Ability, Agility, Anticipation, Adaptability, Ambidextrousness, and Action).

Lesson 3: look at adding customer value, which is the art and science of marketing. Look at value giving rather than mere value extraction.

Lesson 4: look for value waiting to happen.

Lesson 5: put Customer Value data on your balance sheet and make value creation a mantra.

Do not forget the basics of marketing when you go into high tech. Continue to create value. This means you must develop a value creation mindset over a functional mindset, which we are taught at B schools and elsewhere.

Does success come from asking what ideas you feel can disrupt actually create value for your customers over current ideas? Does it create more value than the competitors are creating? Will it continue to create value?

Leaders, be great marketers and avoid disruption, and become value creating disruptors! And do all of this ethically.

* * *

Creating Value Out of Value Destruction by COVID-19

All of us are suffering from the impact and potential future impact of Corona Virus or COVID-19. Such disruptive events happen often. In public life, it is like a world war or the financial meltdown in 2008. In private life, the loss of a job can be disruptive. Someone's death may be disruptive for the survivors. For companies, such as Boeing the 737 Max tragedy was disruptive. They all destroyed value.

What are the lessons we can learn?

1. Often these disruptive occurrences can be destroyers of value, but they are also an opportunity to create value. How do we do this? First and foremost our thinking has to change from bemoaning the disruptive event to seeing how we can convert it to our advantage, without impacting our values (that is doing bad things like charging more for masks or hand sanitizers).

2. We will all have more leisure time and less hectic activity. Is this a wake-up sign that the rat race may not be necessary? Slower economic growth may not be a bad thing. Can we re-invent ourselves and our lives? Can we find more time for each other? Can we become more caring? Can we find time for each other?

   Will this lead to a happier, more balanced society?

   Human beings themselves: will there be a new elite that will come up?

   Will studying at home and on the net make more people more robotic and increase the influence of AI and technology and less on human thinking?

   Will we create a new elite by eliminating middle rows in seats?

3. Our idea of management and work has to change. Why is it necessary for office workers to concentrate in an office? For better communication? Efficiency? Our ability to manage and ensure people are working? Are on time? Are disciplined, are following the rules?

Changing this thinking may bring the same level of efficiency with lower stress. Commute time will be reduced. Infrastructure stress on roads, on mass transport crowds, will reduce. People will learn to do things remotely and probably become more self-reliant.

I am not suggesting this will come with no pain or downside, but this has its positives. Value can be created from value destruction, by changing our thinking and releasing our creativity.

4. Internet payment and services will increase, because people would prefer less personal contact.

5. The idea of globalization modified by glocalization may not be the path for the future. Globalization is more for suppliers and manufacturers. By and large, the consumers are local, although they are made to feel global because they buy goods made globally, in China, India, Mexico etc.

Does it matter if a local product gave the same value?

How do we make that happen? (I have said some of this in a previous section)

Maybe our concept of manufacturing of scale is outmoded. This requires huge manufacturing facilities and even larger distribution and supply chains. Movements such as eat local, grow local; closer to home trade.

What are the products we can make through distributed manufacturing? We may have to use technology such as 3D printing or innovative manufacturing and assembly techniques. An example is machines that can manufacture furniture on demand. They are programmed to manufacture different furniture, a table, a chair, and select the raw materials. Inventory and distribution costs are reduced. Scale is no longer important.

Inventory will reduce, and Just in Time will increase.

6. The political system needs to be relooked. There is no global government per se, and more localization is happening, even in the EU. Moreover, will democracy be the way to go.

Global institutions, what to do, like WTO, WHO etc.

How India should redesign itself through a fresh look, at business, politics, government, society, and environment?

And what happens when economies start to default?

Also, how to look at subsidies to the poorest and not just industry?

7. The environment has improved … how do we take advantage and ensure it does not deteriorate … fewer physical conferences, and meetings, less use of planes and cars?

   Maybe a day of lockdown every week.

8. Everything will need a hard re-look:
   a. In design and architecture, should homes be designed for social distancing, for ease of sterilization, and also how to allow homes to work well for people working from home?
   b. Infrastructure. A great time for us.
   c. Sharing economy, Airbnb, Uber etc.

   Ask yourself, what I can do differently for the future. What is my purpose or what is the purpose of my company? How can I succeed in the future by creating value, and turning value destruction into an opportunity?

This is our global opportunity to re-invent ourselves and move from value destruction to value creation.

Will there be a new normal very different or will we drift back closer to the old normal? Human memory is short and we are prone to go back to our comfort zone, forgetting the good caused by the crisis to pollution, traffic, and our way of working. Will we continue to be investor led? Or value led?

Chapter 14

Marketing and Value Creation

Marketing Must Prevent Customer Value Starvation to Increase Profits

The role of marketing is to create value for all stakeholders according to Phil Kotler. Stakeholders include the owners, customers, employees, partners, society, and environment.

I want to talk about how marketing can create long-term value and not short-term value focused only on selling more. What is bothersome to me is that all of us have horror stories about our experience with our suppliers, be they banks, insurance companies, white goods companies, laptop and mobile companies etc. The problems are payment related, information related (sometimes getting wrong information on the website), service related, complaint related, or are related to solving problems, understanding products, and other difficulties. Why is this? Why isn't this being corrected as a priority? How can companies be Customer-centric and give good experience and value if these problems persist?

One basic problem exists in many companies which is Customer Value Starvation reducing value to customers. And companies don't even recognize this problem as they are too busy chasing highfalutin ideas, such as customer delight. This prevents them from focusing on those niggling issues that all of us consumers face.

To create value for shareholders, companies have to first create value for other stakeholders. You cannot create value for shareholders if there are no

DOI: 10.4324/9781003381624-14

stakeholders: particularly customers. You and your company live in a society and have to pay heed to the good of society and the environment (ESG), and for employees and partners.

The process is that the company creates value for the customer to be profitable. This is where marketing comes in.

What is the value that the customer is looking for from the company? How does the company provide that? Is it on cost or benefits to the customer? What is more important to the customer? What can we make more important to the customer?

When we add value to the customer, he comes back and adds value to us: by buying, buying more, telling others, and re-buying.

Sounds simple. Why does it not work? Why do many customers remain unhappy? Why do some leave? Is it because they cannot reach companies to get help, to hold their hands, to get proper information, for being serviced well, by service people or pickup people or delivery people (who come without appointments), for not being able to complain or having their complaints listened to, attended to?

How many customers have the same problem? Why does the company not solve these problems?

Here lies the major issue.

Generally, these problems seem trivial to the top management, because they are so busy tackling far 'bigger' issues, market expansion, a new plant, financing etc. They ignore Customer Value Starvation.

The people who have to deal with these "trivial" (not so trivial in my opinion) problems are low-level or frontline staff often poorly trained or poorly enabled and with no authority to really solve these problems. And the problems prevail. They never get solved and will cause others a problem.

Ask yourself how many seemingly trivial problems your supplier, your credit card company, or your telephone company causes you, and how much time it takes to do this. This is a waste of time for the customer. Just as much, it uses an enormous time of company reps and costs them money.

Here are some examples.

I am trying to get an additional credit card. The link the company sends me does not work, and I cannot tell anyone that it does not work, because their staff cannot understand and keep insisting the link works … so where am I left? Suspended? To whom do I complain? I ask my relationship manager. She says to get a form from the branch and fill it. After visiting the branch, I fill it out and send it to the branch, with photocopies of address proof and tax information. I am told I have to come to the branch again to prove I am legit, even though I have an account there. Moreover, she could have told me to do this on the net.

Being a senior citizen does not help me with getting special treatment from the bank.

A friend tried to renew a SendinBlue mass mailing account. It did not accept his Amex or Citi card. His associate also tried to renew the account through his debit card. Same problem. They tell SendinBlue about this. They raise a complaint ticket. The answer is to check with your bank. We are perfect.

Finally got through to someone who could listen and she had their account re-set, and we could pay right away (was this magic)? Why is the customer always wrong?

I wrote about my experience with Air India earlier in the book.

Here are my customer value questions. Why doesn't anyone care? Why do they duck the problems? Why isn't there a mechanism to correct these problems and improve? What is preventing it? Do the companies think this is not important? Do they feel it does not matter?

Too many marketers and CEOs opt for new, seemingly good ideas of improving things, providing delight, and fostering loyalty, but they forget the basics. Get the basics right and everything will fall into place. Your customers will not complain. Your complaint handling costs will go down and your customer retention will go up. (This equates to more profits!)

So, my next question is, who is responsible for solving these problems? The answer is no one. This is where marketing should step in. Isn't the role of marketing to create value? Why don't they take over and stop these fundamental, seemingly trivial problems that cause grief to customers?

Many ideas were shown in my chapter on: Air India, Whither Goest Thou, and Tata: How to Create Value (Chapter 4). I will not repeat them except to remind you of what they are

1. Appoint a problem noter and a problem solver, particularly on what the customer sees. For example, does the website work, is the information accurate, and is it easy to navigate? Do my links work? Why is the customer complaining? Can I check if his problem is genuine? How can I solve it?

   Also, do not stop at solving individual problems. If the problem is systemic, **change the system** so that others do not have the same problem.

   Remember, that very few customers complain and even fewer do something about it like I am trying to do.
2. Use Customer-centric Circles to solve employee problems and frustration.
3. Do not run companies with functional thinking but with a heart.
4. Be serious about eliminating Customer Value Starvation and simple, niggling problems.

Customer-centric Circles demonstrated this at Godrej pest control, and

1. Service calls by service people went up from three to four per day
2. Sales went up by 30% because of better coordination and faster response, thereby increasing customer value
3. Less pressure on price
4. Incorporated a courtesy system to be courteous internally and externally
5. Achieved better teamwork and cooperation
6. Call officers achieved a 30% increase in referrals. Call officers better at handling irate customers
7. Better feedback from customers by the technicians
8. Inspection reports are better making it easier for technicians to follow up
9. Less irritation for customers
10. More involvement of top managers

You can see the great value of Customer-centric Circles from the results shown above. These are documented in my book *Total Customer Value Management*.

Next you can help employees and frontline people to become more aware and incorporate the 8As in their work. Don't try to get to customer delight on day 1 that may impact only a few customers. That will come with time. However, get the basics right and you will reach the top in the customers' eyes. Work on this! The 8As are:

Awareness, **A**ttitude, **A**bility, **A**gility, **A**daptability, **A**nticipation, **A**mbidextrousness, and **A**ction

You should read *Customer Value Starvation Can Kill,* a book I have written with Walter Vieira to make marketers understand and prevent Customer Value Starvation.

* * *

Can Marketing Be a Value Destroyer?

At the outset, let me say that I am a marketing person (among my many avatars), and I believe in marketing. So do not view this chapter as an attempt to denigrate marketing. Instead, it is meant for marketers to think, especially in these COVID times and as we go into 2023.

During COVID, 50% of Americans had reported a reduction in household spending along with the collapse of many people's income. Many services have changed and reduced in volumes such as healthcare (non-COVID), education, food services, transport, event management, clothing, and fashion and beauty treatment salons.

Let us start by asking, who does marketing work for? In fact, all employees work for the company. They are paid by the company and they have to do what the company wants. So, marketing works for the company and the good (as defined by the company) of the company. Should they also work for stakeholders and how?

What most companies want is growth, an increase in profits and stock prices. So, the mantra, down the line, is to increase prices and markets (and market share). And so, marketers toe the company line.

Unless the company has a proper purpose in looking at all stakeholders, it cannot inculcate a sense of purpose in marketers and get them to think differently.

However, when the world shifts suddenly in a disrupting and disturbing fashion as it is doing in this COVID crisis, the old norms get thrown out. The Economist calls this (2020) the year when everything changed. They say the sheer scale of the suffering from COVID-19, the injustices and dangers the pandemic has revealed, and the promise of new innovations mean that it will be remembered as the year when everything altered.

Marketing Sherpa says don't run your marketing department with rules. Run the department with a customer-first approach as your guiding principle and a value proposition as your core goal.

Stay focused, but stay flexible. Do not be too narrow in your definition of markets and customers. Crises are a way of life. Find unique opportunities thrown up by viruses ... distancing, mask-like environment, staying at home, more internet, life with different needs. There are other crises waiting to happen: climate change, nuclear war, famines etc.

And when a crisis happens, be ready to move and move fast. Take the example of Zoom and Skype.

Skype was the preferred choice before COVID for chatting and smaller meetings online. But Zoom took over with aggressive marketing when they understood this was a big need for such services and webinars and left Skype which did not change, far behind. Focusing on meetings helped individuals, and later companies, schools, and colleges. Webinars became a big business. Skype did not change, maybe because Microsoft, their owner, was promoting Teams.

Let me give you examples. In many places, doctors are facing a cutback of patients. Most doctors in India have only 30% of the normal patients. Barbers have the same problem. Restaurants, airlines, and others have similar issues.

Instead of looking at the old market as a holy grail, can marketers and companies disrupt their thinking and look at the world differently? New products, new markets for existing products, new delivery methods. An example is restaurants starting home delivery services. Maybe even restaurants at home ... that is, bring in a restaurant feeling with the food at home. Travel is advertising lower COVID risk, and lower occupancy. An example is "Ride the rails from Bavaria to Berlin."

> The clock is ticking on promo code GERMANY50. Try delicious food and beer and immerse yourself in the lively culture of Germany from only ($899) $849 if you book before midnight tonight.
>   Your vacation includes:
>
> Round-trip airfare into Munich, out of Berlin
> 3 nights in Munich
> Standard-class rail from Munich to Berlin
> 3 nights in Berlin
> Breakfast daily

And if they had added you can do this COVID free, and quarantine free, maybe they would have more takers.

The euphoria around Airbnb's blockbuster IPO recently is already long forgotten. Shares have plunged 25% since then, as Wall Street casts a bearish outlook on Airbnb's current valuation.

Uber for example can become a delivery platform and not just a taxi service. Yes, they have Uber delivery, but it could be expanded.

Half measures and incrementalism won't work when your company emerges from a crisis. Marketers have to think about holistic transformation to go all in.

And what will companies do and what will marketing do when the world limps back to "normalcy" away from the pandemic stranglehold and into a new future?

Warren Harding built a campaign for the presidential election in 1920 around his new word "normalcy." It was an appeal to Americans' supposed urge to forget the horrors of the First World War and the Spanish flu and turn back to the certainties of the Golden Age. And yet, instead of embracing Harding's normalcy, the Roaring Twenties became a ferment of forward-looking, risk-taking social, industrial, and artistic novelty.

The positive is that companies and marketers are working to restore confidence and the economy. For this, marketers are value creators.

Brands came out to help the public during the COVID crisis with ads and notifications. They used digital, virtual platforms in a bigger way.

The negative is we might go back into a "Roaring Twenties" situation which can lead to unbridled growth, leading to another crisis. Then marketers will be value destroyers. And this destruction will include waste, demand for unnecessary things, destruction of Nature, and so on.

All this requires marketers to be resolute, resilient, and imaginative. Marketers need the 8As of being aware, anticipating, having ability and agility, and becoming ambidextrous with a great attitude,adaptability and action

They must think of new ways to win and understand customers better, by also looking at non-customers and also better data and analytics, not reforming but resetting according to Mckinsey, and have a renewed purpose for the future.

The future will then admire the way we reacted during a difficult crisis.

So, marketing which can become value destroyers when companies are internally focused can become value creators by changing themselves and their companies.

But it seems to me the urge for companies to grow will force marketers to grow markets, irrespective of the true needs of people. To quote marketing Guru, Prof. Phil Kotler, Marketing is essentially a value creation discipline. He goes on to say in his article in the *Journal of Creating Value*, "The Consumer in the Age of Coronavirus," that we should place more value on the needs of our family, friends, and community. We should use social media to urge our families and friends to choose good and healthy foods and buy more sensible clothing and other goods. Brands must spell out their greater purpose and how each is serving the common good. Marketers and their companies must become more conscious of the fragility of the planet, air and water pollution, water shortages, and other problems.

When the COVID-19 crisis is over, capitalism will have moved to a new stage.

Consumers will be more thoughtful about what they consume and how much they need to consume. And marketing will have to pay heed to this and create value and more value for the consumer and other stakeholders!

Kotler, Pfoertsch, and Sponholz in their book *H2H: The genesis of human-to-human marketing* say that marketing can change the world for the better. During the last decades, marketing experienced many revolutionary changes that added to the quality of life for many people. However, changes have not all been for the better. Due to some unethical practices of over-zealous profit-minded marketers, the current image of marketing, as perceived by employees and customers, has deteriorated to a point where "most people associate negative words, such as 'lies,' 'deception,' 'deceitful,' 'annoying,' and 'manipulating,' with marketing." Public scandals, like falsified market research results, add further aggravation to this bad image. A general lack of trust prevails, which results in the exact opposite of what marketing is trying to achieve.

It is up to us to ensure marketing continues to create more value and destroy less value.

What do you think?

* * *

Pitching Your Value Proposition: How to Focus on What Customers Value

Many sales and marketing people are taught to pitch their value proposition.

Most don't understand what a value proposition is. It is not just benefits. It is not just cost or price. It is the benefits of your offering versus the cost to the Customer contrasted with the competition's proposition.

That's your value proposition. Is that the Customer's value proposition? Here are some examples:

1. We will keep you informed of the project with a weekly update with your people: let's say the Customer doesn't want to be bothered and assumes you have understood what they want and just want a correct product/service at the end of the project.
2. We have terrific service: the Customer just wants a product that will work and will not require service.
3. Our product is so user friendly, that once designed and installed, it will work. The Customer, however, wants his people to be trained and your people to be present. Your value proposition does not have that.

You had, what you thought was a great value proposition. But not what the Customer wanted. So you have to understand the Customer. Let's put this in perspective. Compare the importance of the Customer's needs to your benefits in the value proposition. Mark next to needs the relative importance to the Customer in his view, and also your view of the importance.

Customer needed value	----	Your assumption of value
Total Benefits 70%		*Total Benefits 50%*
Benefits consist of:		Benefits consist of:
Want a finished product		We will liaise with you every week 40%
Want a problem-free product 35%		We have terrific service 50%
Want start-up support 35%		Start-up support (no need for it) 10%
Cost 30%		*Cost 50%*

Numbers in percentages are the perceived importance or impact to the customer in his view or your view.

Look at the above. Your assumed cost was 50% of the value. To the Customer, it was not important and was only 30%. You pitch the cost advantage; the Customer is not interested as much in this. And in the benefits, he is looking for something else. You are proudly pitching your benefits (value proposition).

Beauty and value are in the eyes of the beholder. Look at your proposition from the eyes of the Customer. And to do that you have to understand him completely. How are you doing that with your generic value proposition?

* * *

De-Commoditizing Commodities: Add Value

> Constant reinvention is the central necessity at GE … We're all just a moment away from commodity hell.
>
> – *Jeffrey Immelt, Chairman and CEO, GE*

Like death and taxes, commoditization is a given. So what's a business to do? The answer is to de-commoditize … but not just once … continuously!

Wiki says commoditization is the transformation of the market to undifferentiated products through increased competition, typically resulting in decreasing prices. In economic terms, commoditization is when a market changes from one of monopolistic competition to one of perfect competition. A product essentially becomes a commodity when customers perceive little or no value difference between brands or versions. Price becomes the only differentiation.

If all you can sell on is price, it means you have no other features to sell on. Or that means the purchaser sees nothing other than price to differentiate your product. (You are a commodity and it's the luck of the draw on selling or pricing.)

One certain way to commoditization is the thought of being "Good enough."

In today's Copycat Economy, "good enough" is a frequent response from customers and investors – they're overwhelmed with high-calibre options of goods and services, and customers are no longer easily satisfied. They raise the bar on their minimum expectations of quality and service, and they expect to receive it.

The tentacles of the Copycat Economy extend throughout the market, even into "luxury" sectors. An observer of the private jet market noted in 2002,

> After a huge growth spurt in the jet market, the jet manufacturers find themselves with a ton of capacity and product …. Business jets are heading toward commoditization – meaning they are becoming

essentially interchangeable – because of the large array of models with similar capabilities.

Imitation and commoditization are the most pressing strategic challenges that you will face for the duration of this decade.

Various methods are used to de-commoditize. The most common is to become the low-cost supplier and try to make more profit than competition. This is not true de-commoditization, but just being the best in a commodity market. The other is to reduce prices, and if you go too far, be the first to die.

Differentiation is the other methods such as product, brand, service, relationship, or focus on environment differentiation, brand distinction.

Innovating, bundling (adding a service to it or adding another product), and segmenting are common ways that people use. The real differentiator is value differenting.

Product differentiation is the most popular. This certainly helps, but the advantage is short lived as competition comes up with me too products very soon.

For example, the product 7UP was a commodity for many years. Recognizing the trend for customers to want healthier drink options, 7UP de-commoditized their soda by taking out all the artificial flavours and ingredients and making their product natural. After they launched their new "natural" campaign, sales of 7UP increased.

Segmentation of the market is another method. Natural gas producers were able to segment during an oversupply situation. They used a trained Customer Value team for understanding the "Day in the Life of a Customer" and were able to add value to certain segments leading to a 40% increase in profits.

Water is a commodity. The price of water and perhaps the level of demand will vary when water is scarce, such as in the summertime. You could play that game (wait for scarcity).

Water is water … until you put it in a bottle. Once you put water in a bottle, you can charge for it. You can then put the water in a fancier bottle and charge some more. You can also add some vitamins to it, give it a fancy name, and charge even more. Now you've taken a commodity and you've de-commoditized it. And then you brand to keep your price and market going.

Tata Power differentiated itself by being friendly to the environment and being trustworthy, improving value, and increasing customers.

But the best way to differentiate is to add Customer Value and this is with better service, customer experience, and customer relationship. Marketing Professor John Quelch of the Harvard Business School says the most overlooked investment a marketer can make in advance of inevitable commoditization is a customer relationship.

You have to create value for the customer. First understand what a customer values and deliver it and keep track of his changing value needs. Look even at "Uncharted value," the late Professor Oren Harari of University of San Francisco said. And companies looking at uncharted value are not aspiring to satisfy customers. "Satisfaction is a commodity response to a commodity transaction," Harari said. What you want is the "wow!" approach to increase value.

We have helped clients in businesses as commoditized and diverse as fertilizers, pest control services, and power distribution to de-commoditize by providing an emotional connect to the brand and by creating value. We have found that values create value and help de-commoditize businesses. We have helped them differentiate themselves and look at next practices and superiority.

Make your employees your internal partners, who will raise the bar and make customer interactions moments of truth. And the only way out of the Commodity Hell is to add value. So learn to measure what a customer values and deliver more of it than competition. And value can be product, service, brand image, and customer relationship. Or you can play the price game and die.

Remember, when you start turning your products into commodities, you start treating your customers like commodities.

* * *

Customer and Value Migration

Your customers move where they perceive they get better Customer Value, causing your company value to migrate to competition (Figure 14.1):

Why do some Customers migrate? And why don't others?

Many Customers remain with a company because of convenience and inertia. They are just too lazy to move. Just because they stay on, they are not essentially loyal.

And loyalty is not necessarily a long-term or lifelong phenomenon. Loyalty has to be gained and maintained by providing higher Customer Value.

And as your competitors start to provide better Customer Value, there is consequent Customer and value migration away from your company towards competition.

In 1996, Adrian Slywotzky described value migration. Bala V. Balachandran in a 2007 article, "Customer-centricity Drivers: Driver for Sustainability Profitability," cautions that failure to keep up with Customer Value migration is a key reason for a reduction in the performance of a company.

Value Migration of Customers happens because your business model is outmoded and Customers are finding companies which create more value for them

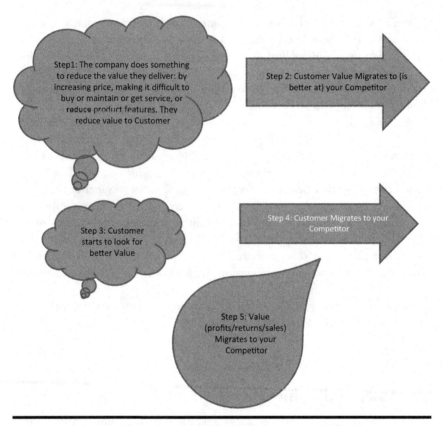

Figure 14.1 Customer and Value Migration

and probably through a better business model. The competing value-creating forces have moved beyond your company's offerings.

And Marketing strategy, according to Adrian, is the art of creating value for the Customer. This can only be done by offering a product or service that corresponds to Customer needs. In a fast-changing business environment, the factors that determine value are constantly changing.

A business model describes the rationale of how an organization creates, delivers, and captures value.

We have seen the shift from landlines to cell phones

From teletype to fax to email/scans

From full fare to discount airlines

From Lotus 123 to Excel

The various storage and replay devices, spool tapes, cassettes, video tapes, floppies, CDs, iPods, and pen drives

Thus, value can flow between industries, between companies, and within a company. And this happens in stages.

Value can be absorbed by different industries or companies, iPhone and the Samsung clone (the inflow stage). Then there is a value equilibrium stage where there is some stability. And as companies fail to innovate and move ahead and do not create Customer Value, there is the value outflow stage.

Since we are looking at the value your firm creates versus competition, Customer Value Added is always relative. This is a necessary measurement for you to make.

Unfortunately, marketing and CxO thinking is focused more on the acquisition, and sometimes retention. But the Customer is growing, evolving, and changing. He graduates from being a student to an earning member of society and acquires a family and affluence. His needs are changing, and just trying to get him to remain loyal is not enough. How do we get him to buy the things he was never buying before? Or he will migrate.

And more importantly, when he migrates, you might ignore him. That is why your data has to show when a person moves from being a heavy user to an influencer and a light user. Take someone who stays in a hotel chain and acquires titanium status and then gets promoted and travels less but influences the use of the chain within his company. But he is ignored because he no longer is a heavy user of rooms!

Therefore, beware when you reduce Customer Value. It will hit you because as your actions reduce Customer Value, you are causing Customer Value to migrate to your competitor, and consequentially Customers migrate and value migrates with them away from you. Be careful when you reduce Customer Value. You might be reducing your profits!

* * *

Value of Being Anonymous?

I often look at the business world and wonder. What are they all about? They spend oodles of money on branding (in simple terms to be recognized by potential Customers, to distinguish themselves in the marketplace).

Companies also profess they wish to present a human face. They want to be seen as caring, friendly, and concerned.

Why is it that when the chips are down, they behave like inanimate behemoths with anonymous officers?

Isn't this a dichotomy? Isn't this against what they seemingly want to portray?

Try to find responsible executives in a company to tell them what is happening to you as a Customer or your experiences. (Companies will find you to ask questions, but they do not want you to find their executives.) Try finding an executive's telephone number, and if you do, you start to go through corporate watchdogs (receptionists, secretaries, and assistants if you can get past the answering systems, those wonderfully inert inventions that corporates love). Elsewhere I had written that companies, while they pretend they are inanimately anonymous to Customers (the only time they appear distinctive is in branding exercises), they are composed of real people, real live people. Companies are in the people business (they comprise people, even though the voices come across as tinny IVR tones), and they deal with people (read Customers, employees, partners, and society).

Why then do they come across as anonymous? (Smaller stores and mom-and-pop businesses may have a more human face.) Is it convenient to do so? Cheaper? Is this because the next quarter's results are lurking around the corner? Or is it because they do not care (I do not believe anyone would be that crass)? Or is it that the convenience of the Customer is secondary to the convenience of the company? Or because Customer focus is only a corporate myth, which they try to dispel through brand building? Or is it that the CEO will be crucified to look at Customer ease and corporate accessibility before profits? And is it because the number one thought that comes to them for increasing profit is a cost-cutting strategy? Not a Customer strategy to boost profits (can corporates see this? It means creating value and giving a great experience in the shortest possible journey).

I quote from Prof. Luiz Moutinho, a world famous Marketing Guru, who has been unable to get any help from Vodafone on some serious issues. He says,

> All the other possibilities lead towards a paradigm where Service should be called "Make the Give Up…" a policy of total Corporate Anonymity … as opposed to corporate transparency and engagement through a "brain to brain" intelligent dialogue with Customers.

I rest my case.

But wait, I have something even worse. Most companies talk about a 1-to-1 interaction, they talk about customization and a Customer segment of one! The fact is for most companies, Customers are anonymous. Many companies have no idea how many Customers they have. The company knows what and how much they sell and through which channel. They can tell you about the profitable products, and the profitable segments of Customers. But who are these faceless people? The answer is we do not need to know. How then will they customize?

Granted this is changing. Social media and big data give them the opportunity to interact with Customers. It gives them the chance to put a name to some of these people, and to access them, but at the company's terms. Big data gives some personal information, but much of it is still masked through the anonymity of a huge unrelated mass of information that companies have to delve into, clarify, and make sense of. But they are more comfortable doing this than really knowing Customers.

And what will happen when we go away from a physical retail store to a virtual one? Companies have to ask if Customers want to be anonymous, or if they are offering their personal data, their likes, and their dislikes, do they want to be anonymous or do they want to make themselves known? And do they want to deal with anonymous people in companies?

Look at the net. You will see article upon article on making Customers anonymous, but very few on making them known. I just did a Google search and found nothing! And of course the reader will say, we can make the Customer known, he just doesn't want to be known. Others will say, we are taking photographs, making records, and soon they will be known Customers.

I would suggest a strategy to change. The change will start with the CEO and the CxOs getting to talk to Customers and get to know them (their needs, their likes and dislikes, what creates value for them. Knowing their names may not be as important), and likewise for other executives. In a digital environment it may be difficult, but the winner will be the companies that try and succeed. Some companies already do this and executives spend one day a week with anonymous's (a.k.a. Customers).

Will you be able to create more value for a known or anonymous one? Will you create more value or less if your people were not anonymous? Or are you destroying value?

* * *

Does Planned Obsolescence Destroy Value?

I wrote in my article on the new normal, and on Phil Kotler's suggestion that marketing should focus on the more useful and the more necessary than on selling more. In the new normal, I suggested planned obsolescence should be examined, and perhaps more repairs and re-use. Why should a cell phone last two years and cost so much? Product obsolescence destroys value for consumers and the environment and creates value for manufacturers.

Some smartphone manufacturers stop supporting two-year-old models. Planning includes poor quality components or software that can fail in 2 years, not providing upgrades, and worse still making hardware changes to attract switching like a better camera. My camera works well on my Oneplus 5 and my friends say it is great. But now I am tempted by the camera of the Oneplus 8* because it is probably better (this move to buy the Oneplus 8 is not because my

---

* Now there are Oneplus 11 phones also. No more thinking of the Oneplus 8.

old phone camera has obsolesced. Yes, its battery has weakened. Is that due to planned obsolescence?).

Software failure happens on printers also. So apart from contrived durability, we also have prevention of repairs, both value destroyers. Other examples are:

Light bulb manufacturers spent years getting light bulbs to fail after 1000 hours.

Having irreplaceable batteries in phones that die after a year or so causes value destruction.

Not being able to re-fill an ink cartridge, or showing a cartridge needs replacement triggered by a microchip or a light sensor forcing premature replacement.

College textbooks, nylon stockings, fashion items, and video games are all planned to become replaceable.

Morris B. Holbrook who is W. T. Dillard Professor Emeritus of Marketing, Graduate School of Business, Columbia University, wrote to me:

I was thinking, in particular, of Microsoft's habit of introducing a new operating system every couple of years, obsoleting the old ones. Lately, we've had Windows 7, 8, 10, and so forth. I had a laptop that was about ten years old but still working just fine. But Windows stopped "supporting" its operating system. Then my PC with Windows 7 stopped functioning. I've had to buy new computers. And – when that happens – I also have to buy replacement versions of Word, PowerPoint, Excel, and so forth. Microsoft just rakes in the money. And ... it's annoying. For a while, I was furious with Bill Gates. But I notice that he's become quite a generous philanthropist. So, in a way, when I get robbed by Microsoft, I'm supporting some worthwhile charities. At least, that's my rationalization.

Lack of durability is another method of planned obsolescence ... durability of toys, of clothes, are examples.

Another case in point is luxury items that take advantage of customer desire and affordability strategized by planned obsolescence. Customers will opt to pay a substantial premium for products that often have finer craftsmanship, greater durability, and resale value. That takes us to another extreme: last forever and pay a premium.

But what happens to the luxury buyer, when the manufacturer starts to put the product and the name in the mass market? It makes the luxury buyer want to buy something else which is exclusive! This is perceived obsolescence!

The auto industry also practices phased obsolescence, as you all know, by coming up with new models.

Tesla, by updating software, is reducing obsolescence.

Lastly, product obsolescence is wasteful, it increases landfill, and it uses more resources. Post-COVID can we have more re-use and create value? It goes against what Kotler is suggesting (in the Journal of Creating Value), sell more useful and more necessary and NOT MORE.

Thus, buy durable brands in the first place that do not need extended warranties that cover products should they fail (unless they are designed to fail). Buy products where spares such as batteries are easily available. Look for retailers who repair and recycle old products safely. Buy used products that will last.

France has a law against planned obsolescence and went after iPhone and Apple, who admitted software slowed down older models! They also said older batteries slowed down the phones.

One solution is to make products a service. They do that for cell phone services in the USA, but they too ask you to upgrade to a better, newer phone. Service is a good idea if not linked to planned obsolescence. We need more ideas.

Can new manufacturers or existing one disrupt this practice by coming up with durable long-lasting products and create more value? Remember Kotler saying marketing is all about creating value.

* * *

My Terms or Yours: What Creates More Value?

We are all brought up to follow rules. Sometimes we are forced to … when we buy something, we find that we have to follow the terms of the seller. When we enter school, we have to toe the line with the terms of the school (both parents and children).

When we play with kids and animals, we often want to play with them on our terms; play when we want to, and how. We pay scant attention to whether the kid or the pet wants our attention then, or prefers to be alone or sleep. We want to play ball with them, and they want to read … who will prevail?

In the end parents and authority prevail, and the kids get used to following the terms, because they cannot change the parents, or the system.

The most enduring love is when it is on the loved one's terms and not just on the lover's terms. Yet we try to impose our terms on the loved one.

Lessons to be learnt:

Stakeholders do not want to live just with your terms. They want their terms to be taken into account. This is true whether you are an employee or a customer. Neither wants only your rules to prevail. For example, have you thought of the customer's rules? If the customer is much larger than you, you tend to follow the customer's terms.

This has best been brought out in Firms of Endearment by Raj Sisodia, Jag Sheth, and others. We all should have terms of endearment. Terms that give rather than take and are customer friendly.

Government and bureaucratic organizations are the worst. It is my way or the highway. Countries with economic strength always try to deal with you on their terms.

Companies have rules so that there is no confusion and they can exercise control, and these rules are made for their convenience (to hell with the customer's convenience). Health care is an example of not really caring about the customer's importance.

I understand you cannot make individual rules to suit individual stakeholders. Perhaps you can segment the customers by those who need more handholding, those that are savvier, those that have less time, and those that have a serious problem.

Even more serious is the issue of what terms do you dictate to AI. What can AI dictate to you? Should AI be allowed to dictate to you? And on what issues?

The least today's leaders and corporate chiefs and customer people should be understanding the other person or customer's terms and thinking about how to accept them. This thinking is the first step towards redesigning your own terms, because if you only think your terms are correct and will prevail you will not be able to get customers' eyeballs and differentiation.

All of us have to embrace the two-way door concept to create value. You can create value by accepting the terms of the other person completely. This is what true love is, true caring is. But it cannot always be a one-way street and has to be two ways to create the most value.

Chapter 15

Value Creation and Technology

Why Creating Value Is a Skill Needed for the Future with AI and Technology

McKinsey in the article "Defining the skills citizens will need in the future world of work" has said, and I quote that they will need to:

1. Add value beyond what can be done by automated systems and intelligent machines
2. Operate in a digital environment
3. Continually adapt to new ways of working and new occupations

While I agree these are necessary, I feel McKinsey has defined skills too narrowly in terms of the future of work and life. First and foremost, the skill needed is not just adding value but *creating* value to be able to manage and address the future of ourselves, our lives, our way of life (or what is left of it in the changing environment), and our work, to think of rewards and risks of AI.

One of the skills necessary is to understand that creating value also means creating the future. While digitizing and bringing in AI, one must:

1. Create value for, and ensure that the environment is managed and designed for the betterment of life, and not just for efficiency and for giving up our control because AI can do it better

2. Ensure our values and human values are incorporated
3. Have controls and checks for human intervention and control. And I add
4. Be continually adaptive to create continuing value
5. Become multi-disciplinary and multi-aware

These might sound trite, but the lure of technology is to do more with less, and that seems to be the technologist's endeavour becoming eventually the human endeavour. We cannot allow this.

Ejaz Ghani thinking of India in 2030 says there will be a rise of the middle class and there will be a demographic dividend; India will be part of the global talent race; an urban awakening; and India will be close to the largest digital economy; with a changing face of globalization. There will be green growth and gender will be a growth driver. The problem is managing the transition.

So, we need to re-skill to manage the future and do so by creating value. Digital democratization will make people more equal unless our AI does not allow it. How can this happen? By poor design. By letting AI discriminate (and this can happen by not giving the tools or training to or re-skilling people and many other factors).

Quickly, AI is now embedded everywhere.

OpenAI's GPT-3 engines and others generate texts that cannot be distinguished from human expression. And AI is becoming ubiquitous.

More reason for humans to be alert and on top of all this by value creation.

Denis Rothman states, you can either be the tool of AI or use it as a tool. Millions of micro-decisions will be made every day, and all humans put together will not be able to slow this down.

You have to have the right mindset and creating value is a mindset that can set you ahead and design smartly. Cross disciplinary thinking becomes imperative.

We have to manage the risk versus the value creation potential of AI. Only people with a creating value mindset of risk and value destruction potential can do this if they are AI savvy.

Another risk is being driven by the lure of technology without understanding the fundamentals:

A famous case of innovation gone terribly wrong is the Silicon Valley start-up *Juicero*. This company had raised $120 M from investors like Google Ventures. The company sold juice boxes and a $400 press machine meant to be the only way to squeeze the juice out. The start-up claimed the machine wielded four tons of force, but they were profoundly humiliated as *Bloomberg News* reported that a person could easily squeeze the juice only using their hands. In this case, a start-up created a very costly solution for a problem that did not even exist in the first place. See https://latamlist.com/how-to-create-value-for-your-customers -through-technology-and-innovation/.

Risks of artificial intelligence as told by Mike Thomas states there will be:

Automation-spurred job loss
Privacy violations
"Deepfakes"
Algorithmic bias caused by bad data
Socioeconomic inequality
Weapons automatization

"Once computers can effectively reprogram themselves, and successively improve themselves, leading to a so-called 'technological singularity' or 'intelligence explosion,' the risks of machines outwitting humans in battles for resources and self-preservation cannot simply be dismissed."

Thus, skilling is necessary not only to use and understand AI but to manage it and prevent a run-away AI catastrophe. People, governments, institutions, and companies need to combine to mitigate AI risks in the future.

The real risk is that greed and profits may make some people take shortcuts and not prevent the possible risks that can de-humanize the system.

* * *

Technology as a Potential Value Destroyer

Technology is ubiquitous. It dangles many advantages such as costs, speed, fewer human interventions etc. Technology is taking over the CEO's thinking, and influencing him/her.

Take, for example, bank CEOs. However, in adopting technology, they should not forget that they are first and foremost bankers and not technologists; that they should not be lured by technology to think technology first but must think of banking, customers, partners, delivery chains, and society first. Stakeholders and banking must come over technology. Fundamental thinking is important, i.e., a focus on banking. Then technology becomes a slave and not the driver of their banking business. Technology can become a value destroyer when CEOs think they are running technology companies. This thinking has to be avoided, and banking traditional thinking must endure, using technology as a tool.

Bill Winters, CEO of Standard Chartered, says that technology is delivering more products and that they have to be sure to understand the product is a banking product and not technology. If CEOs do not understand the banking product, technology cannot deliver the right solution.

Technology has become a business disruptor, giving rise to opportunities for many banks and start-ups. Artificial intelligence is also becoming a core function of technology, all potential value creators. Using Fintech and third-party software is often attractive for banks for apps, products etc. Blockchains, biometrics, cloud banking, chatbots, and zero trust systems are all being used now.

Technology inputs are dependent on human intervention, and often these technological wizards do not understand banking, customers, context etc. For example, my neighbourhood club requires a very complex login password, and I wonder why? Are the family jewels at risk? But the designer is not concerned and has put in a most difficult-to-crack criterion when not needed. Or he decides your phone number cannot be used for more than three or four services, requiring you to get a second phone!

Focusing on your core areas and zero trust may be a starting point for managing technology.

Unfortunately, today, people are forgetting that products are meant for customers and that the customer focus is more important than the product focus and definitely more than the technology focus.

Bill Winters focuses on customer convenience more than all the other factors a customer may value such as the product and understanding it and its cost, the relationship, the feeling of safety, and not being taken for a ride.

Customers may not care for technology unless the technology creates value for them, other than just a do-it-yourself solution. Very often net banking is much more cumbersome than paying cash. But paying cash requires people to get the cash, and keep it safely, and these trade-offs must be understood. On the other hand, paying bills automatically, getting online services for entering nominations, and transferring funds for understanding financial products to use them are useful results of technology.

Value disruption with technology can include:

- Technology and Service Interruptions. These include service interruptions physically for customers visiting banks.
- Security and Identity theft Concerns.
- Limitations on Deposits.
- Convenient but Not Always Faster.
- Lack of Personal Banker Relationship.

The scope of service is limited to what is on the menu and nothing else.

I deal with the State Bank of India and love human interaction, and whenever there is something on the online systems I do not understand or do not work, I get help from them. I have the best of both worlds! Unfortunately, two days ago at the Friends Colony Branch in Delhi, I had an unpleasant experience, because the technology was not working, and I needed human intervention which was so surly and reluctant. The combination of bad service and poor technology is the worst!

Big Technology is asking regulators for a level playing field with traditional banks, a level playing field required for fintech, big technology, and banks. Sure, big technology can improve efficiency and come up with new ideas (source: Chris Skinner's blog).

The key takeaways from a regulator's report are:

The introduction of the Regulator's report begins:

> *Technology firms such as Alibaba, Amazon, Facebook, Google and Tencent have grown rapidly over the last two decades. The business model of these "big techs" rests on enabling direct interactions among a large number of users. An essential by-product of their business is the large stock of user data which are utilized as input to offer a range of services that exploit natural network effects, generating further user activity. Increased user activity then completes the circle, as it generates yet more data.*

> *Building on the advantages of the reinforcing nature of the data-net-work-activities loop, some big techs have ventured into financial services, including payments, money management, insurance and lending. As yet, financial services are only a small part of their business globally. But given their size and customer reach, big techs' entry into finance has the potential to spark rapid change in the industry. It offers many potential benefits. Big techs' low-cost structure business can easily be scaled up to provide basic financial services, especially in places where a large part of the population remains unbanked. Using big data and analysis of the network structure in their established platforms, big techs can assess the riskiness of borrowers, reducing the need for collateral to assure repayment As such, big techs stand to enhance the efficiency of financial services provision, promote financial inclusion and allow associated gains in economic activity.*

> *At the same time, big techs' entry into finance introduces new elements in the risk-benefit balance. Some are old issues of financial stability and consumer protection in new settings. In some settings, such as the payment system, big techs have the potential to loom large very quickly as systemically relevant financial institutions. Given the importance of the financial system as an essential public infrastructure, the activities of big*

techs are a matter of broader public interest that goes beyond the imme-diate circle of their users and stakeholders.

There are also important new and unfamiliar challenges that extend beyond the realm of financial regulation as traditionally conceived. Big techs have the potential to become dominant through the advantages afforded by the data-network-activities loop, raising competition and data privacy issues. Public policy needs to build on a more comprehen-sive approach that draws on financial regulation, competition policy and data privacy regulation. The aim should be to respond to big techs' entry into financial services so as to benefit from the gains while limiting the risks. As the operations of big techs straddle regulatory perimeters and geographical borders, coordination among authorities – national and international – is crucial.

And ends with a call to change how firms are regulated.

Traditionally, financial regulation is aimed at ensuring the solvency of individual financial institutions and the soundness of the financial system as a whole. It also incorporates consumer protection goals. The policy instruments used to achieve these goals are well understood, rang-ing from capital and liquidity requirements in the case of banks to the regulation of conduct for consumer protection. When big techs' activity falls squarely within the scope of traditional financial regulation, the same principles should apply to them.

However, two additional features make the formulation of the policy response more challenging for big techs. First, big techs' activity in finance may warrant a more comprehensive approach that encompasses not only financial regulation but also competition and data privacy objectives. Second, even when the policy goals are well articulated, the specific policy tools should actually be shown to promote those objectives. This link between ends and means should not be taken for granted. This is because the mapping between policy tools and the ultimate welfare outcomes is more complex in the case of big techs. In particular, the policy tools that are aimed at traditional financial regulation objectives may also impinge on competition and data privacy objectives, and vice versa. These interactions introduce potentially complex trade-offs that do not figure in traditional financial regulation.

You decide if technology is a value creator or a value destroyer for banks.

* * *

CIOs Can Be True Value Creators

CIOs can be true Value Creators. Why aren't they and why are they not viewed as business value creators?

Adjunct to these questions is: why are they considered staff people? In a day and age where IT and ITES are so relevant and key to businesses, shouldn't they be line people?

A "line function" is one that directly advances an organization in its core work. This always includes production and sales, and sometimes also marketing. A "staff function" supports the organization with specialized advisory and support functions (Wiki definition).

Sadly, CIOs are not known to directly advance the organization's core work. Why? Why do they play second fiddle? The bigger leadership on big data, digital media etc. is taken by the marketing people, who are ill equipped to understand and use the technology. CIOs should be taking the lead, and holding Marketing's hands in using such technologies. They should take an evangelizing role in internet, intranet, and web-based solutions, in digital media and in big data, to mention a few areas.

Is this because traditional functions remain traditional? Or is it because the concept of Value Creation has not caught up with CIOs? Or do CIOs view efficiencies and controlling software development spends as Value Creation?, they should view leadership, in bringing in new technologies and getting others to use these wisely and usefully as value creation? How much time would be saved if they took the lead, and marketing followed their advice? Today CIOs get involved when there are IT problems or when someone asks them to address a particular software or digital media-related issue, or when they are instructed to build a platform.

An example of a proactive CIO is HP Global CIO and senior vice president Ramon Baez who explains in an interview with CIO publisher emeritus Gary Beach how the new business drivers of cloud and mobile contribute to the bottom and top lines. He also discusses IT costs, security, the need for top IT talent, and the increased speed necessary to compete in today's business environment. It used to take three weeks to provision a database. Now it takes five minutes in a cloud environment, says Baez.

Why can't he be considered a line guy?

Vishal Bindra, CEO of ACPL, a security and service firm in IT, had the following comments:

1. Many CIOs are not sure they can add any value. They listen to people like Gartner and KPMG and follow them "almost" blindly.

2. They are technology and not process/customer driven. Better processes and customer focus will have a more direct impact on business.
3. Unfortunately, in the last few years they have become a much-pampered lot by IT Product companies and they are becoming too biased in their decision-making.

On the other hand we have some great CIOs who have contributed and become an integral part of the organization's business, such as people at Apollo Tyres, Perfetti, and Maxlife. They have all been contributing to business and using "Information," not Technology.

Jeanne W. Ross and David F. Feeny of the Centre for Information Systems Research at the Sloan School of Management reached the conclusion that the Chief Information Officer has emerged as a critical executive position in most organizations. Increasingly, CIOs sit on firms' executive teams and help shape organizational strategy. His role is to be a Business Visionary.

Do CEOs need to re-assess their old-fashioned ideas of business organizations and give CIOs a line role? Do CIOs need to understand that creation of value is their job, or do they need to understand what value they can create? Do business schools need to teach Value Creation for CIOs, and leadership roles? The answer is an emphatic YES.

CIOs need to ready themselves for leadership and Value Creation roles. They have to move from being functional to business mindsets.

Your comments are welcome.

Chapter 16

Value Creation for Suppliers and Partners

Are You Adding Value to Your Suppliers and Partners?

You don't get paid for the hour. You get paid for the value you bring to the hour.

Jim Rohn

Purchasing professionals are focused on adding value to their companies, and so are sales and marketing professionals selling to them.

Both of these professionals, however, focus on price or cost as the major source of value creation for their companies. Sales professionals want to discuss their value proposition, but the discussion often deteriorates into a price one.

Assuming both purchasing and selling companies recognize that mutual value and partnership have to be created or co-created, could they not discuss and negotiate this? Could they not discuss how to co-create value? Could they not agree that value creation is what additional the supplier should give at what price?

Let's start with generally what the thinking is:

I am adding value to the supplier by buying from him (helping him fill out capacity, helping him make money); how much can we get by outsourcing to the supplier versus making on our own (and we do not fully price our self-manufacture).

DOI: 10.4324/9781003381624-16

My role is to increase total profit (not just reduce the total cost of acquisition). Shouldn't I look at the total value added? Shouldn't the supplier do this? Does the supplier understand what creates value for the buyer?

Both these negotiating parties must understand that there has to be a sharing of value, and a co-creation of value.

How do you go about doing this? A Value Co-Creation Model is shown in Figure 16.1.

The Financial and non-Financial benefits are shown below:

The Financial benefit chart shows higher profits due to better collaboration and fewer delays and mistakes, sharing of profits (reduced price to start with profit incentives), lower costs for changes, spares, inventories etc. (Figure 16.2).

The Non-Financial benefits include happier employees/bosses, reduced time to market, happier customers, better acceptance, and so forth (Figure 16.3).

Strategic Partnership: Purchasing-Supplier Value
Co-Creation Model (Purchaser View)

Figure 16.1   Value Co-Creation Model

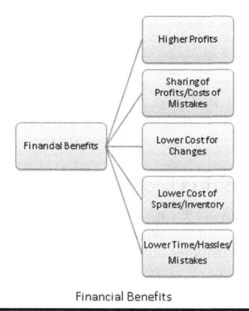

Financial Benefits

Figure 16.2   Financial Benefit Chart

Figure 16.3   Non-Financial Benefits

Isn't this a better model than just beating down the supplier on price, and trying to commoditize his offering? And building a value chain.

Go from a supplier evaluation to a partnership collaboration.

If you cannot do this, then maybe an artificial intelligence system to buy and sell based on value (benefits –price) should replace the human purchasing person, as co-created value and collaborations are not required and price is king!

* * *

The Supplier Strikes Back

As Customer advocates, we tend to see the Customer's viewpoint. We want the supplier to understand and pander to the Customer and provide Customer delight!

But do we ever consider how Customers treat suppliers? Suppliers (whether they have B- or C-type consumers) may have been mistreated, or their people ill-treated. An example is a service person who visits a customer at an appointed time and the customer is not there. Or a customer gives a cheque that bounces. Or he returns an item, after using some of it to get a refund. Some of these are repeat offenders.

In my book *Customer Value Investment: Formula for Sustained Business Success*, I quote Carlos Cordon of IMD who says that the crude reality is that he knows of no company that measures whether it is an attractive Customer to its suppliers, although most companies measure and re-measure every single action of suppliers. Chief purchasing officers can tell you about the "on-time delivery" or "quality track record" of, and other information on a supplier. Chief purchasing officers if asked about how attractive they are to their suppliers as a Customer will probably answer, "Yeah, that's important, but we do not measure it." Companies talk about "relationship" and sometimes that meant "relation-shit," or about "win-win" and that meant the same guy (the Customer) winning twice. No wonder some suppliers are now calling for revenge.

Thus it is important to treat a supplier like a Customer and understand his needs if you want to get the best out of him. We want to control our Customers and our suppliers. Really, we should remember to understand their needs and treat them right.

Cordon gives the example of a steel outage at Nissan causing them to shut down for 5 days. He wonders if this happened because Nissan was too tough with suppliers.

I spent time on a Customer Value course for the Indian Army on creating value for suppliers, so that the suppliers would work hard to ensure the Army was never shorted of supplies.

Thus business is all about getting to know the needs of Customers, employees, and suppliers, and adding value to and consequently getting them to do their best for you.

I have many other B2B examples. For example, Dow caused a resin outage at Continental Can years ago.

I had a reverse example. I made a deal with a resin supplier at 34.5 cents a pound for an annual supply, when the going rate was 33–33.5 cents a pound. Three months later due to oil prices and shortages, the spot price went up to 60 cents a pound. The supplier honoured our price for the longest time possible because we had been lenient and understanding when negotiating. They increased prices fast for our competition.

I had a boss, who taught me the art of reverse negotiation. He said always be nice to suppliers and they will work their b ... s off for you. And so we were not the toughest negotiators, but in return we got their loyalty, and the best service and support.

Do we want supplier loyalty? To do so create value for the supplier.

Is this important for Customers to understand? And that a relationship is a two-way one?

Chapter 17

Value and Values

Driving Businesses from Values: Values Create Value (And Higher Profits)

Values and governance are often the motherhood part of corporate statements.

Management often does not realize that values indeed create value for all stakeholders and essentially increase shareholder wealth. Raj Sisodia, David Wolfe, and Jag Sheth, in their book *Firms of Endearment*, demonstrate the power of values and value, and caring for enduring business success. Firms of Endearment outperformed S&P 500 indexes, 10 to 1 over a 10-year horizon and outperformed Jim Collins's "Good to Great" companies 3.1 times in this period. In fact, companies move up a Maslow-like hierarchy to capital actualization or corporate actualization where the company's values create value for employees, customers, partners, and shareholders. Building your values into strength requires the implementation of Total Value Management.

Total Value Management helps you create value for all stakeholders and increase loyalty and referral sales, market share, and profitability. It makes the company a better place to work and increases teamwork while reducing pressure on price. It helps you focus on your value systems.

In today's e-age, and increasingly aware and educated Customers, companies must reinvent themselves to be leaders for the future and to co-create value. Managers must forget conventional learning to equip themselves for their own personal and corporate sustained success.

Total Value Management (TVM) is about value creation for all stakeholders and balancing them to gain competitive advantage. While the Customer has

DOI: 10.4324/9781003381624-17

centre stage, adding value to the employees, suppliers, and associates (supply and delivery chain, including dealers and retailers) becomes important. TVM examines whether the old norms of business must change, and a focus on the "endearment" of the stakeholders should be espoused. It helps companies understand the true value of having real values.

We have found through various studies with Tata Fertilizers, Tata Power, Godrej, and others that Values create value, apart from immediate results in reduced complaints, better teamwork and output, better pricing, improved loyalty and sales, market share, and profits. Firms like Tata Power that emphasize environmental friendliness have higher scores from customers on image and brand and on buying decisions by them. At Tata Fertilizer, a sense of belonging to the Tata family built the image and buying propensity. In both cases, price became less of an issue!

Expanding the Tata Power example, we found that about 60% of why customers preferred their power provider was its image, and 65% of the image was based on sustainability, health and environment, and the company's efforts to reduce the cost of electric supply. The rest of the image was based on being trustworthy and reliable. Thus working on all these issues would increase the image of the company and therefore, the preference (and the desirability to do business with), thereby increasing customer value, attractiveness to customers, and possible price. Thus focussing on ESG is important for sales of power companies.

Thus, Values create value.

Unfortunately, Values of a company adorn the walls of a company or the annual report. Management thinks these are nice-to-do statements. Companies think of Values such as being environmentally friendly and trustworthy as nice things to do and treat Values issues as cost centres. Our value studies show that Values create value for the customer and the stakeholders and can increase the image of the company and its own value creation.

Often customers will pay more to a trustworthy, more environmentally friendly, and well-governed company. This increases the bottom line, and companies should look at implementing Values as a revenue centre.

My advice to corporations is to build on your values. Also create employee, customer, and other stakeholder value, and when you do so assiduously, you will find this will create value and wealth for all stakeholders. Corporate Values become really an important part of doing business and lead to corporate actualization and increased shareholder wealth.

Total CVM is enunciated in Gautam Mahajan's book: *Total Customer Value Management: Transforming Business Thinking.*

* * *

Value and VBA

Chris Baker, Peter Stokes, and Jessica Lichy wrote in EFMD Global Focus: Volume 09 Issue 02, 2015 about *Values, beliefs and attitudes: The implications for organizational culture:*

> We find that the implications of Values, Beliefs and Attitudes (VBA) are much wider. VBA can create or destroy Value, depending on whether they are positive or negative. What Value means, and the importance of relevance of VBA in creating or destroying Value through VBA is examined. Lastly, we discuss how creating Value can impact VBA.

The VBA article suggests sources of VBA as education, family values and experience, peer pressure, culture, the media, company ethos, business practices, personality, wisdom with maturity, friends, religion, and spiritual values and expectations by others.

These are in sync with the Value thinking on Values and Attitudes supporting Value Creation.

"Values are principles, standards or qualities that an individual or group of people hold in high regard. These values guide the way we live our lives and the decisions we make," they said.

According to them, Value is a belief of what something is worth, or whether it is important to us, which we consider to be of worth. They gave an example,

> Some people may see great value in saving the world's rainforests. However, a person who relies on the logging of a forest for their job may not place the same value on the forest as a person who wants to save it.

Values can influence many of the judgements we make as well as have an impact on the support we give clients. It is important that we do not view client's decisions based on our values. We should always work from the basis of supporting the client's values. https://sielearning.tafensw.edu.au/MCS/CHCAOD402A/chcaod402a_csw/knowledge/values/values.htm

We define Value as creating good for and improving the wellbeing and worth of ourselves and others. Value and value creation are natural to and basic in human behaviour and endeavour and should be at the centre of our attention (Mahajan, 2016 Value Creation; Mahajan 2017, Journal of Creating Value (JCV) 3.2 Value Dominant Logic).

Value Creation is a process that is easier to define than value which is generally intangible, though we try to define and label it as tangible. Our definition of Value Creation is executing pro-active, conscious, inspired, or imaginative and even normal actions that increase the overall good and wellbeing, and the worth of ideas, goods, services, people, or institutions including society, and all stakeholders (like employees, customers, partners, shareholders, and society), and ideas waiting to happen. In fact, value creation is a basic requirement for sustained human flourishing (Mahajan JCV 2015; Mahajan, JCV, 2016a, 2-1; Mahajan, Value Creation, 2016b).

Mahajan 2017 framed eight principles of Value Creation. We examine these to see how VBA impacts these principles:

The first principle: Value and its creation are a basic requirement or a necessity for sustained human flourishing (Mahajan, 2016a, 2016b) and the advancement of human activity, caring, wellbeing and behaviour, and progress and creativity. Value and its creation are important in all fields, education and academics, society and government, and social work, innovation, entrepreneurship, and business. It impacts humanity and society. It is an essential trait for executives and leaders. It goes beyond the classic business/social ecosystem. It can be latent value or value waiting to happen, which when perceived could provide the basis for greater value.

Your traits such as caring and your Values (integrity, ethics) and attitudes (VBA) impact Value.

The second principle: Value is proactively exceeding what is basically expected of you or your job. It is going beyond your functional and routine roles to adding and creating value in your ecosystem. Value creation can be planned or spontaneous, and in both functional and emotional thinking, and should be consciously created.

Values go beyond your job and hence create value, and you are known as a person of Value. Your attitude impacts the Value you create. Thus VBA impacts Value.

The third principle: just creating value for yourself is not enough. True value comes from creating value for others who turn around and say you have created value. Value is created and co-created for you by others using your potential value or your potential to see value (this, in a sense, is the real reason why companies are in the marketplace, because creating value for customers co-creates value for their stakeholders). What is interesting is that such value is not just the realm of the producer; it is also the realm of the user. Co-creation is where mutual value is expanded together.

Your attitudes towards others create Value. When people see you have Values, they think you are a person of Value.

The fourth principle: Value and its creation impact all stakeholders, that is, you, your colleagues, your employees, your partners (supply chain, delivery chain, unions), and society to create resounding value for the customer and thereby for the shareholder (Kumar & Reinartz, 2016). Customers tend to buy or use those products or services that they perceive create greater value (or greater relative value) for them than competitive offers. It is essential for executives and leaders to create higher value for their customers than competition can.

VBA by impacting Value creates Value for others and society.

The fifth principle: Value and its creation leverage a person's or an organization's or an actor's potential, learning, and creativity while making it meaningful and worthwhile for people and actors to belong and perform, both physically and emotionally.

Value increases with a creative and innovative mindset and attitudes.

The sixth principle: Value and its creation presents a very powerful decision-making tool for companies to select actions, programmes, strategies, and resolutions of dilemmas and choices for individuals and the actors that can increase the actor's longevity (prevention of destruction) and profitability.

The seventh principle: Value and its creation must exceed value destruction or reduce negative value and be done consciously (not just done unconsciously as often is the case today). You must create more value than you consume, or else the process will become destructive. The sharing of value has to be equitable; otherwise, value will be destroyed for one or more actors. Often by not being caring, governments and people negate the impact of the value they are trying to create.

Sometimes companies try to extract more value than they create (for employees, partners, customers, and society), and this is destructive.

This again depends on an individual's VBA.

The eighth principle: Values (what you stand for, integrity, honesty, fairness etc.) create value. This holds for all actor-to-actor interactions (Mahajan, 2016b).

This is the main reason VBA impacts Value Creation.

VBA is important because your values influence your actions. One must not let our values prevail over customers, but we should try to adjust to their values, as long as they are legal.

The VBA article states, "In recent years, human capital (the skills and knowledge for operating in the workplace) and social capital (the value-creating relationships in the workplace) have received considerable attention."

We prefer to use the definitions below:

Human capital is a term popularized by Gary Becker, an economist from the University of Chicago, and Jacob Mincer who refer to the stock of knowledge, habits, social, and personality attributes, including creativity, embodied in the ability to perform labour so as to produce economic value.

Another definition is the collective skills, knowledge, or other intangible a ssets of individuals that can be used to create value for individuals, their employers, or their community. To us the value does not have to be economic, it could be emotional for example.

Social capital is defined by the OECD as "networks together with shared norms, values and understandings that facilitate co-operation within or among groups." In this definition, we can think of networks as real-world links between groups and individuals. Think of networks of friends, family networks, networks of former colleagues, and so on.

Social capital provides the glue which facilitates co-operation, exchange, and innovation and gets us to think about the New Economy.

We mention social and human capital since Value creates all kinds of human and social value. Hence it is important to create value. VBA plays a role in creating value.

VBA drives Value which creates human and social capital. The VBA article goes on to define the drivers of behaviour:

> *Drivers of behaviour*
> These centred on issues of the bottom line; employee satisfaction and happiness; spiritual capital (doing things well and in a good spirit); relating all the aforementioned into the "bigger picture" – macro-global changes and pressures on the micro-individual dimensions.

The VBA article goes on to discuss the Impact of VBA *on individuals and the corporate.*

Behaviour: Illustrations of working together and sharing to get through hard times – for example, taking and sharing reductions in hours to ensure people keep their jobs albeit on reduced incomes during order downturns. Identifying and reporting deceitful or dishonest behaviour. Being mindful of how to talk to each other and clients.

Thus, by impacting culture, behaviour, and attitudes, VBA impacts Value.

One important driver of Value is Values. In VBA, integrity is outlined as an important "value(s)." We have found that in many business objectives values are used and propounded as core values which in truth are no more than traits. Enron for example has communications, respect, excellence, and integrity as traits (though called values. Only integrity is a true "value(s)").

Core Values and Traits

Companies and individuals need to develop a Sense of Value. The sense of value includes the feel and intuition and insight of value. Intuitions depend on expertise, experience, and knowledge. Insights help us develop new thinking.

We know from experience and data that Values create Value (Mahajan 2012).

Leaders must have values: morals and ethics etc. It is not to say that leaders without values and morals are not successful. Or those who bend values are not successful.

Morals and ethics are different. Morals are one's own principles and thinking about what is right or wrong. Morals are about our own codes of behaviour. These depend on what we think is right or wrong, based on our faith systems, and the society and environment we live in.

Ethics is what is seen or expected by external rules. Ethics are the code of conduct we apply to others and society. Values are about doing good and being good.

There is an overlap in ethics and morals. Often, morals and ethics can be the same. Killing someone falls into this. However, in war, killing an enemy may be ethically sanctioned.

As an example, your morals may include being honest, being religious, and being truthful.

Ethics could include integrity, honesty, transparency, fairness etc.

Many leadership ideas focus on core values and they confuse values and traits:

George Mason University cites traits (and calls them core values):

Respect, as demonstrated by self-respect and respecting others regardless of differences; treating others with dignity, empathy, and compassion; and the ability to earn the respect of others. Making a Difference, integrity, authenticity, courage, service, humility, wisdom etc.

A larger list of traits is:

Ambition, competency, individuality, equality, *integrity*, service, responsibility, accuracy, respect, dedication, diversity, improvement, enjoyment/fun, loyalty, credibility, honesty, innovativeness, teamwork, excellence, accountability, empowerment, quality, efficiency, dignity, collaboration, stewardship, empathy, accomplishment, courage, wisdom, independence, security, challenge, influence, learning, compassion, friendliness, discipline/order, generosity, persistence, optimism, dependability, flexibility.

These are all traits. The only item that fits into values is integrity. Others are ethics, honesty, morality, and fairness.

So leadership training does not focus that highly on values. Traits are often called core values and shape the mission and style and the culture. But the culture and style must reflect basic values.

In business jargon, values are called ethics, and traits are core values. In our definition core values are not traits but actually the ethical and moral framework of what is right and what is wrong, fair, and not fair.

"Values" refer to moral standards, as we have learnt earlier. Value indicates that which is important to people, those things and conditions that enhance the experience of living. As the term is used in the Soka Gakkai International (SGI), value points to the positive aspects of reality that are brought forth or generated when we creatively engage with the challenges of daily life.

Attitudes

What are attitudes? We look at the values, and how they are upheld. By an underlying culture, and attitudes.

Attitudes are based on what we like or do not like. They are impacted by our training, background, and environment, and sometimes by our emotions and feelings, mainly our likes or dislikes, though they do not remain restricted to our emotions and feelings. Attitudes impact our behaviour and how we are seen by others, and how we behave towards others.

Attitudes can change and can be impacted by our reflection and future learning, awareness, and observations.

Attitudes and mindsets are similar.

The Dictionary suggests that a person's usual attitude or mental state is his or her **mindset**. If **you** have an environmentalist **mindset**, **you** probably bring your own bags to the grocery store. ... Sometimes, a **mindset** spreads between people in a group and colours the entire group's outlook – psychologists call this groupthink.

https://www.vocabulary.com/dictionary/mindset

In a **fixed mindset**, people believe their basic qualities, like their intelligence or talent, are simply **fixed** traits. They spend their time documenting their intelligence or talent instead of developing them. They also believe that talent alone creates success – without effort. They're wrong.

https://mindsetonline.com/whatisit/about/

Alternatively, "in a **growth mindset**, people believe that their most basic abilities can be developed through dedication and hard work – brains and talent are just the starting point. This view creates a love of learning and a resilience that is essential for great accomplishment," writes Dweck (August 29, 2013, edglossary.org/growth-mindset/).

A **positive** person never wants to give up trying. A **negative** person is so cynical they toss their hands up in the air and say, "What's the use?!" A person with a **positive attitude** (welcomes) tomorrow as an opportunity to change things for the better.

Hence an attitude is important to have and maintain positive Values. A negative mindset can lead to disaster of values or a destruction of values.

Encapsulating this into a chart of VBA and Culture, we can see how the organization and its culture and climate and the attitudes/mindsets of individuals can impact the Values of an organization (Figure 17.1).

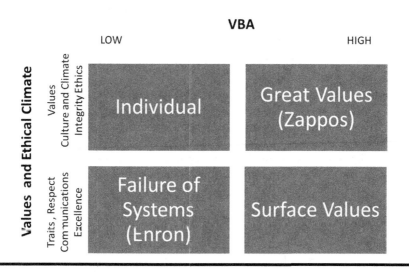

Figure 17.1   Value Beliefs and Attitudes versus Values and Ethics

* * *

Corporate Unconsciousness: A Wakeup Call

Have you asked yourself:

> Will I make more money by being dishonest or not being customer friendly?
> Am I at risk and my company at risk by having lower value standards?
> Will my values make customers prefer me and/or pay more?
> Will I be more successful as a firm of endearment (firms that endear themselves to their stakeholders)?
> What stops me from being one?
> Am I afraid my competition will overtake me by doing something unethical?
> Should I have a conscience, should my company have a conscience?
> Why? Read on.

Naturally, you should wonder if corporate consciousness makes sense or if we should remain in a state of corporate unconsciousness. Corporate consciousness, the very soul of a company, is generally missing in many companies, though it is masked by things like CSR and motherhood mission statements. In the book *Firms of Endearment*, the authors (Sisodia, Wolfe, and Sheth) espouse share of heart over a share of wallet, the emotionally intelligent leader, and the new Capitalism of Caring. Surely enough returns for you to think about corporate consciousness. Is eight times higher returns good enough reason for you to read on and think of changing?

Think of politicians seeking more power, and the impact of greed and corruption. We all look at greed and corruption (depending on who we are and where we are) with disregard and shrug them away as being necessary, or with contempt or even sometimes with revulsion. We do little about it because success is measured in money, position, and power. So is a corporate success. The ends are often more important than the means.

Think of companies such as Godrej and Tatas, Costco, Johnson & Johnson, Traders Joe, Whole Foods, and Google (and I am sure you know others). Are they disadvantaged for being honest and ethical or at least trying to be?

The economic downturn is a result of greed and selfishness in business – and the times are definitely changing. The public is standing up against the ethical and moral bankruptcy of certain corporations guilty of a "what's in it for me" mentality throughout the western world. The consumer is less likely to accept irresponsible business practices, quoting from Streinbrecher. He says: In my mind, corporate consciousness can be broken down into the three "R"s: **Reverence, Respect, and Responsibility for people and the environment.**

So what is corporate consciousness about? Is it about being honest and straightforward, or is it about bending the rules to get ahead? Does it mean making less money?

The answer is simple. Corporate consciousness means building a culture of consciousness and awareness and doing the right thing for stakeholders, and as leaders in culture consciousness. Doing this is called conscious capitalism and it means *making more money in the future.*

The phrase "conscious capitalism" was coined by Muhammad Yunus, recipient of a 2006 Nobel Peace Prize for his creation in 1983 of Bangladesh's pioneering microlender, Grameen Bank.

What we are finding is that conscious capitalism or corporate consciousness builds a culture of trust, ethics, and teamwork of caring for people. In such an environment, value creation flourishes, where you create value for people: employees, customers, partners, and owners.

We have learnt from my previous articles that:

Values Create Value (see my article *CSR or Capital Consciousness,** and my article *The Legal Case against Shareholder Capitalism*†).

We learn that creating value for people is important. We learn that our business is a people business and if we create value for the people we deal with such as employees, customers, and partners, we create greater value (read profits) for ourselves.

So forget profit capitalism, stop corporate unconsciousness, and build a company with a soul and start conscious capitalism.

Conscious capitalism, conscious leadership, and conscious culture become the norm (or core values).

Corporate capitalism and the stakeholder perspective become a result rather than the motive.

Corporate consciousness culture is the real bottom line. A company with a well-developed culture, open to all that its members want to bring, easily outperforms competitors. They will create value for stakeholders and themselves. Culture and consciousness are powerful new partners that will decide sustainability and profitability and value creation in the new economy.

I hope you will say: I promote the creation of a Statement of Corporate Consciousness. I will not masquerade by using buzzwords and by doing business as usual. You agree this will not work. The thriving, high-performing environment is transforming the hearts and minds of leaders to generate a new mindset

---

* https://customervaluefoundation.wordpress.com/2012/05/22/csr-or-capital-conscious ness/

† https://customervaluefoundation.wordpress.com/2012/07/09/the-legal-case-against-share holder-capitalism/

in business that will see us using the right tools and the right values for prosperity and universal wellbeing.

Bottom line – if you aren't on the Corporate Consciousness bandwagon, you'd better hop on quickly. These issues aren't going away any time soon – at least not in the foreseeable future. Let us help you become true value creators

Be the change you want to see in the world.

(Mahatma Gandhi)

Chapter 18

Value Waiting to Happen and Innovation

Value Waiting to Happen

What you can do about creating disruptive value for yourself?

This elusive word value, which we all seek but do not always find … Is it there, is it discovered, or is it created?

Is it a two-edged sword, where on the one hand it is created and on the other side it is diluted?

Or is it a win–win situation? Value is created for both sides (or co-created?)

In my definition, there is latent or potential value. Value that exists but is not noticed. This is value waiting to happen.

I am going to give a few examples:

1. Where value is shared with the customer and the provider gets little value

Google search, free: creates great value for us customers, and very little for the company or disproportionately less (at least when it started, and for a number of years after that). Is it a win–win? Is this because Google had a long-term policy?

Giftivism and pay what you like: restaurants (Karma Kitchen in Berkeley) or eye clinics (Arvind Eye Hospital) are an example, where you pay what you want, and your payment could fund or pay for others who come after you. The high throughput this causes lowers the cost per patient and payment to doctors per

DOI: 10.4324/9781003381624-18

patient, increases value for customers, and reduces costs of supplies like medicine, stent etc.

Nipun Mehta in a Ted Talks said instead of showing value we were creating value. What can we give rather than what can we get? (https://www.youtube.com/watch?v=kpyc84kamhw).

2. Where value is created for the customer and the provider and simultaneously destroying value for someone else

Uber: cars are being used sparingly (they stand idle for most of the day). Uber increases utilization, and so fewer cars will be needed, a loss situation for car makers, and a win situation for consumers who get transportation on demand.

3. Where value is not noticed but emerges

Steve Vargo talks about value emerging. We sometimes do not notice it but it emerges in unexpected ways. He gives an example of hydrogen and water, both not moist; but when combined water emerges, an entirely different form from the inputs. We must look for such value emergence possibilities.

Look around you. Do you notice value that is staring us in the face and waiting to happen? Examples are:

In India, the helpless service people like independent plumbers and electricians who could not own phones can now be in touch with their customers, do more with their lives, and be reached by the customer (sharing their time effectively). This was waiting to happen and did not happen by design but happened as these people acquired cell phones and became connected.

Audhesh Paswan, Associate Dean of Northern Texas University, talked about the value creation of Bollywood culture. It exposes India and Indian culture to countries in Asia, Europe, the Middle East, and the Americas. People are now learning Bollywood dance.

Had the Indian Foreign Service/Indian Government looked at this as a way of making India known and Indian culture popular, they would have promoted Bollywood in these countries and converted latent value into real value years ago, rather than latent value evolving as a matter of course.

A similar example is the Indian brain drain, which was bemoaned by everyone including the Government, because educated Indians were leaving India. Today, everyone says wow! How smart. We have Indians around the world contributing in so many different spheres and becoming recognized. Most send money back to India. Others come back and contribute to India. Latent value was not developed and not harnessed. It just happened.

When driverless cars happen, where can you create value? In parking solutions, in making cars available where needed, in refuelling/re-energizing options, in downsizing cars, in making single-person modules or pods, and by redesigning roads. The ideas are endless, the value can be huge. And what do you do with unemployed drivers?

Or in the future your personal drone that can carry luggage and convert into a seat flying from your home into a plane to your assigned area. No waiting time, no check in. Everything is pre-checked. Imagine the savings in time and the increased convenience. The planes are parked for shorter times and can be utilized for longer times. And imagine the exit from the planes. Your drone flies off to your destination.

And security systems, to add value for those seeking security or those seeking to penetrate security. From invisibility solutions to overwritten videos, from molecular keys for locks to … (let your imagination run. See what you'd like to see, and ask why it isn't there).

And when this latent or potential value is noticed, we call it disruptive technology or innovation. Be aware of potential value (learn to become aware, because value exists but it has to be seen, it has to be noticed and appreciated, like beauty). Latent value has to be nurtured and built into real value by you. It then has to be shared (or co-created with customers).

Examples include adhesives used in surgery to close wounds, based on observing how lizards stick to walls and using this technology.

Observing how leaves 200 feet high in a tree get nutrition: MIT scientists designed a pump using virtually no energy.

Understanding cat's eyes and ability to see in the dark to make road reflectors. Percy Shaw noticed that cat's eyes were reflecting light and discovered a mirror like substance in cat's eyes that reflected light.

Or how Velcro was created after its inventor noted how a dog taken on a walk through a forest got burrs on his coat.

Disruption is the waking up of people, becoming aware of the latent value.

You can be a disruptor and an innovator, too. Look for potential value. Value is everywhere around you. You have to notice it and build the latent value into real value. You can use any of the techniques above.

Appendix A

Guide to Customer Value Creation Definitions

Some of these are taken from *Customer Value Investment: Formula for Sustained Business Success* by Gautam Mahajan. The reader can replace customers with stakeholders also.

Add Value to the Employee	Employees consider Value to be the benefits they get (such as the association with the company, what they learn, what they can contribute, and the relationship with management), and what they earn and what perks they get. Value added employees tend to stay with companies and can add Value to the Customers and the company.
Attribute Trees	These are developed after the Customer waterfall of needs (also called Customer journey), pinpointing attributes of importance to the Customer. Attribute trees have a price branch (actual price, cost of doing business, and cost of ownership) and a quality branch (of goods, brands/relationships, and services).

Avoid Commodity Hell	Understand the key drivers of Customer business success. Discover new methods and opportunities for Customer benefit. Build these into a strategy and implement the strategy. In effect, increase the Value to Customers, thus co-creating the Customer experience. Prevent your Company from going into a commodity death spiral. De-commoditization starts with increasing Value.
Brand Equity	Brand equity is not only the advertised brand but also is impacted by the brand equity of the employees. The brand equity of employees when they do things well will improve the total brand equity.
Brand Loyalty	Initially it meant Customers being loyal to a specific brand. Today, the brand has to be loyal to the Customer! The brand must deliver on its promise. The brand must meet the Customer's expectations and Values if the organization is to expect loyalty and repeat purchases.
Build a Relationship Which Is About:	Accessibility, responsiveness, knowledgeable people, promptness, promises kept, being kept informed, follow up, no surprises, doing it right.
Business of a Company	Eventually, the business of any corporation is to create Value for its stakeholders, the investors, and the Customers. The Customer Value investment is the best outlay you can make for sustained business success and for increasing ROI. So, you need a chief Customer Value Creator and a chief investor Value Creator reporting to the CEO, and thus you build a Customer-focused organization. There is a higher purpose described later.
Business Processes	Often designed from the point of view of the company and purely for their own convenience. Processes should be for the convenience of the Customer. Processes should be Customer-centric.

Chief Customer Officer	Companies' chief customer officer, who is a Customer champion and should cut across all functions to make the company, its processes, and its Customer interaction custom centric, should be a board-level person. The purpose is not to take complaints but to ensure the entire company is working together to eliminate Customer complaints. Departmental Silos have to be broken to promote Customer-centricity.
Communication	Communication of Customer data within the organization. Communication with employees and touch points is important for making them think through Customer issues and aligning them and motivating them to focus on the Customer. Communication of data to the Customer is important, particularly where you are better than competition.
Companies Should Work On	Making Customers own the relationship. Building a partnership with the Customer. Giving the Customer a worthwhile experience. Co-creating the Customer experience. Developing Customer DNA (do not annoy) into the design of processes and touching.
Competitive Profiles	Facilitate tabulating the CVA (Customer Value added) scores on various attributes. Enable you to see where you are better or worse than your competition, and where you need to improve.
Concept of a Business	No longer business selling to consumers (**B2C**). Now, it is consumers buying from business (**C2B**). How easy is it for the **Customer** to interact with the **Business**?
Cost of Retaining Customers	It is far less than the cost of acquiring new Customers. This cost of acquiring and retaining can be determined and the Value for the Customer can be calculated.

Creating Value	Value Creation is a necessary step for management transformation to Customer orientation. Value Creation means doing good and increasing the wellbeing of people and institutions etc. Creation is executing proactive, conscious, inspired, and imaginative actions that Create better gains or value (costs or benefits or both) for Customers and all stakeholders.
Creating Value Alliance	A global alliance of creating value professionals and of learning and networking to get more value creation education and understanding and usage.
Customer Advocates	Customer advocacy is a specialized form of Customer service in which companies focus on what is best for the Customer. It is a change in a company's culture that is supported by Customer-focused Customer service and marketing techniques.
Customers as Ambassadors	A good Customer Ambassador recommends you to his network. A great Brand Ambassador also has a virtual social network where he can and does refer you.
Customer as Assets	Customers are assets because, if treated properly, they can ensure an ongoing stream of revenue. The Customer assets can appreciate or depreciate; depending on how it is maintained and handled, the Customer assets can be shown on your balance sheet, which impacts the way an investor views you. Companies need a specific strategy to grow and nurture Customer assets (as the Customer is indispensable to our business, as without him, we have no business).
Customer Attractiveness	How attractive Customers are to the company.
Customer's Bill of Rights	They are important for the Customer and the employees, because they set the direction of what to expect. Should be visible and available to Customers. Should be implemented. A circle of promises is needed within the company to ensure the promises in the Bill of Rights are kept.

Customer Capital	Asset Value of current Customer's Value of existing relationship (number of relationship times the average Value of each relationship + Value of potential future earnings from existing Customers + Value of referral power – cost of retention).
Customer-centricity	Customer-centricity is a euphemism for "creating customer value." All parts of the company fccused on the customer, who is priority number 1.
Customer Champion	Companies need a Customer champion who is a senior officer. In a perfect Customer-oriented world, you'll have a Chief Customer Officer and many Customer champions.
Customer Collaboration	Customer Collaboration is a form of loyalty as the Customer collaborates and co-creates with you.
Customer Conduits	Are generally top driven by the CEO and his staff and are designed to have a common thought process in the company on the Customer. All people in the company need to be sensitized to the importance of the Customer and be led by a Customer mission statement.
Customer's DNA	What annoys Customers? Do Not Annoy (DNA) Customers.
Customer Effort	The effort a Customer has to expend on interacting with, thinking of, or working with a product and the company.
Customer Experience	All of the interactions a Customer has with a company and its products, as perceived by the Customer. Includes conscious and subconscious and emotional feelings.
Customer Equity	It is similar to Customer capital.
Customer Franchise	Value of present and future Customer relationship, or Customer Capital + Customer Momentum.

Customer Hugging and Touching	Everyone in a company who comes into direct or indirect contact with a Customer is a touch point, "hug" your Customers, and care about them. Very often "touching" is outsourced to call centres or downstream in the chain to retailers and agents, whereas companies need to find a way of touching Customers directly, CEOs should spend a day a week with their Customers discovering if they are meeting Customers' expectations and how service and other offerings can be improved.
Customer Journey	The journey that the Customer has to make to deal with the company. It is also the journey seen by the Customer as the company reaches out to the Customer. Company employees often have to make a journey within the company to fulfil the Customer's needs; often this journey is forced onto the Customer (for example, call so and so). Used to be called the waterfall of needs.
Customer Lifetime Value	The Value of, or revenue from, a Customer in terms of the business potential he represents for you over the life of your relationship with them. The revenue from potential referrals from that Customer.
Customer Metrics	Measure what is important to Customers. Obtain information from him or on him, and ask him what is important to him, directly or indirectly, in order to measure what he deems important.
Customer Momentum	The ability to attract and sustain a new Customer. The ability to increase wallet share for existing Customers.
Customer Relationship Management Program	Essentially process-oriented, passive, and don't touch Customers. Must move ahead to CVM. Often thought of as "loyalty programs," which they aren't.
Customer Relevance	What is relevant to the Customer, when, and where. Instead of selling what you have, you sell him what is relevant to him at a point in time and depending on his needs.

Customer Responsibility	While this can mean many things, in this context it is the responsibility that the company takes for the Customer. So if the company has a Bill of Rights for the Customer, then it has a responsibility to uphold the rights. Or if they bring out a product, they have a responsibility the product will perform and be repaired if it does not. In an overall sense, the company must feel responsible to the Customer.
Customer Satisfaction	It is a necessary condition for loyalty but not a sufficient condition. Higher Value than competition will lead to loyalty. Satisfaction is a subset of Value. Normally measures transactions and is not generally compared to satisfaction our competitors' Customers get.
Customer Service	One definition of service is that it is a convenience and should build a relationship.
Customer Share	Your company's share of Customers' purchases of your products. Also referred to as "wallet share."
Customer Share Marketing	The way you increase your share of a Customer's business. Increasing your share of the Customer's wallet.
Customer Strategy	Customer strategy looks at the Customer and Customer opportunity, whereas the Business strategy looks at the marketplace opportunity. Helps align the organization to the Customer and gets top managers to be part of the Customer process. Makes the organization Customer-driven and Customer-centric.
Customer Value	The Customer's perception of the benefit he gets for his perception of the cost (price and non-price) versus competitive offers. Value for money means the Customer is price conscious. Money for Value Means he is quality conscious. Value Measures embedded perceptions. Customer Value is an investment, and Value to the firm (Value of Customer) is the return on investment.

Customer Value Added (CVA)	The ratio of the Value you add to your Customer versus the Value your competitors add to their Customers. Providing higher Value than your competition will lead to increased Customer loyalty. Relative Value wins market share and increases return on investment. CVA is a leading indicator of market share. If you get the "heart share" of your Customer by increasing the Value you provide, market share will inevitably follow. Higher CVA scores lead to increased market share, ROI, and wallet share.
Customer Value Index	This is the Customer score and ranks companies on how Customeric and attractive they are to the Customer.
Customer Value Management	Customer Value Management is a strategy to attract and retain Customers by building on the Value they assign to goods and services. CVA scores are comparative and are the ratio of the score you get from your Customers divided by the score your competitors get from their Customers. Proper Customer Value Management involves everyone in the organization. Product development and technology should flow from the Customer's needs and desires often through competitive studies, i.e., a CVA for each function in the company such as product development is necessary. Customer Value-based pricing models should be followed. Should consider putting Customer assets or Customer capital on balance sheets.
Customer Value Management Program	Integrate all Customer efforts in a holistic manner. Make the initiatives more efficient and Customer-driven. Lead to a wider spectrum of competitive advantage.
Customer Waterfall of Needs	Refers to the business processes that make up the Customer's experience with the company. Is interconnected and sequenced. Now called Customer journey.

Customer Circles/ Customer-centric Circles	Are a company-sponsored group of people who have regular contact with Customers, may not necessarily include Customers in them, and will focus on Customers. Develop tactics and tasks for dealing with Customers at a local level. Devise ways and means to make it easier for the Customer to do business with the company. Find ways to touch the Customer and give them a great experience. Customer data, information, input, complaints, or plaudits should be provided to the Customer circles as and when it is available, or an effort should be made to collect such feedback. Customer circles will come up with better ways to handle a Customer. Through this process, Customer awareness will invariably increase (and the Customer's awareness of the company will also improve). Since the initiative starts with and belongs to the members of the Customer circles, they will take ownership of it and be more Customers focused. Members of Customer Circles are touch points, back-end managers, and other employees who can influence processes, systems, and policies. This is a bottom-led Customer initiative.
Customer Experience (CX)	Customer experience (CX) is the sum of all **experiences** at various touch points a **Customer** has with a supplier of goods and/or services, over the duration of their relationship with that supplier. This can include awareness, discovery, attraction, interaction, purchase, use, cultivation, and advocacy.
Customer-in-Centre Approach	Customers should be at the centre of your business strategy; Customers should drive your strategy rather than being used to fulfil your goals.
Customer Value Investment	The investment you have to make in improving Value. Value increasing ideas include doing things right (and cost nothing). Others like major product redesign could require higher investments.

Customer Touching	Wherever you touch the Customer, you have the potential to improve your scores. Scores improve not only for benefits but also for price, as the same product appears cheaper to a Customer when he is being touched (or is happier). Customer-focused action can be used to change the importance (or weights) of various attributes. Customer hugging is a term that is also used.
Customer Value Added Data	Should be reported at the CEO level along with financial data. Should be communicated to key personnel, and selectively to Customers. Should lead to the implementation of CVM. Should be used to inform measure that ensures longevity for program and Customer focus.
Customer Value Added Design	The design of the CVA Study starts with segmentation: by product, by geography, by Customer segment, etc. Your company's targeted competitors are needed along with their market share, which are used to normalize the data. A waterfall of needs and attribute trees have to be developed. A questionnaire is developed on this basis and then vetted by the Customer through in-depth interviews or focus groups. The sample size has to be selected: these are based on significance levels that one is aiming for the confidence levels. The sample includes competition's Customers. Typically sample size of CVA is one-third to one-fourth of the sample size required for normal surveys where the frequencies of responses are compared. In the CVA score, we are comparing average, which allows us to reduce the sample size. Questions are normally based on a ten-point scale anchored at either end of the scale. Careful analysis of the data will yield usable and useful results.
Customer Value Added Follow-Up	Prioritization of action steps. "What-if" analysis and an analysis of where we want to be and what action steps to take and how. Who is responsible for the action and the time frame?

Customer Value Added Results	The results will yield the following: individual scores for each of the attributes. Importance weight for each attribute. Competitive profiles: the relative score of your company versus: the industry, the competition (competition is the industry minus yourself), and individual competitors. You could get similar scores for your competitors. You can plot slippery slopes and Value Maps.
Customer Value Management Implementation	It is important to understand the implementation of Customer Value Management: Steps for implementing CVM include data analysis, prioritization of actions, setting of score increases to be expected by the action, and putting responsibilities.
Customeric	Customeric is a word coined to show that a company has the Customer-in-Centre. The Customer is the centre of its strategy, its focus. The company is Customer-centric, takes Customer responsibility, measures Customer data, and lets Customer thought lead the business.
Customerised	Customized for each individual Customer.
Dealing with Customers	Talk to Customers because you learn a great deal by doing so. Try to get known by Customers, as often buy from anonymous people/suppliers. Make it easy for Customers to find you. Make them feel less anonymous. Companies should be loyal to Customers if they expect Customer loyalty. Take Customer complaints seriously and have a complaint resolution mechanism in place. Avoid erosion touches.
Eliminate Customer Defection	Meet their expectation. Do not ignore the Customer. Improve touching by the company. React quickly to complaints. Make the process of registering a complaint easy for him. Make the company easy to contact. Build good knowledge of/information on Customers. Develop an emotional bond with the Customer. Improve experience with the company. Respect the Customer by not talking down to him.

Frontline Employee/ Touch Point	Generally the lowest on the totem pole but the most important to the Customer. Face of the supplier/company.
General Company Beliefs	They are doing "everything" for the Customer. They have programs underway to impact the Customer. They have insufficient bandwidth or are too busy to start a Customer Value program.
How Do We Move to Customer-centricity?	Customer circles, Customer conduit, Customer-in-centre philosophy, have Customer champions, reporting CVA, and Customer asset data.
How Do You Satisfy Your Customer?	Think in terms of **C2B** (Customer to business), rather than **B2C** (business to Customer), then think of **C2C** (Customer to Customer), where you build a community of Customers, understand the end-use experience your Customers are looking for, provide your Customers with the products and services that provide Value, and give them the experience they want.
Keep Your Promises	Exceed Customer's expectations and build trust and confidence. Remember Customer satisfaction = perceived performance/Customer expectations.
Managing Suppliers	Suppliers should be treated like Customers; you should develop a true relationship with your suppliers.
Ombudsperson	The concept of an ombudsperson to resolve disputes will reduce complaints going outside the company. Should be easy to find, reach, and work with. Should resolve problems fast.
Path to Competitiveness	To achieve strategic management, companies and their executive have to embrace Customer Value and Customer-centricity. These build a competitive advantage.
People Value Added/ Employee Value Added	This is the ratio of what your company adds to the employee versus what your competitors are adding to their employees. You want this ratio to be greater than one to get a competitive edge.

Processes, Services, Customer Value, and Customer Perception	As the quality of processes, services, and products improve, Customer Value increases, and perception of price improves. The price perception improvement for improved service can be studied, putting a monetary Value on service.
Purpose, Vision and Mission	Purpose is the *Why the company is in business*: to help humanity, to save the environment, to improve nutrition, etc. Vision is *What to achieve* and Mission is *How to reach the goal.*
Put the Customer in Control	Provide him with the ability to communicate directly and painlessly with the company. Realize that the Customer should have it his way. Build a community of Customers and allow them to communicate with one another and with your company, and to blog or set up a message board thereby: letting him get easy information on products, shipments, and specials. Giving him delivery his way (maybe he can call in and his grocery bag is ready for pick-up). Remember, that if we think it is right to want to control our suppliers, we should let our Customers control us, because we are their suppliers.
Relevance of Work Effort from a Customer's Viewpoint	Divide your work into categories that the Customer would think of as: necessary and relevant, necessary and irrelevant, unnecessary and relevant, and unnecessary and irrelevant. Concentrate on the necessary and relevant tasks from the Customer's viewpoint.
Reporting Customer Data	Customer data should be reported on balance sheets. This is being proposed by the Security and Exchange Commission, which wishes investors to know a company's Customer assets and how the Customer assets are growing/deteriorating.

Resistance to Embracing Customer Value and CVA	Organizational inertia or executives feel they are doing enough for the Customer or they are into too many initiatives, and there will be a resource drain. Executives feel they understand the Customer and the marketplace. Executives worry about correlating Value data and satisfaction data. Value studies are not well-understood or that well-advertized or pushed as satisfaction studies, which are generally run by market research companies that push satisfaction over Value. Top executives are not exposed to Value globally as they are exposed to satisfaction.
Return on Customer	It is the Value of the Customer divided by Customer capital. This is the firm's current cash flow plus a change in equity divided by the equity of the firm at the start of the period.
Satisfaction vs. Value	Satisfaction is measured soon after an event or transaction. Unlike Value, satisfaction does not measure embedded feelings. Satisfaction is a necessary condition for loyalty but not a sufficient one, whereas Value is. Satisfaction does not equate to loyalty unless you have competitive data. People buy because they perceive better Value from your products.
Slippery Slopes	This is the graph (generally S-shaped) of re-purchase intent versus Value or satisfaction with price and quality. It is called slippery because once you get past the very satisfied Customers, you tend to lose Customers very rapidly even with minor Value score losses.
Stated vs. Implied Weights or importance	Stated weights are received directly by asking the Customer to weight attributes. Derived or implied weights are obtained by statistical means and give a better idea of the importance of different attributes in the buying decision.

Tools of Customer Value Management: Where Are We?	Qualitative tools: what attributes are important to Customers? The Customer waterfall of needs to derive transactional attributes and Benefits and Price Attributes Trees to derive Benefits (including the product)/price attributes. Quantitative tools: where do we stand versus competition? Competitive profiles, Slippery slopes, and Value Maps.
Total Customer Value Management	Total CVM is designed to have Value Created for Customers and managed by the total company (by everyone in the company). Total CVM shows how this is to be done (see Gautam Mahajan's book: *Total Customer Value Management: Transforming Business Thinking*).
Third-Party Touching	Often touching is outsourced through retailers, call centres, etc. We must examine third-party touching and see if your company can touch the Customer directly, or better.
Traits of Winning Companies	Obsessive about knowing, even better than Customers themselves, what Customers want. Create and manage Customer expectations. Design their products, services, and processes to maximize Customer satisfaction. Make Customer Value everybody's business. Maintain a business philosophy to add ever-increasing Value to the Customer. Have a culture driven by a vision that creates a strong Customer focus. Constantly ask if their proposed action will benefit the Customer, or adversely impact them.
Using CVA for Business Decision: Product, Service, and Technology	CVA is used for a business decision on products, services, and technology offerings. CVA help make a business decision using the Customer's input and point of view for pricing, new product introduction etc.

Using CVA for Pricing	CVA techniques can be used for pricing of products and services and for deciding on the various features to put into products. CVA pricing looks at costs from a Customer's viewpoint and is based on the relative benefits you create vs. competition, and the importance of each benefit to the Customer. As benefits increase, the price can be increased depending on the importance of each benefit the company provides. Brand is also a benefit.
Value	It is the balance between cost and quality. The more the Customer perceives what he gets for his money, the higher his perception of the Value. It is what a product is worth to the Customer, and how he perceives the benefits of the product, given what it costs him to buy or own it.
Values (Of People, Companies)	The Values, standards, morals ethics, beliefs, and ideals principles that a company has and are reflected in its culture, and its approach towards Customers and employees, and the environment safety and sustainability and to society.
Value Creation	Executing proactive, conscious, inspired, and imaginative actions that do more good and create better gains or Value for Customers and all stakeholders.
Value Illness	The main role of an executive is to create Value for himself, his employees, and his Customers and thereby for his investors. The role of a company is to create Value for its employees and Customers, suppliers, and partners and thereby for shareholders, which prevents people from following the right things.
Value Maps	Position of your company relative to the Customer's rating of your company and the competitors on price and quality. Help you make a sound strategic decision. Useful in pricing and in what-if analysis on whether to improve/reduce price or benefits or both.

Value of Customer	The Value of your relationship with your Customers. The average Value of each relationship can be measured by the following: revenue per Customer, the average length of a Customer relationship, the total number of referrals who became Customers divided by the total number of Customers plus one (the original Customer). Can be referrals to as R, Average spent per Customer per annum multiplied by relationship length with R (a measure of referrals), Customer Value is an investment, and Value to firm (Value of Customer) is the return on investment.
Value Deprivation	Where people are deprived of value availability, opportunity and fairness
Value Starvation	When Customers are starved of value through small niggling problems the company ignores to correct.
Voice of Customer and Voice of Competitor	CVM is akin to the voice of the Customer (and the voice of competitor). Many companies use CVM studies for this purpose.
What Investors Want to Know?	How many Customers do you have? What is your profitability per Customer? How well do you treat your Customers? How fast you are growing a Customer franchise?
What Is a Customer?	An indispensable part of your business, without which there is no reason for your business to exist.
What Is the Goal of a Company?	To satisfy stakeholders (employees, Customers, suppliers and partners, unions, and shareholders) and to create Value for them.
What to Do for Customers	Convert anonymous Customers into known ones. Understand and incorporate Customer Do Not Annoy (DNA) into any Customer initiative. Avoid erosion touches.
Where Do We Want to Be?	Value Map prioritization and focus areas to build competitive advantage.

Who Is a Customer?	A Customer is someone who buys from you, or is a consumer, or someone who could potentially buy from you, or is someone else's Customer.
Zero Complaints	Zero Complaints is a similar concept to zero defects. It should be the intention of any company to get to zero complaints by examining hygiene factors, Customer journey, Customer experience, and everything to do with product reliability, usability, and service. Leads to Customer-centricity.

Index

A

8As, xxi, 20, 36, 57, 85, 86, 135, 196, 235, 236, 245, 247, 249, 250, 252, 253, 260, 263

Abney, David, 120
Adams, Michael, 33
Air India, 83–87, 259
Akihiko, Konagaya, 191
Amazon, 27, 80, 120, 122, 123, 153, 208, 216, 228, 251, 252, 279
Ambidextrousness, 8, 36, 55, 57, 86, 135, 196, 235, 236, 247, 250, 252, 253, 260
American Customer Satisfaction Index (ACSI), 68, 198
Anonymous value, 12, 269–271
Apex Customer Circle, 77
Apple, 109, 110, 120, 123, 153, 157, 178–180, 207, 208, 216, 251, 273
Arnold, Craig, 120
Artificial intelligence (AI), 34, 83–86, 134, 154, 164, 168, 188, 248, 274–278, 286
    risks of, 275, 277
    and technology, 168, 188, 248, 275–277
Ashta, Ashok, 206
Avoid destroying value, 214, 230

B

B2B (Business to Business), 27, 41, 287
B2C (Business to Customer), 27, 38, 307, 316
Baez, Ramon, 281
Bagehot, Walter, 200
Bajaj company, 185
Baker, Chris, 206, 291

Balachandran, B. V., 267
Bank's effort, customer-centric, 150–151
Barriers to customer experience, 131
Bazerman, Max, 246
Becker, Gary, 294
Bezos, Jeff, 120, 208
Big brother syndrome, 178–180
Big technology, 279–280
Bindra, Vishal, 282
Bottom line, 50, 66, 67, 113, 290, 294, 299–300
Brand assets, 117, 118
Brand Keys. 153
Brand equity, 103
Brecher, Christian, 134
British Standards Institution, 19
Bruvold, N. T., 103
Building/breaking silos, 130–132
Businesses and institutions
    building silos/breaking silos, 130–132
    companies misunderstand price, 140–141
    companies not creating value, 125–130
    customer value constellations, 118–120
    customer value creation evangelist, 143–145
    four types of companies, 120–125
    loyal companies, 115–116
    management by creating value, 132–137
    need financial incentives, 138–140
    output/input, 113–115
    real sources of value, assets and performance, 116–118
    value creation centres, 141–143
Business Roundtable, i, xvii, 5, 120, 132, 188, 190, 209, 223, 227, 228, 229, 235

Business schools, 21, 156–158, 170, 198, 246, 266, 282
Business strategy, 55, 59, 72, 101, 130, 148–151, 186–187, 189, 190

C

C2C (Customer to Customer), 27, 38, 316
Cáceres, Champetas, 171–172
Carlisle, Madeleine, 222
Carpinella, Paul, 141
Carras, Jim, 139, 218
Case study, SME Packaging company, 61–63
CCIP, *see* Continuous Customer Improvement Program
"The CEO's Balancing Act," 219
Chief creating value officer, 208–211
Chief Employee Value Creator, 98, 99, 102–105, 118, 210
Chief Financial Officer (CFO), 168, 173, 208–210
CIOs, 281–282
Circle of Promises, 9–11, 59, 70, 73, 75, 131, 154
Co-creation of value, 170–174
Co-destruction
    collaborative process, 171
    deceptive marketing, 174
    overview, 170–171
    risk of, failure/external disruption, 172
Co-innovation, 171
Collins, Jim, 289
Commodity, 266–267
Communication, 76–77, 108, 122, 154, 195, 216, 228, 237, 245, 248, 255, 295
Companies transformations, 215–216
    two goals, 219–220
    value creation *vs.* value destruction, 218–219
Company
    Fourth Industrial Revolution, 223–225
    four types of, 120–125
    misunderstand price, 140–141
    new purpose of, 227–230
    World Economic Forum, 222–223
Companystan, 143–145
Conley, Chip, 37
Conscious capitalism, xix, 21–22, 229, 299
Conscious/unconscious value destruction, 180–182

Consumer behaviour, 48–50
Continuous Customer Improvement Program (CCIP), 10–12, 16, 17, 36, 56, 69–71, 74, 154
Cook, Tim, 120, 208
Copycat Economy, 265
Core Customer Circle, 77
Core values and traits, 295–296
Corey, Irwing, 201
Corporate consciousness, three Rs, 298
Corporate unconsciousness, 298–300
COVID-19, 20, 180, 188, 215, 247, 260–263, 273
    crisis, 185, 261–263
    destruction, 254–256
Creates value
    economics, 156–159
    purpose, 225–226
    trust, 194–195
    wellbeing, 30
Creating disruptive value, 301
Creating value, 183–184, 231–233, 238; *see also* Value creation
    definition, see Creating Value definition
    management, 132–137
    stakeholders, 208–209
    for yourself, 1–2
Creating Value Principles
    first principle, 292
    second principle, 292
    third principle, 292
    fourth principle, 293
    fifth principle, 293
    sixth principle, 293
    seventh principle, 293
    eighth principle, 293
Crosby, Phil, 139, 218
Culp, Larry, 208
Customer advocate, 59, 286–287
Customer and value migration, 267–269
Customer assets, 117, 209
Customer centric circles, 8–11, 57
    case studies, customer value foundation, 76–78
    Customer Bill of Rights, 74–75
    experiential learning and mindset changes, 69–71
    lessons for management, 78
    rollout and composition, 72–74

Customer-centricity culture, 66
Customer Churn Rate, 65
Customer circles, 11, 16, 17, 36, 68–70, 72;
    see also Customer centric circles
Customer culture, 67
    CCIP, 10
    Circle of Promises, 9–10
    Customer's Bill of Rights, 9
    zero complaints, 10–11
Customer delight, 10, 73, 76, 86, 257, 260,
    286–287
Customer department, 55, 76, 130, 144
    function, 56
    importance, 55
    new ideas, 57
    products and features, 56–57
Customer Effort Score, 65
Customer experience (CX), 10–13, 23, 40,
    44–46, 55, 63–68, 70, 79, 92, 112,
    131, 152, 154, 266
Customer-first approach, 261
Customer Health Score, 65
Customer life time value, 59
Customer loyalty, 8, 63, 64, 130, 153
Customer network, 60–61
Customer Renewal Rate, 65
Customer reporting, 55
Customer responsibility, 144
Customers as ambassadors, 59
    creating value for customer, 60–61
    with social value, 58–59
Customer satisfaction survey, 64
Customer's Bill of Rights, 9–12, 36, 56, 69,
    70, 73–76, 119, 131
Customerstan, 143–145
Customer strategy, 6, 11, 55–56, 59, 78, 131,
    148–151, 153, 186, 228, 270
Customer value, 16, 39–40
    constellations, creation and destruction,
        118–120
    consumer behaviour, 46–50
    create real value, 40–42
    customer centric circles, 57
        business philosophy, 72
        case studies, customer value
            foundation, 76–78
        Customer Bill of Rights, 74–75
        experiential learning and mindset
            changes, 69–71

lessons for management, 78
rollout and composition, 72–74
customer department. 55-57
customer experience, 44–46, 63-68
customers as ambassadors
    creating value for customer, 60–61
    with social value, 58–59
give away too much to customer, 51–54
SMEs benefit, case study, 61–63
value starvation, 257–260
    more value not much cost, 87–89
    nuisance value, 93–94
    value creation implementation, avoid
        value destruction, 89–91
    value deprivation, 95–96
    zero customer complaints, 92
    zero defects, 91
Customer Value Added (CVA), 51–53, 58,
    72, 78, 97, 103, 105, 175, 187, 209,
    250–251, 269
Customer Value Foundation, 37, 63, 76–78,
    152, 232
Customer Value Investment, 159, 192
*Customer Value Investment: Formula for
    Sustained Business Success*, 286
Customer value management (CVM), 11, 113
Customer value starvation, 55, 63, 80, 83–96,
    236, 249, 257–260
CVA, *see* Customer Value Added
CX, *see* Customer experience

D

Dann, Chris, 166
Daskal, Lolly, 197
Davidow, Moshe, xix, 26, 28, 49, 50,
    138, 139
Davos Manifesto 2020, xiii, 5, 132, 180, 188,
    190, 222, 223, 227, 235
Death of profit, 154
Debates, 28, 205–206, 229
De-commoditizing commodity, 265–267
de Mestral, George, 246
Destroyed value, 254–256
    intellectual dishonesty, 181–182
Diamandis, Peter, 134
Differentiation, 128, 265, 266, 274
DiGioia, Steve, 13
Digitizing, 165, 275–276

Dillard, W. T., 272
Dimon, Jamie, 208
Disrupted marketplace, 245–250
    destruction by COVID-19, 254–256
    marketing and disruption, 250–254
Disruption, xix, 172, 245–247, 249,
        253–255, 278, 303
DNA (Do Not Annoy), 17, 70, 73, 76, 87,
        307, 309, 321
Drivers of behaviour, 294
Drucker, Peter, 30
DTH company, 12
Dunham, Bob, 198
Dunn, 164
Dweck, 297

E

Economics, 3–5, 18, 29, 44, 50, 85, 94, 115,
        118, 132, 155, 173, 178, 206,
        222–224, 233, 234, 238, 239, 254,
        265, 274, 279, 294
    creates value, 156–159
Emerson, Jed, 243
Employee value, 2, 56, 118, 199, 210
    assets, 117
    attribute tree, 98, 99
    build market place foresight, 107–110
    employee journey, 105–107
    EVA, 98–99
    relationship truth, 37
    specialists create more value, 110–112
    value creation, 107–110
        by employees, 100–101
        tips, HR professionals, 101–105
Employee value added (EVA), 98, 103–105, 210
    advantages, 98
    use for benefit, 98–99
Empowerment, 179–180
Endowment Effect, 50
Environment, Social and Governance (ESG),
        xiii, xx, 118, 137, 191, 231,
        236–237, 258, 290
Environmental, sustainability and governance
        issues, 137
Environmentalists, 238, 296
Environment value, 238–239
Epstein, David, 110–111
EVA, *see* Employee Value Added
EYeka, 171

F

Favaro, Ken, 136, 142
Fear, 22, 49, 50, 188, 193–194, 197, 216
Feeny, David F., 282
Financial benefit chart, 103, 284–285
Firms of Endearment, 22, 131, 137, 274,
        289, 298
Fourth Industrial Revolution, 223–225
Fowler, Curt, 151
Friedman, Milton, 229, 235
Functional thinking, 100, 192, 252, 259
Fundamental commitment, stakeholders, 208
Furquhar, 164
Future innovation, 303
Future skill need, AI and technology,
        275–277

G

Galbraith, J.R., 122
GE, 28, 165, 208, 265
George Mason University, 196, 295
Ghani, Ejaz, 276
Ghosh, Sunanda, 93
Gillespie, Nick, 229
Gleeson, 197
Globalization, 223, 248, 255, 276
Global opportunity, 249–250, 256
Glocalization, 248, 255
GNP, *see* Gross National Product
Google, 4, 97, 101, 153, 178–180, 216, 228,
        253, 271, 279, 298, 301
Gordon, Gregg, 219
Gorman, James, 120
Gottfredson, Ryan, 193, 195
Graves, Michael, 156
Greenwashing, 233, 240–241
Growth mindset, 297
Guide to customer value creation, 305–322
Gulati, Ranjay, 13
Gunderson, Garrett, 15
Gurdjian, Pierre, 198

H

*H2H: The genesis of human-to-human
        marketing*, 263
H2H, 35, 38
Hagel, John, 135

Halbeisen, Thomas, 198
Hall, Brian, 21, 195
Harari, Oren, 266
Harding, Warren, 262
Hassan, Carla, 13
Hastings, Hunter, 156
Hewson, Marillyn, 120
High-tech marketing, 250
Hiller, Nathan J., 196
Holbrook, Morris B., 272
Holzwarth, Greg, 150
Hughes, Paul, 20
Human capital, 294
Human–machine interface, 169
Hussain, Faisal, 15
Hyde, Lewis, 121

I

Ibarra, Herminia, 197
Immelt, Jeffrey, 265
Implementation ideas, avoid value
    destruction, 89–91, 211–212
Increase customer net value *vs.* retention, 152
Innovation,
    councils, 141–143
    proprietary information, know-how,
        intellectual property assets, 118
Intangibles, 5, 37, 38, 68, 105, 114, 117–118,
    138, 243, 292
Intellectual dishonesty, 181–182
Internal customer, flawed concept, 130–132
Internet payment and services, 248

J

Jackley, Jessica, 35
Journal of Creating Value, xx, 39, 49, 83,
    183–184, 211, 217, 232, 234, 245,
    263, 273, 291

K

Kahneman, Daniel (Prof.), 44, 50
Kegan, Robert, 201
Knowledge, creating value 34
Know value, 100, 232, 234
Kohda, Youji (Prof.), 34, 35
Kordupleski, Ray 44, 72, 79, 114

Kotler, Phil, 63, 85, 183–184, 189, 232,
    245–246, 250, 257, 263, 271, 273
Kotler World Marketing Summit, 183

L

Lane, Kevin, 198
Larsen, Gitte, 104
Leaders, not always lead, 191–193
Leaders create value, xix, 159, 184–185,
    192, 193
    mindset, 185–186
    not taught, 185
    performance goals, 184–185
    strategize and innovate, 186
        look at value destruction, 186–187
        value waiting to happen, includes
            innovation, 187
Leadership, xix, 5–6, 21, 55, 66, 70, 71, 77,
    115, 131, 143, 184, 188, 192, 281,
    282, 295–296, 299
    development programs fail, 198–199
    and education, 195–198
    skill, able to unlearn, 201–203
Lee, C. H., 103
Lee, Dick, 144
Lichy, Jessica, 291
Life's purpose, 29–30, 221–222
Lihaz. 21
Liozu, Stephan, 141
Long-term value, 3, 96, 120, 136, 173, 208,
    224–225, 231, 257
Loyal company, 18, 115–116, 119, 195
Lucas, Gerardus JM., 20

M

Mackey, John, 229
Magnuson, Jim, 33
Mahajan, Gautam, 18, 20, 36, 42, 57, 164,
    238, 239, 245, 290, 292, 305, 319
    8As (Mahajan), 36, 135, 235–236, 260
    Air India, value creation, 85–86
    culture, 7
    giving and taking matrix (Mahajan), 124
Maher, David, 250
Maidique, Modesto A., 196
Management,
    creating value, 132–137

learn to transform, 212, 216
lessons for, 77–78
Manufacturing, 28, 55, 68, 100, 109, 117,
    132–135, 144, 191, 237, 248,
    252, 255
    suppliers and partners, 283–286
    supplier strikes back, 286–287
Marketing
    creates value, 273–274
    customer and value migration, 267–269
    de-commoditizing commodity, 265–267
    and disruption, 250–254
    getting organizations, 253
    orientation, 245–246
    planned obsolescence destroy value,
        271–273
    prevent customer value starvation, increase
        profits, 257–260
    value destroyer, 260–263
    value of, being anonymous, 269–271
    value proposition, focus, 264–265
Market share *vs.* value, 52, 53
Marshall, Barry, 202
Marx, Karl, 3–5
Marx Utility value, 2, 3
Mazzucato, Mariana, 204, 206, 207
MBA programs, 195, 196, 230
McArthur, 227
McCracken, Elizabeth, 33
McKinsey, 23, 65, 198, 205, 263, 271, 275
McMillon, Doug, 120
Measure value, xiii, 6, 20, 27, 47, 118, 139,
    140, 232, 234–237
Measuring customer value, 228, 250
    CEO pay over years, 127
Mehta, Nipun, 298, 302
Mehta, Pavi, 21, 22
Menger, Carl, 156–158
Michener Center, U of Texas, Austin, 31–33
Microsoft, 28, 178–180, 228, 261, 272
Military, 163, 192
Mindset, 11, 21, 29, 36–38, 195–199, 235,
    236, 296
    change, 68–71, 235
        attitude, 236
        awareness, 235–236
        customer centric circles, 236
        customer retention and profits, 154
    fixed mindset, 296

growth mindset, 297
    value creation, 184–185
Mission, 226–227
Modern marketing orientation, 245
Mogan, Gary, 4
Money and power, 180–182
Montier, James, 126
Moutinho, Luiz, 270
Moynihan, Brian, 120

N

Narayanamurty, 121
NATO, 162, 163
Natural resources, preserved, 233
Neale-May, Donovan, 100, 101
Necessary work, 175, 204
Negative attitude, 297
Net value creation, 239
New purpose, 120, 188, 208, 227–230
New York Times magazine, 147, 155, 241
Nine reasons, companies not creating value,
    125–130
Nishinaka, Miwa, 29
Non-customer, 40, 56, 263
Non-financial benefits, 103, 284, 285
Non-owner stakeholders, CEOs, 190–191
Non-value-added tasks destroy value
    businesses, 175
    customers, 175
    relevant and necessary tasks, 175–177
    value co-creation, 174
    value co-destruction, 174
NPS, 44, 64, 200
Nuisance value, 93–94

O

Organization
    of future, 130, 210
    purpose and culture flow, 237–238
Organization, transformational growth,
    215–216
    balancing act, 217–219
        two goals, 219–220
    future leaders, transform through value
        creation, 217
    steps to transform, 217
    value creation and leaders, 216–217

Orphaned customer, 12–14
Orts, Eric, 100, 101

P

Parker, Doug, 120
Paswan, Audhesh, 302
Patagonia Textile company, 180
Peleg, Danit, 134
People skilling, 167
PET bottles, 166
Pfoertsch, 263
Picasso, Pablo, 164
Pinto, Eddie, Dr., 223–225, 227–229
Planned obsolescence destroy value, 271–273
Plant and machinery assets, 117
Plant fuel cells, 253
Ple, 171–172
Polman, Paul, 22, 138, 168, 188, 211, 233
Positive attitude, 297
Potential leaders, 198, 199, 293
Power and value, 179–180
Prahalad, 170
Premji, Azim, 121
Prevent customer value starvation, increase
    profits, 257–260
Pricing strategy, 155
Primary role of leader, 184
    getting a value creation mindset, 185–186
    leaders create value, 184–185
    not taught to create value, 185
    value helps you strategize and innovate
        better, 186
    value waiting to happen includes
        innovation, 187
    you start to look at value destruction,
        186–188
Pro-activeness, 16, 18, 78, 100, 106, 125
Producer-consumer exchange, 158
Product offering assets, 117
Profit centre, xx, xxi, 231–233, 235, 239
Profit motive destroys value, 147–151
Profits and value
    balancing act, increase profits, 151–154
    economics creates value, 156–159
    mindset change, improve customer
        retention and profits, 154
    profit motive destroys value, 147–151
    value added stories, increase price,
        155–156

Purchasing professionals, 283
Purpose
    of company
        dealing fairly and ethically with our
            suppliers, 120
        delivering value to our customers, 120
        generating long-term value for
            shareholders, 120
        investing in our employees, 120
        new purpose of, 227–230
        supporting the communities in which
            we work, 120
        World Economic Forum, 222–223
    creates value, 215–226
    in life, 221–222
    sense, vision and mission, 226–227
Putin, Vladimir, 162–163

Q

Quelch, John, 266
Quincey, James, 120
Quinn, Robert E., 15

R

Ramaswamy, 170
Rand, Ayn, 95
Real sources of value, assets and performance,
    116–118
Regulator's report, 279–281
Reina, Chris, 193, 195
Relevant work, 175, 204
Rodgers, T.J., 229
Rohn, Jim, 283
ROI, 53, 87, 114, 209
    vs. relative customer value, 53, 54
Rorty, Richard, 94
Ross, Jeanne W., 282
Rothman, Denis, 276
Ruggeri, Kai, 2
Russia–Ukraine war, 161–163
Ryan, Don, 150

S

Sampson, Scott, 206
Sanghvi, 164
Schwartz, Jeff, 135
Schwarzman, Stephen, 208

S-D logic, 170, 173
Self-healing and self-powering systems, 167
Sense, vision and mission, 226–227
Sense of value, 7–8, 295
Service Level Agreements (SLA), 130
Shafer, Michael, 206
Shareholder value destruction, 164–165
Shaw, Percy, 303
Sheth, Jagdish, 85, 113, 137, 274, 289
Sierra, Kathy, 203
Singh, Namrata, 229
Sisodia, Raj, 137, 229, 274, 289
Skafdrup, Erica, 104
Slym, Karl, 219
Slywotzky, Adrian, 267
Smart city
    people skilling, 167
    physical transportation, 167
    self-healing and self-powering systems, 167
    smart lighting, 166–167
    value creation/destruction
        insolvency, 168
        plastic bottles, 168–169
        short-term focus, 168
        technology and artificial intelligence
            (AI), 168
Smart lighting, 166–167, 187, 234, 237
Social assets, 118
Social capital, 294
Social media and public relations programs,
    114
Sorenson, Arne, 120
Soussloff, Gregory, 143
Spielberg, Steven, 143
Sponholz, 263
Stakeholder, 1, 5, 20, 22, 42, 55, 97, 112,
        115, 120–121, 186–188, 243, 261,
        273, 290
    culture, 6–7
    strategy, 6, 55, 148, 151, 186
    value, 6, 18, 129, 132, 140, 148, 189, 190
Stokes, Peter, 18, 20, 164, 172, 291
Strategize and innovate, 186
Sudarshan, D., 179
Sugai, Philip, 239
Suppliers and partners, 283–286
Supplier strikes back, 286–287
Sustainability, 190–191
    creating value, 231–233, 238

know value, 234
measure value, 234–235
mindset change, 235
    attitude, 236
    awareness, 235–236
    customer centric circles, 236
natural resources, preserved, 233
opportunity, 236–239
synopsis, 239
value washing, 239–243
Sweet, Leonard, 30

T

Task Matrix (Mahajan), 203, 204
Tata Chemicals Crop Nutrition and
        Agri-Business, 71, 77
Tata Consulting Services (TCS), 219
Tata Power, 76, 232–233, 290
    customer circles, 76–78
    image, 232–233
Taylor, David, 120
Technology, 132, 143, 144, 152, 154, 163,
        181, 188, 203, 215, 251
    artificial intelligence (AI), 168
    disruptor, 251
    potential value destroyer, 277–281
Thomas, Mike, 200, 277
3D printing, 134
Tip the balance, increase profits, 151–154
Toffler, Alvin, 201
Total Customer Value Management (Total
        CVM), 11, 70–72, 95, 97, 285,
        290, 319
Total Customer Value Management, 86, 159,
        192, 208, 260
Training
    vs. development, 200
    does not create great leaders, 200–201
Transformation, 215
    balancing act, 217–219
        two goals, 219–220
    companies, 215–216
    future leaders, transform through value
        creation, 217
    steps, 216, 217
    value creation and leaders, 216–217
Trust creates value, 194–195
Tversky, 50

Types of people and companies
balanced (long-term thinking), 122–123
givers and mostly takers, 123
takers (extractors), 124–125
true givers (altruistic), 121–122

U

Universal purpose of company, 223–225
Unlearning, 32, 111, 201–203
Unlock customer Value, 109

V

Value, xx, 1–3; *see also individual entries*
being secure to create value, 16–18
co-creation, 18, 20, 23–28, 118, 171, 174
councils, 141–143
creating value for yourself, 1–2
customer culture
CCIP, 10, 12, 16, 17, 36
Circle of Promises, 9–11, 75, 131, 154
Customer's Bill of Rights, 9–11, 36,
69, 119, 131
zero complaints, 10–11
destruction, 5, 18, 20, 87, 89–91, 93–94,
132, 151, 161–182, 254–256
extraction, 124, 129–130, 173, 206, 253
grabbing, 21–23
sense of value, 7–8
value creation, xx, 18, 21
and culture, 5–7
framework, 19
value grabbing to value creating, 21–23
value of belonging, 12–14
and VBA, 291–295
attitudes, 296–297
core values and traits, 295–296
wellbeing and value creation, 28–30
"What's in It for Me" syndrome, 14–16
Value added stories, increase price, 155–156
Value attribute tree, 88, 98, 99
Value co-creation model, 18, 20, 23–25, 26,
118, 171, 284
platform, 26–28
Value creating behaviour, 21
Value creation, xx, 18, 21, 107–109; *see also
individual entries*
and culture, 5–7

definition, xx
education
with knowledge, 33–35
at Michener Center, U of Texas,
Austin, 31–33
training *vs.* learning mindset, 35–38
by employees, 100–101
financial incentives, 138–140
framework, 19
implementation ideas, avoid value
destruction, 89–91
and leaders, 183–184
leaders must have values, 187–188
leaders of the future and value
creation, 188–189
Phil Kotler, value creation and
marketing, 184
primary role of a leader is to create
value, 184–187
mapping, 57
mindset, 185–186
output/input, 113–115
positive *vs.* destroyed, 133
principle, 292–293
tips, HR professionals, 101–105
and wellbeing, 28–30
Value Creation, 208
Value creation/destruction
customer value constellations, 118–120
of plastic bottles, 168–169
of society, technology and artificial
intelligence (AI), 168
Value creator/destroyer, leaders, 193–194
Value creator/value taker, 205–207
Value deprivation, 94–96, 321
Value destroyer, 22, 42, 87, 94, 178, 193–194,
260–263, 272, 277–281
Value destruction, 18, 186–187
ace value creation
Google, Apple and Microsoft, 178–179
co-destruction, 170–174
creation of value, 164
smart cities, 166–169
strategy, 164–166
synopsis, 169–170
desire of two superpowers, stronger, 161–162
insolvency, 168
lack of understanding, 163–164
money and power, 180–182

non-value-added tasks destroy value, 174–175
positioning and posturing before war, 162–163
power and value, 179–180
relevant and necessary tasks, 176–177
short-term focus, 168
Ukraine war, 161
Value disruption, technology, 278
Value Dominant Logic (VDL), 18, 33, 59
Value Dominant Logic, 175, 205
Value matrix, 7
The Value of Everything, 206
Value proposition, focus, 264–265
Values, beliefs and attitudes (VBA)
    drivers of behaviour, 294
    human capital, 294
    impacts, 293–294
    individuals and corporate, 294–295
    social capital, 294
    sources, 291
    vs. values and ethics, 297
Values, beliefs and attitudes: The implications for organisational culture, 291
Values create value, 19, 43, 118, 137, 267, 289–300
Value waiting to happen, 29, 50, 112, 121, 183, 184, 186, 187, 189, 229, 234, 237, 241, 246, 247, 250, 252, 253, 292, 301–303
Value washing, 233, 239–243
Vargas, Rosa, 135
Vargo, Steve, 85, 298, 302, 303
Vaughan-Nichols, Steven J., 178

VBA, *see* Values, beliefs and attitudes
VDL, *see* Value Dominant Logic
Vision, 226–227

W

Walker, Rob, 155–156
Water as a commodity, 266
Webb, Tobias, 50
Weed, Keith, 48, 50
Wellbeing, 3, 16, 18, 28–30, 58, 96, 101, 106, 112, 116, 121, 148, 150, 151, 167, 168, 171, 172, 183, 184, 189, 193, 196, 205, 217, 220, 224, 225, 229, 234, 239, 241, 246, 250, 253, 291, 292
"What's in It for Me" syndrome, 14–16, 298
Williamson, Kevin D., 5
Winters, Bill, 273–274, 277–278
Wolfe, David, 137, 289
Woods, Tiger, 227, 243
Wooll, Maggie, 135
Working Identity, 197
World Economic Forum, 132, 222–225
    purpose of company, 222–223
Wyatt, Watson, 104

Z

Zappos, 108, 109, 122, 142, 153
Zelensky, Volodymyr, 162–163
Zero complaints, 10–12, 17, 38, 65, 128
Zero defects, 91, 151

Printed in the United States
by Baker & Taylor Publisher Services